Community Music Therapy

of related interest

Beginning Research in the Arts Therapies
A Practical Guide
Gary Ansdell and Mercédès Pavlicevic
ISBN 1 85302 885 1

Groups in Music
Strategies from Music Therapy
Mercédès Pavlicevic
ISBN 1 84310 081 9

Music Therapy – Intimate Notes
Mercédès Pavlicevic
ISBN 1 85302 692 1

Music Therapy in Context
Music, Meaning and Relationship
Mercédès Pavlicevic
Preface by Colwyn Trevarthen
ISBN 1 85302 434 1

Music for Life
Aspects of Creative Music Therapy with Adult Clients
Gary Ansdell
ISBN 1 85302 299 3

Music Therapy in Children's Hospices
Jessie's Fund in Action
Edited by Mercédès Pavlicevic
Foreword by Victoria Wood
ISBN 1 84310 254 4

Music, Music Therapy and Trauma
International Perspectives
Edited by Julie P. Sutton
ISBN 1 84310 027 4

A Comprehensive Guide to Music Therapy
Theory, Clinical Practice, Research and Training
Tony Wigram, Inge Nygaard Pedersen and Lars Ole Bonde
ISBN 1 84310 083 5

Community Music Therapy

Edited by
Mercédès Pavlicevic & Gary Ansdell

Foreword by Even Ruud

Jessica Kingsley Publishers
London and Philadelphia

First published in the United Kingdom in 2004
by Jessica Kingsley Publishers
116 Pentonville Road
London N1 9JB, UK
and
400 Market Street, Suite 400
Philadelphia, PA 19106, USA
www.jkp.com

Library of Congress Cataloging in Publication Data

Pavlicevic, Mercédès.
Community music therapy / Mercédès Pavlicevic and Gary Ansdell; foreword by Evan Ruud.— 1st American ed.
p. cm.
ISBN 1-84310-124-6 (pbk.)
1. Music therapy. 2. Music— Social aspects. I. Ansdell, Gary. II. Title.
ML3920.P2278 2004
615.8'5154— dc22

2003028264

British Library Cataloguing in Publication Data

A CIP catalogue record for this book is available from the British Library
ISBN 1 84310 124 6

Printed and Bound in Great Britain by
Athenaeum Press, Gateshead, Tyne and Wear

To those music therapists
– past, present, and future –
who dare to follow where people and music lead.

Contents

PART III: Is Community Music Therapy a Challenge to the Consensus Model?

PART IV: But is it Music Therapy?

PART V: What has Culture got to do with it?

Acknowledgements

First and foremost we would like to thank our community of authors, who have been a joy to work with – and who have survived the rigours of their chapters being editorially massacred, and their favourite ideas expunged. They have not complained (publicly) about this, and we thank them for their tolerance. We admire them and the originality of their work.

There are several intellectual and clinical godparents to this book, who may or may not agree with, or approve of, what we've done here. They have been vital in our getting to the point of saying what we've got to say. In no particular order we'd like to thank: Even Ruud, Brynjulf Stige, David Aldridge and Rachel Verney.

Then we would like to thank our 'supporters', without whose aid the book would not have come together: to Pauline Etkin, Managing Director of the Nordoff-Robbins Centre, London, and Professor Chris Walton of the Music Department of the University of Pretoria.

Finally, thank you to two people whose forbearance is a little closer to home: Tania and Keith.

Editors' Note

Musicking/musicing

Several authors have used the term *musicking* with direct reference to Christopher Small's (1998) influential book of that name. Another author, David Elliott (1995) also came to a similar concept independently, using the term *musicing* (see Chapter 3 by Ansdell for a discussion of these terms). Along with other unconventional usages such as 'musicers' or 'musics' we have chosen not to italicise or put inverted commas on these terms at every appearance, unless specifically emphasised by the author.

Foreword
Reclaiming Music

Even Ruud

When music therapy was reinvented as a modern profession in the middle of last century, it became affiliated with established institutions and ideologies. Music therapy was incorporated into university programs, and research was initiated within a natural science paradigm. Music therapy was constructed as a treatment profession where the individual relation between a client and a therapist was foregrounded. Therapy was performed within medical or special educational frames, and music became a means to establish and regulate the basic therapeutic relationship. For many years, music therapy seemed less preoccupied with larger social forces or cultural contexts. Music therapists insisted upon the boundaries between their discipline and others, such as music education, community musical practices or alternative healing medicines.

Thus, music therapy was performed inside the institution, in the music therapy room. There were few links to the world outside; sometimes even other children, parents and siblings were not involved in the therapy. The biomedical model of illness did not allow therapists to consider or challenge social and material conditions, social networks or cultural contexts when therapeutic measures where taken. Also, at the time, systemic thinking was not developed within music therapy.

Gradually, music therapists have come to realize that ill-health and handicaps have to be seen within a totality, as part of social systems and embedded in material processes. People become ill not only because of physical processes, but also because they become disempowered by ignorance and lack of social understanding. Music therapists have come to see how their tool, music, may be unique in involving other persons, to empower and make visible those who, because of ill-health and handicap, have lost access to the symbols and expressive means so important in every culture. Music therapists are now on the way to using music to bridge the gap between individuals and communities, to creating a space for common *musicking* and sharing of artistic and human values.

A whole new discourse labeled 'Community Music Therapy' is gradually evolving. In this anthology, we are offered for the first time a collection of articles that documents this new practice as it has developed in a number of countries. Some readers may look for what is new in these reports, and perhaps only see the links to conventional practice of music therapy. Others may notice how this community-oriented approach is changing not only the goals, vocabulary or language of doing music therapy, but also the actual practice. An approach to the use of music in therapy that is sensitive to cultures and contexts speaks more of acts of solidarity and social change. It tells stories of music as building identities, as a means to empower and install agency. A Community Music Therapy talks about how to humanize communities and institutions, and is concerned with health promotion and mutual caring.

This is a book that challenges traditional boundaries and definitions of music therapy. It takes seriously how culture informs our ways of perceiving therapeutic needs, and seeks to develop new perspectives, role identities and ways of doing music therapy. It is essential reading for the socially engaged music therapist.

For some of us who entered music therapy during the 70s, we had an idea of how music might become an important factor in social change. We saw music therapy as an orientation towards life, as a social movement, in addition to a treatment profession. Although we had no way to express this idea clearly, it informed our ways of doing and theorizing music therapy. Today, we are witnessing music therapists crossing the boundaries between 'therapy' and 'community music making'. We can see how music therapy takes part in reclaiming some of the original functions of music in our culture.

Music ethnography has claimed that music in some form or another exists in all human cultures. It also seems that music has always had a regulative role concerning the individual's place in cosmology, in healing rituals, educational settings or in building relations and networks. In contemporary society, although many of the earlier functions of music may have become less obvious, music seems to serve a whole array of functions ranging from social control to ideological maintenance within the institutions of religion, politics and art. Increasingly, music sociologists and psychologists also report the power of everyday *musicking* to energize our lives, to prepare us emotionally to cope with the technologized world (DeNora 2000; Juslin and Sloboda 2001).

Although music always served everyday needs in our culture, such needs and functions were gradually placed in the background. From the eighteenth century onwards, we saw the installation of an aesthetic of music that insisted upon the pure and uncontaminated contemplation of the musical artwork as the paradigmatic relation to music: music was taken away from everyday life and cultivated in concert halls and conservatories. The result has been a highly elitist art form, ideologically separated from 'low culture' through an aesthetic discourse where music is constructed as autonomous and universal, complex and original.

Something was lost when music became an art-form within an aesthetic that became disentangled from everyday life and separated into its own sphere. Music became non-instrumental and not intended to serve any practical purposes in life. This process may have come to its end. Within the post-modern climate, the process of differentiation and fragmentation that characterized modernity are met with processes of integration and search for wholeness. We are witnessing how the arts are corroborating with the economic spheres; how music is being taken into marketing as well as medicine.

The post-modern climate, which challenges much music education as well as public support for the arts, has led to a more inclusive attitude towards the value of popular musical forms. The boundaries between high and low are not any longer easily justified.

At the same time, music sociologists and music psychologists are discovering how people are using music to regulate and control their emotional behaviour (DeNora 2000) and take care of their health needs through music (Ruud 2002). Music is used for identity building (Ruud 1997), relaxation, to cope with stress, to release pain or to regulate sleep patterns. People bring their own soundtracks and personal stereo into the urban landscapes to regulate their moods and attentions (Bull 2000). As this book demonstrates, music therapy is aligning with this research.

Music therapists are increasingly more often working with whole communities. They not only work with individual problems, but also focus on systemic interventions: how music can build networks, provide symbolic means for underprivileged individuals or be used to empower subordinated groups. Music has again become a social resource, a way to heal and strengthen communities as well as individuals. Music therapists may soon become health music psychologists, and start teaching people to take care of their own health needs through music. *Musicking* thus will be seen as a kind of 'immunogen behavior', that is, a health performing practice, in the same spirit as when Pythagoras practiced his music at the root of culture.

Maybe this is the time for music therapy to leave its marginal site, and to take on a more central role in society. Music therapy may come to express the same spacial politics as other groups, like new social movements, youth subcultures and identifications associated with the 'New Age' who have come to artic-ulate alternative futures for society (Hetherington 1998). Could it be that music therapy, in aligning with other practices of music making, could vitalize the healing, empowering, self-regulatory functions of music? Thus music therapy could reclaim music for everyday life as a central force in humanizing the culture.

References

Bull, M. (2000) *Sounding Out the City. Personal Stereo and the Management of Everyday Life.* Oxford: Berg.

DeNora, T. (2000) *Music in Everyday Life.* Cambridge: Cambridge University Press.

Hetherington, K. (1998) *Expressions of Identity. Space, Performance, Politics.* London: Sage Publications.

Juslin, P.N. and J.A. Sloboda (eds) (2001) *Music and Emotion. Theory and Research.* Oxford: Oxford University Press.

Ruud, E. (1997) *Musikk og Identitet.* Oslo: Universitetsforlaget.

Ruud, E. (2002) 'Music as a Cultural Immunogen – Three Narratives on the Use of Music as a Technology of Health.' In I.M. Hanken *et al. Research in and for Higher Music Education.* Festschrift for Harald Jørgensen. Norwegian Academy of Music 2002:2.

Introduction
'The Ripple Effect'

Mercédès Pavlicevic and Gary Ansdell

An ex-client calls 'hello' to a music therapist in the courtyard of a drop-in centre, and five minutes later they are jamming with violin and guitar outside the café. People start gathering around the musicians. Someone turns the radio off in the café and the diners have live music with their lunch.

In a remote African village a large group of women who are care workers on a support course start singing spontaneously. Children appear at the windows as the sound leaks out into the village, and other people come in to sing and dance. They don't need a music therapist to start the music.

In a 'Music for Health' group for volunteer workers in the Northern Ireland 'troubles' other workers in the building comment on how the music sounded this week through the walls. Elsewhere, a music therapist finds herself doing spontaneous musical groups in the car park, or in a corridor. They happen when and where they happen – as music catches people's spirit.

A music therapist in a top hat and playing a trombone leads the children of a paediatric oncology ward (along with parents, some staff and visitors) around the hospital in a musical procession – a modern-day Pied Piper.

Patients and staff in a psychiatric hospital rehearse a musical about patients in a psychiatric hospital, then get on a coach and perform it at the annual conference of the British Royal College of Psychiatrists.

A music therapist takes a group of patients to an art gallery where the exhibits can be played like instruments. They improvise there as they do back at the centre. Elsewhere, a music therapist invites in local community musicians to do workshops with his patients in jazz and in drumming.

A music therapist finds himself on the stage with Maria, who's got together a show of her 'therapy songs' about her battle with cancer. Elsewhere, a music therapist plays with his band for the rehabilitation hospital's 'Happy Hour' – where the staff serve patients drinks and the musicians provide the entertainment.

A music therapist stands in the middle of a church in Berlin and conducts a spontaneous musical event for 80 culturally diverse refugees, connecting these disparate individuals into an energetic, spontaneous musical community.

What is going on here?

Our curiosity about these seemingly unusual practices in music therapy (which we also find ourselves part of) led us to plan and edit this book. We want to investigate this phenomenon which is becoming known as Community Music Therapy[1]. In recent years, music therapists have been cautiously presenting their newer practices, along with their thoughts about them. We invited a selection of these therapists to describe their work and how they think about it.

So what *is* going on? The cover image of this book gives our tentative preliminary answer: the 'ripple effect'. The vignettes you have just read lead to many thoughts, but one in particular: music naturally *radiates*, like dropping a pebble in a pond and seeing the waves of energy spread out in concentric circles. This could be a metaphor for many aspects of CoMT.

First, music's sound and energy naturally leaks out from its source. Anyone who's ever tried to soundproof a music therapy room knows they're on a fool's errand. Music is not designed for privacy or containment – it naturally reverberates, permeates, goes through boundaries and walls. And in doing so it calls to others, attracts, gathers, connects people together. It creates community. As in the examples we started with, you can often see how a musical event has a widening impact. Music therapist Stuart Wood writes: 'The power of music to connect people has an impact which can extend far into a participant's life, like ripples in a pond' (p.61).

Here the 'ripple effect' has a slightly different meaning – not just the sound moving out from its source, but also the idea that the impact of music therapy can work 'outwards' for an isolated person towards community, and it can also bring the community in, and can create community within a building. Here the concentric circles of the ripple model socio-cultural life, and also suggest a way

---

1   Community Music Therapy is abbreviated to CoMT throughout.

of thinking about music therapy that includes a socio-cultural agenda for the people and communities it works with, and the places it works in.

As we edited the chapters in this book the ripple metaphor kept turning up, with different connotations, but with a central message: that music therapy always takes place *in context*; in the nested concentric circles of our socio-cultural life. No patient or music therapist is an island – our work unavoidably takes place in social, cultural and political contexts. After a period when music therapy has been modelled on the private needs of the psychological individual, music therapists seem again to be following where music also naturally leads – towards creating community and a cultural home.

'Whatever Next?', part of the title of Anna Maratos' chapter conveys some of the recent professional reactions to CoMT. The scenarios at the start of this Introduction are not very conventional, and, to some music therapists, can even seem dangerous as practices.

And yet we have also been getting different, and interesting reactions, to CoMT as we've talked about it in various places around the world in the last few years. People approach us and say 'It's like coming out of the closet! I do x, y or z practice because that's what I think my client, or my institution needs. But I've always thought *that's* not music therapy – and I certainly wouldn't present it to my colleagues! I might get struck off! But now I feel I can talk about it.' For these people the idea of CoMT has given them permission to discuss what they do and how they think about what they do – it's given a 'conceptual umbrella' for legitimating and exploring a wider variety of music therapy practices. Also for thinking theoretically in different ways – about culture, society and politics in relation to music and music therapy.

Another variant of the story people tell us is that they once worked as community musicians, or in music education, then trained as music therapists and assumed a new identity – conceiving of music therapy as a relatively narrow practice, and apparently unrelated to their past work. For them, CoMT seems to be a way of 'coming out' with a broader identity of what it is to work musically with people – integrating their past and present professional identities in new ways.

One message in this book is loud and clear: CoMT is a different thing for different people in different places. Otherwise it would be self-contradictory. You can't have something which is context and culture sensitive but which is a 'one size fits all anywhere' model. So you will not find authoritative definitions in this book – or recipes for practice, or techniques, as such. What you will find is a wide and colourful range of examples, alongside stimulating thinking, discussion and speculation – with a little added provocation and challenge.

Rather than summarise the chapters, in this Introduction we'd like to contextualise them by discussing them in terms of some of the major questions which music therapists (and other professionals) are asking about CoMT in the fairly short time it has been circulating internationally. Our answers are, of course, open to debate and dialogue.

If nothing else we all hope that CoMT will stimulate thinking about what music therapy *can* be, and what it perhaps *needs* to be in the twenty-first century. Perhaps CoMT is more a question than an answer...

Some questions and answers on Community Music Therapy

New name, old game?

There is of course nothing new under the sun, and a common response to CoMT is to ask whether it is just re-naming an established international practice – and, moreover, re-naming from a eurocentric and ill-informed basis. Are we, then, re-spraying an old car to sell it as new? David Aldridge said to one of us that it might be more useful to re-name narrower music therapy practices 'clinical music therapy' rather than re-branding the broader practices of most of the world's music therapists 'CoMT'. These are fair and urgent questions. Are we just reinventing the wheel?

After all, didn't most of the pioneer music therapists – Mary Priestley, Nordoff and Robbins, Juliette Alvin, Florence Tyson – work in flexible and broad ways, which included both private and public work? Alvin wrote in 1968 of the need for 'a flexible program of music therapy [which] may give the patient an incentive to continue music activities when he returns to the community' (in Stige 2003). Florence Tyson was probably the first music therapist to use the term 'Community Music Therapy' in 1971, in connection with her New York centre (though she may not have meant by it the same as we are suggesting today). Equally, the Scandinavian tradition of music therapy has taken a community-oriented, socio-cultural stance since the 1970s under the mentorship of Even Ruud. Brynjulf Stige has been calling his work 'Community Music Therapy' since 1993 (and working in this way for ten years before this). Certainly some of this work is well-documented and discussed within music therapy discourse. However, this doesn't seem to justify the view that CoMT is merely an old game. If other music therapists have indeed always been working in broader ways, and thinking in a culture-centred way, then there is very little evidence of them presenting this work, writing about it, theorizing or research-ing it. This work seems to have been, until recently, a marginal tradition.

Some of the complexities of this history are being filled in now – with a major survey of the 'roots and routes' of CoMT in the first doctoral thesis on the area by Brynjulf Stige (2003).

History will surely sort out some of the facts. What is interesting at the moment is how individuals and regional traditions of music therapy arrived at practices or notions of CoMT for themselves, in relative isolation from others. Several of the contributors to this book tell this kind of story. Rachel Verney and Gary Ansdell arrived at the term 'Community Music Therapy' in an excited moment in Rachel's kitchen in 2000, following a conversation about the interface between music therapy and the British 'community music' tradition, and how their work seemed to draw from both these sources.[2] They then discov-ered a whole tradition of 'Community Music Therapy' in Scandinavia – reached by quite a different route. David Stewart describes how he too came up with the term quite independently to describe *his* work in Ireland – bridging as it does musical and social work.

So perhaps it doesn't matter where CoMT comes from, or whether or not it's 'new' in a strictly historical sense. The more interesting question is: why is it a practice and a concept that seems to have found its season *now*? Why are people suddenly interested in talking and writing about it? David Stewart suggests that this situation highlights how particular ideas and practices make themselves available at certain times and within certain contexts.

Another response by therapists annoyed by CoMT is to claim that they've always done it and it stands within the mainstream practice of music therapy – as such, CoMT does not need a new name. In a recent introductory text to music therapy, CoMT is acknowledged under a list of 'models of treatment':

> Although the term 'Community Music Therapy' is relatively new, the work it refers to has constantly been developed pragmatically by music thera-pists, addressing issues of culture, community and society together with needs that are personal, individual and private. (Darnley-Smith and Patey 2003, pp.10–11)

Brynjulf Stige makes the following comment on their assimilative strategy, taking us back to our opening question, 'New name, old game?'

---

2   See Ansdell (2002) – also the chapter by Wood, Atkinson and Verney in this volume – illustrating work that followed these ideas.

What I have tried to demonstrate…is that something more is going on than simply a new naming of an old game. Community Music Therapy as an emerging area of practice in professional music therapy represents something different than pragmatic adjustments of the work of individual music therapists. It represents adjustments of the conception of music therapy as discipline, profession and practice. Lately, a growing body of literature has suggested that a turn is on its way; from music therapy in community to Community Music Therapy, that is, from adjustments of (more or less) conventional practices located in community settings to new and context-based community practices. (Stige 2003, p.392)

Stige throws his hat in the ring with a definition here, which leads us to our second question.

Is Community Music Therapy an area of practice, a model, a theory or a paradigm?

We said earlier that you should not expect an authoritative definition of CoMT in this book, and the contributors feel this would not be helpful at this stage. We must confess, however, that we formulated a working definition which we initially sent to our contributing authors. Other early publications on CoMT, such as Ansdell's (2002) discussion paper, perhaps got too excited with their description of CoMT as a 'paradigm shift' in music therapy. We are glad in retrospect that few authors took the definition very seriously, and some challenge the whole notion of defining CoMT within their chapters – or indeed of defining music therapy in general. Mercédès Pavlicevic states: 'We can no longer simply state that music therapy is "such and such" a practice, described with the help of "such and such" theories, without addressing a crucial third bit: context' (see p.45). Simon Procter agrees: 'It is time to stop trying to define music therapy prescriptively: it is simply musicking in pursuit of well-being' (see p.230). Brynjulf Stige writes: 'I cannot tell you what Community Music Therapy is, only what it is for me', and David Stewart (Chapter 14) wants to go beyond defining himself in relation to a theory – calling himself a 'no label music therapist'.

These opinions underline a crucial point: that to define CoMT would be to define it for other people, other places, other contexts. It would be to assume that one set of practices, skills, techniques or theoretical models could be transported across situations and cultures without problem. Partly then (as we'll see in the next section), these attitudes of Community Music Therapists are a reaction to the previous generation of music therapists' desire to establish a consensus of good practice and good theory for all times and all places.[3] In a more recent text, Ansdell reformed his previous definition as follows:

> Community Music Therapy is an anti-model that encourages therapists to resist one-size-fits-all-anywhere models (of any kind), and instead to follow where the needs of clients, contexts and music leads. (Ansdell 2003)

Perhaps, however, Stuart Wood has coined the best and pithiest definition yet: Community Music Therapy is *joined-up music therapy*. This last definition may mean more to you as you read this book.

Is Community Music Therapy a challenge to the 'Consensus Model'?

In several of the chapters you will find reference to, and discussion of, the 'Consensus Model', formulated by Ansdell in an article called 'Community Music Therapy and the Winds of Change' (2002). The consensus model was presented as a thinking tool to contrast the practices, theory and assumptions of music psychotherapy with the newer practices and ideas of CoMT.[4] Ansdell referred to the model as a 'consensus' in that a sizeable international body of music therapists seem to have arrived in the last 20 years at an understanding of what music therapy is, and how it should be practised, in relation to one theoretical model (which has been written about, presented, taught and generally legitimated). Significant differences in opinion between the consensus model and CoMT in the following areas could lead to fruitful dialogue and debate:

Identities and roles: Who *am* I as a music therapist? What am I expected to *do* as one?

Sites and boundaries: Where do I work as a music therapist? Where are the limits to this work? What are the limits on what I *do* there?

Aims and means: What am I trying to do as a music therapist and *why?* How do I go about achieving these aims?

---

3   See for example the article by Elaine Streeter (1999) and the replies to it by Aigen, Ansdell, Brown and Pavlicevic (all 1999).

4   The original article was published on the *Voices* webjournal (www.voices.no) and the responses and subsequent dialogue can be followed on the site. A briefer version of the article can be found in Kenny and Stige (2002).

Assumptions and attitudes: On what theoretical assumptions are all of the above questions based? How do these ideas affect my attitude to both people and music?

Variations on these questions are entertained and grappled with by most authors in this book: some explicitly in terms of Ansdell's formulation, some in their own terms. Some think that the CoMT/psychotherapy debate is peripheral, others consider it central, but all are involved in some kind of reflexive re-thinking about the identity of music therapy. Stuart Wood considers his project to be a dialogue with prevailing music therapy values; Anna Maratos (Chapter 6) grapples honestly with her desire to continue using her psychoanalytic perspective within her work, whilst questioning the difficulties her newer practices raise for this in terms of boundaries of place, privacy and therapist role; David Stewart tracks his journey through various 'templates' of theory and experience – from calling himself a 'psychodynamic music therapist', to his training as a social worker, and currently to his identity as a 'no labels music therapist'. His shifts of practice have led to shifts of experience and thinking – courageously challenging his own orthodoxy. For him, adopting new perspectives does not necessarily mean losing older ones: rather than displacing a psychodynamic perspective, could a CoMT perspective re-orient it? He writes:

perhaps music therapy – indeed psychotherapy in general – could be seen less in terms of re-composing the past and more as a means of composing a future, creating something new with what is available to the person within his or her context. (see p.298)

Dorit Amir also traces a shift in her practice and thinking – from what she calls 'individualized music therapy' which keeps to the 'rules' of music psychotherapy, towards her version of CoMT where she follows her clients and music beyond the therapy room.

Several others find themselves re-thinking their identities, roles, sites and boundaries, aims and means, attitudes and assumptions as they simply follow the needs of clients and situations. For many, it is performance situations which provide the pause for thought: as when Alan Turry, in Chapter 9, performs with Maria singing her 'therapy songs' there is a recalibration of the inside/outside therapy boundaries; when Zharinova (Chapter 11) opens up the 'safe space' of individual therapy to the 'open public space' of performance with her refugee clients; when Procter finds himself jamming with an ex-client outside the centre café... These events and processes of performance have led music therapists to ask themselves what they are doing – professionally, ethically. As Simon Procter writes: 'What would my professional association say about this? Am I doing this for my own pleasure or can I really get away with calling it music therapy?' (see p.220).

Two overall points come out of this complex situation. Mercédès Pavlicevic emphasises that an unconventional situation for music therapy shows up just how socially and culturally constructed are its *conventions*. As we have emphasised before, there is no good reason for assuming that the consensus that may have built up in one time and place has any more than a relative value and truth. Music therapy is very much a child of culture and context.

Secondly, CoMT does *not* mean (as sometimes assumed) stopping individual work with clients. Far from it! As many chapters show, there is often a valid need for the traditional 'safe space' of the therapy room and the boundaried therapeutic relationship – at some stage in the therapy. And this is the vital point: that CoMT invites thinking about individuality (and privacy) within the context of culture and community. To put it another way: there is often a time to be private, and a time to be public in music therapy; a time for the nurturing of intimate communication; and a time for the performance of the fruits of achieved communication, skill and confidence.

Several authors refer to Ansdell's *Individual-Communal Continuum* (Ansdell 2002), which suggests that music therapy work can happen flexibly along a continuum *between* individual and communal possibilities, along with client and institutional needs. The community music therapist's thinking, ideally, needs to contain the whole continuum, and entertain the possibility of both client and therapist moving across it, as and when appropriate.

The argument, then, is not whether psychodynamic thinking might be sometimes necessary, but rather, whether it is *sufficient* as a guiding theory for music therapy practice. The debate will doubtless continue.

What has Culture got to do with it?

Brynjulf Stige's (2002) definitive book, *Culture-Centered Music Therapy*, presents a systematic perspective on contemporary music therapy practice and theory, building on a particular Scandinavian tradition of work. Kenneth Bruscia, in his Foreword to Stige (2002), calls this perspective the 'fifth force' in music therapy, and we share the view that Stige's ideas will set much of the debate on music therapy for some years to come.

Stige's main message is shared by most authors in this book: 'culture' is not an optional add-on, and *any* music therapy is naturally shot through with culture. There is no choice but to be culture-centred or culture-sensitive as music therapists: our practice, theory, conventions, assumptions and attitudes are all products of a time and a place; they are *cultural constructions*. This relatively recent perspective in music therapy has been fuelled by, first, the interest of outside academics in the *history* of music therapy (e.g. Horden 2000), which shows the historical relativity of practices and ideas about the relationship between music and healing; and secondly, the anthropological work done on music/healing practices (including twentieth century music therapy) by Even Ruud, David Aldridge, Mercédès Pavlicevic, Carolyn Kerry and by 'outsiders' such as Penelope Gouk (2000) in her book *Musical Healing in Cultural Contexts*. Again, the message is that practices and theories are contextual. Music therapy is made, not found!

In our book, this perspective is highlighted by Mercédès Pavlicevic (Chapter 1), who describes her professionally disquieting experience of ending up in a remote African village, unsure, suddenly, why she is there, how she can help and what on earth 'music therapy' can mean in that situation. Her honest self-reflection on this situation leads her to some even more professionally disquieting conclusions about the culturally constructed nature of our treasured tradition of music therapy – or rather, it is disquieting for a music therapist who may think his or her carefully constructed model suits any time, any place, anywhere. Mercédès intends to make one point very clear: the fact that her experience takes place in an exotic 'other' context does not mean that music therapists working in 'conventional' settings and the comfortable confines of their own cultures can sit back and think that culture has no implications for *them*. Rather the opposite: the exotic context merely highlights her conclusion:

> the geographical and cultural setting for this chapter needs to be set aside,
> so that we can retain the freshness of our questioning as music therapists:
> *who* are we in terms of where we are, and *what* are we doing here? (see p.47)

So far we have focused on music therapy as a *cultural enterprise* and on the need for culture to be central to our thinking. This sensitizes us to the music therapist as potential *cultural worker*, and to musicing as a *cultural force and resource* available to the community music therapist. Both Oksana Zharinova and Mercédès Pavlicevic describe themselves as 'music therapy ethnographers' in their work: enculturing and attuning themselves to their clients' music – how they play, what music means to them, how music can be shared. From this sensitivity, music somehow leads them into the work that is needed, and into the appropriate role for both therapist and music in *that* situation, in *that* place. By taking a cultural view of the situation, both are able to mobilize the cultural resources music holds for their work to be effective and helpful.

It seems to us that these and other examples in this book are paradigmatic of many music therapy situations in the twenty-first century: society both in Europe and elsewhere is rapidly changing from a monoculture to a multiculture.

The refugees, immigrants and asylum seekers are both socially and culturally disempowered and disenfranchised. But importantly, music mobilized in particular ways (ways in which a music therapist could have particular expertise) is a key way of building cultural bridges, or helping re-socialisation, acculturation and integration into new cultural homes. As Simon Procter writes, in a time of social and cultural violence, CoMT holds the promise of being a 'recuperative cultural enterprise'.

What have Society, Community and Politics to do with it?

As music therapy has become a respectable profession, so too have music therapists become respectable (and some would say establishment) people. Some are now professors, quite a few have doctorates, others are rising up the professional ladder in health or social service settings – all a far cry from music therapy's origins. Some authors would clearly like to re-establish music therapy's more radical edge – its capacity for what Simon Procter calls 'radical acts of musicking'. For him 'music therapy – like other forms of musicking – is a political act. To deny this is simply to side with the powerful.' Arguably these sentiments lie at the heart of where a lot of music therapy came from – a challenge to the establishment, for people's freedom to create and to express themselves, to be listened to and not medicated into submission. Has music therapy lost this aspect? Has its long-awaited baptism by the state[5] neutralized, as Procter contends, its potential as a force for change in society?

The sense that music therapy *can* have an agenda of social politics and social justice seems characteristic of a vein of CoMT. Brynjulf Stige in this volume writes: 'Community Music Therapy is about changing the world, if only a bit' (see p.107). Stige's chapter begins the task of providing appropriate theoretical tools for thinking around CoMT practices by suggesting the connections between culture, care and welfare. Music and musicing is used to empower and enable others, 'balancing music's potential as integrative and subversive activity in relation to a community and society'.

Many chapters illustrate strongly the point that simply working as a music therapist in certain contexts, with certain people – and daring to follow their needs, necessarily involves an engagement with cultural politics. Peter Jampel, interviewed by Kenneth Aigen, uses music as a way of negotiating with his patients through the ups and downs of the politics of the changing provision for psychiatric patients in New York City. Similarly, Simon Procter's work in

---

5   In the UK, state registration for music therapists is as recent as 1996.

non-medical psychiatric settings prompts him to a socio-political analysis of
how people are disempowered by 'the psychiatric system' and how music therapists can work as 'radical musicians' in creative opposition to this. Then there is
the very contemporary worldwide problem of refugees and asylum seekers.
Ignoring cultural politics here is simply not an option. Oksana Zharinova's
chapter is a courageous and insightful account of how a sensitive response to the
cultural dimension of the situation can lead to music being truly a force for
social action – where it can lead to the creation of *new* community for those who
are socially and culturally isolated and disenfranchised. Dorit Amir illustrates a
similar situation: how a socially isolated musician refugee in Israel can use music
and music therapy to gradually find her social and cultural place in an adopted
land.

This takes us to the concept of *community* – a multi-faceted idea central to
the new movement of CoMT. 'Community' can be seen as part of the wider
discourse on social identity and social policy (which Stige and Ansdell discuss,
amongst other authors). David Stewart opens his chapter by describing his
gradual sensitization to the way in which people's problems are contextualized
in the communities they live in. For him, the discourse on 'community' places
talk of music therapy within contemporary notions of social policy (within the
UK particularly, but doubtless elsewhere). This of course is a two-edged sword.
As several authors point out, 'community' is both a feel-good 'cuddly' word,
with quasi-utopian connotations – and also a politically manipulative
euphemism. So-called 'community care' of patients in the UK has often been
quite the opposite!

A second important strand in the use of 'community' here is to convey a
sense of *place* to be worked with (notice we say *with*, not *in*). This is probably the
defining difference between previous 'conventional' models of music therapy –
which took music therapy work *into* 'the community' – and CoMT, which
explores ways of working *with* communities, and ways of thinking about this
work. A community effectively becomes a client here. Trygve Aasgaard's work,
which he calls 'milieu music therapy' or 'environmental music therapy', shows
how a musician can work to enhance a place, to make an environment feel more
healthy – which of course makes people feel more healthy within it.

A third meaning of 'community' is *connection*. Trygve Aasgaard, the Pied
Piper of a paediatric oncology hospital, talks of *homo conexus* – we are beings
who naturally take part with others, and with our surrounding environment.
Trygve shows us how music and musicing helps, in his challenging context:

> New 'musical friendships' between patients, relatives and hospital staff
> occasionally develop during the period of treatment. A Community Music

Therapy approach in the paediatric hospital involves working towards creative networks wider than the patient/therapist dyad ... Human beings are social species – and a social being is an active being. The Pied Piper treats his followers with this in mind. (see p.162)

The term *communitas* perhaps sums up these thoughts. An anthropological concept suggested by Victor Turner, it was first introduced into the music therapy discourse by Even Ruud (1998). *Communitas* evokes the experience of musical community created through music (especially in improvisations and in socially charged settings). It combines the notions of connection, changing identity, liminality and transformation – all somewhat marginalized phenomena within the consensus model. For several authors, communitas is both the means and the end for CoMT work.

What has music to do with it?

Everything of course! The Pied Piper calls the tune – but it's the tune which draws his followers. Stuart Wood writes that '... the main feature of the path that participants took in the programme was their commitment to musical activity' (see p.60). This realization is congruent with the experience of quite a few of the authors: of the re-asserting of the power of music in and of itself for people. David Stewart writes of the impact not only of clinical experiences, but of musical experiences in his personal life: witnessing how music helps put the buzzing world of his five-day-old son back together helps him to re-think some of his assumptions about the role and meaning of music within music therapy: '...music can create a world as well as represent it. It can both reflect and shape experience. Music can be a source of attunement and transformation.' (see p.300)

Stewart's rediscovery of music as an active, transformative social force is a common theme in this book. The ways in which music can be something which not only reflects emotional life but *creates it* and as such can be vital in health promotion, personal and cultural identity building and re-building. How music can be an attractor, a connector, a motivator for the sometimes unheard-of to happen.

What else but music could lead to the heart-warming scenario Harriet Powell describes (see Chapter 8): where people with Alzheimers' find themselves within the magic of the performance of *A Dream Wedding*? Alice sings about her blue wedding gown, time falls away, and she walks over to her son for a tender meeting. Not a dry eye in the house, as Harriet says. Here is music connecting, attracting, transforming. For Oksana Zharinova, music bridges not just the barriers of illness, but also of culture and social isolation. Music allows forms of togetherness, not available in other ways. But, above even this, it is music's *humanness* which is key to her work in creating trust between people – where trust has been destroyed by violence. Here she describes music as an antidote to inhumanity.

Along with these experiences of music and community is a growing theoretical support for thinking about music as personal and social action, as a cultural and political as well as an aesthetic force. The three more theoretical chapters in this book – by Stige, Ansdell and Davidson – as well as the Foreword by Even Ruud, all outline aspects of the sea change in thinking about music within the academic disciplines of musicology (in particular the so-called 'new musicology'), music anthropology and the 'new' social psychology of music. If one were to put this varied work into one concept it would be perhaps this: that music is no longer thought of as 'over there', but 'in here' – woven into our personal, social, cultural and political being-in-the-world: music is a socio-cultural ecology. CoMT has emerged just as there is a perfect support structure of thinking about music for it. Perhaps this is no accident!

Overall, the connection between music and community is the simple fact that music creates community. Stuart Wood writes that the concept of communitas was the central inspiration to the project he describes in a neuro-rehabilitation hospital. Perhaps the central organizing concept of CoMT is *musical communitas*.

But is it music therapy?

Music therapy has been quite successful in forging itself as a discipline in the last 40 years. Music therapists have benefited from the well-articulated systematic knowledge that the profession has gathered and promoted. It seems to know what it is and what it does. In these days of demand for 'clinical effectiveness', who could argue with that? Well, *us* actually – and many authors in this collection. The shadow side of a discipline is that it, quite literally, *disciplines* its knowledge, and its practitioners (the latter through professional associations, state registrations and so on). The danger, we feel, is that newer therapists become inducted into a pre-existing order of what is and is not 'proper' (i.e. ethical) practice, and which theories and practices are 'right' and 'wrong'. Our position is that any perspective that claims an authoritative and non-relative stance on music therapy is dubious, given what we now know. One function of CoMT is, perhaps, to suggest that confidence in the consensus model has been premature.

All these issues are part of the background to many of the sometimes questioning, sometimes nervous, comments peppered throughout this book. Trygve

Aasgaard, perhaps thinking of himself as the Pied Piper leading his 'troupe' through the corridors of the hospital in top hat and with trombone, asks 'When am I, first of all, an entertainer, and when am I a "serious" therapist?' (see p.149). He thinks it may be possible that he is 'Jack-of-no-proper-trades'. Similarly, Kenneth Aigen's interviewee, David Ramsey, has a nervous moment, thinking of his work providing music for the hospital 'Happy Hour': 'It's me being a bit of a recreation therapist – God forbid – but it is!' (see p.190). To re-iterate Simon Procter's thoughts as he's jamming with an ex-client outside the centre café: 'What would my professional association say about this? Am I doing this for my own pleasure of can I really get away with calling it music therapy?' (see p.220).

These examples show that therapists' questioning of themselves revolves not just around issues of identity, but also of practice; in fact, they involve all of the categories identified earlier as areas of contrast between CoMT and the consensus model: identities and roles, sites and boundaries, aims and means, assumptions and attitudes. For example, Anna Maratos explicitly asks herself, of her work on the musical *The Teaching of Edward* with her psychiatric patients, 'Is this music therapy?' (see p.139). For her, there are issues of boundaries between patients and staff, the moving out of the therapy room, the work towards a musical product, the doing of a performance…all of these challenge what she understood music therapy 'should be'. David Ramsey, on the other hand, worries that he's going back to the good old bad old days of American remedial music therapy, before music psychotherapy legitimated music therapy as proper therapy. Other therapists such as Dorit Amir and David Stewart simply admit that their ideas about what 'proper music therapy' was, what a 'proper music therapist' does, changed with the needs of their clients in the social and cultural contexts they found themselves working in.

Some authors gently illustrate that there are quite different ways of thinking about what music therapy is, and what a music therapist does, than have become conventional in the last 20 years. Trygve Aasgaard sees his work as having little to do with illness and normal conceptions of therapy. Instead of a *pathogenic* position – treating the problem – he suggests a music therapy that is *salutogenic* – working for health and fun – musicing – being a 'health performance' even for the sickest children.

It is noticeable that the chief issue around which questions about 'is this music therapy' revolve is that of *performance*. The consensus model suggested strongly that musical performance was inappropriate to therapy: patients instead needed confidentiality, privacy, a musical search for emotional authenticity. Modern thinking is challenging this assumption but, of course, with the proviso that performance is an *option when appropriate* for music therapy, not something that is foisted upon clients. Music therapy theorists such as David Aldridge have long championed the idea that our identity and our health are *performed* in the world. And as Oksana Zharinova points out, if we work in culture-sensitive ways it follows that we acknowledge that for many clients from non-Western traditions, performing music is natural and a key part to performing their cultural identity. How could it not be part of the possible agenda of music therapy?

As many chapters of this book show, performance situations often grow pragmatically out of the needs of patients and institutions. They have their benefits and their risks, and a good thing about the CoMT debate is that there is a new venue for thinking responsibly about the role and benefits of performance in music therapy. Stuart Wood is puzzled that activities which are central to musical culture – composition, performance and learning an instrument – are *not* central within music therapy. His work with Joy involves composing, performing and learning, and he playfully writes, 'Like her fellow musicians, she did not share our theoretical concerns about learning and therapy. Her pathway was one of music-making' (see p.60). Likewise Trygve Aasgaard's 13-year-old client is disappointed when she finds Trygve is a *therapist*. 'I had hoped we could just make music together,' she whispers (see p.157). As Brynjulf Stige comments, there's no reason why a music therapist should always think she has to do 'therapy'.

Perhaps this is the key: what unites all authors in this book is their courage to throw theoretical concerns to the wind when appropriate, to follow the needs of people and circumstances, asking not 'what is music therapy?' and 'what is a music therapist', but 'what do *I* need to do *here, now?*' They dare to follow where people and music lead.

Brynjulf Stige too asks of CoMT: 'But is that music *therapy?*' (author's emphasis). His answer is: 'Yes, it is music therapy, but maybe it is not "therapy" the way you define the term' (Stige 2002, p.182). He goes on to explain:

> If we do not consider the term music therapy to be an exact label naming a predefined territory, but rather a banner that a group of people with shared interests have chosen to hold up while marching, we may understand that as they march both the landscape and the members of the group may change considerably. (Stige 2002, p.185)

This is a useful way of thinking about CoMT: a sign of the marchers approaching new territory.

Pretoria
September 2003

References

Aigen, K. (1999) 'The True Nature of Music-centered Music Therapy Theory.' *British Journal of Music Therapy 13*, 2, 77–82.

Ansdell, G. (1999) 'Challenging Premises.' *British Journal of Music Therapy 13*, 2, 72–76.

Ansdell, G. (2002) 'Community Music Therapy and the Winds of Change' [online]. *Voices: A World Forum for Music Therapy.* http://www.voices.no/discussions/discm4_03.html

Ansdell G. (2003) 'Community Music Therapy: Big British Balloon or Future International Trend?' In *Community, Relationship and Spirit: Continuing the Dialogue and Debate.* London: BSMT Publications.

Brown, S. (1999) 'Some Thoughts on Music, Therapy, and Music Therapy.' *British Journal of Music Therapy 13*, 2, 63–71.

Darnley-Smith, R. and Patey, H. (2003) *Music Therapy.* London: Sage.

Gouk, P. (2000) *Musical Healing in Cultural Contexts.* Aldershot: Ashgate.

Horden, P. (2000) *Music as Medicine.* Aldershot: Ashgate.

Kenny, C. and Stige, B. (2002) *Contemporary Voices of Music Therapy: Communication, Culture and Community.* Oslo: Unipub.

Pavlicevic, M. (1999) 'Thoughts, Words and Deeds: Harmonies and Counterpoints in Music Therapy Theory.' *British Journal of Music Therapy 13*, 2, 59–62.

Ruud, E. (1998) *Music Therapy: Improvisation, Communication and Culture.* Gilsum, NH: Barcelona Publishers.

Stige, B. (2002) *Culture-Centered Music Therapy.* Gilsum, NH: Barcelona Publishers.

Stige, B. (2003) 'Elaborations towards a Notion of Community Music Therapy.' Unpublished Ph.D. thesis. Department of Music and Theatre, University of Oslo.

Streeter, E. (1999) 'Finding a Balance between Psychological Thinking and Musical Awareness in Music Therapy Theory – A Psychoanalytic Perspective.' *British Journal of Music Therapy 13*, 5–20.

PART I

New Name, Old Game?

CHAPTER 1

Learning from *Thembalethu*: Towards Responsive and Responsible Practice in Community Music Therapy

Mercédès Pavlicevic

This chapter describes work over a period of three days at *Thembalethu*[1] in South Africa. *Thembalethu* is a non-governmental organization (NGO), that is, not for profit and relies on donations, and is based in Mpumalanga, which is the South African province that borders Mozambique on the east, and the kingdom of Swaziland in the south. Traditionally, this corner of the country is poor, unemployment is rife, and the HIV/AIDS statistics horrifying. *Thembalethu* trains home-based care-workers and also oversees home-based care for hundreds of persons who are ill at home, as well as HIV/AIDS orphans who often need help in managing their households. The work was part of a community arts project set up by the Dedel'ingoma Theatre Company, which is committed to developing a community arts model in disadvantaged communities across South Africa.

> We arrive at Thembalethu hot and thirsty, nauseous from the anti-malaria medication, and late. We are taken to the case conference in the pre-fab building, in which are seated around 70 women, in rows behind tables. We sit on the chairs set out to face the women, and listen. There is a song to welcome us, and then we are formally addressed, through an interpreter, and thanked for coming all the way from the city to be here, in this tiny forgotten rural corner of the country. Each of the women then introduces herself, and we take this as a cue to introduce ourselves: Kirsten is the drama therapist, Lauren the clinical psychologist, Hayley is the art therapist, Maria is to do massage, and I am the music therapist. For the

---

1   Thembalethu's website can be accessed at http://www.keyplus.org/

following hours, the five of us listen to various stories from the women, to do with their work as home-based care-workers, caring for people dying of HIV/AIDS. After the 'case conference' we are taken to surrounding villages, accompanying the care-workers as they visit their 'patients'. In small dark huts we see and smell thin bodies, some blind, some coughing, some covered with sores, and we witness the care-workers talking, holding a hand, washing a wound and, simply, being there, with the dying person. After the visit, we five drive to the lodge, where we will spend the evening discussing how, as arts therapists, we can contribute something to Thembalethu's work.

This may sound melodramatic and sensationalist. It is a tiny window into the days that follow.

During the next three days, we hear constant sawing, drilling and hammering in the wood workshop across the small parking area. Occasionally, a coffin is carried out of the workshop and loaded onto a waiting van: another HIV/AIDS statistic in South Africa.

This vignette suggests unfamiliar territory in terms of conventional[2] contexts for music therapy practice. The unfamiliarity is to do with regional and physical space, the large group number, language, ethnicity and discomfort (the temperatures are searing). In thinking about Community Music Therapy practice, the assumption might be that it is this unfamiliarity that invites a re-considering of music therapy practice and a critique of the consensus model. That would be too easy, and also imply that music therapy practice that is embedded in more familiar socio-cultural and work contexts need not concern itself with re-visiting conventional norms, theory and intentions. While other chapters in this book describe Community Music Therapy within established – if not always traditional – working contexts, this chapter uses a context where at first nothing about the territory feels familiar or adaptable. My experience, here, was that the basic tenets of music therapy needed constant re-thinking and re-assessing, and it was this experience of having my professional ground profoundly shaken that I use in this chapter, to re-visit some assumptions and norms in all music therapy practice: those of skills, health, roles and timing.

---

2   Throughout the text I use the term 'conventional' music therapy to describe both historically established practices of music therapy (e.g. analytical, improvisational, medical, vibro-acoustic, educational and GIM), and more familiar contexts within which music therapists work (e.g. educational, health, rehabilitation, forensic, private practice and charity-funded organizations).

Coding the cultural contexts

Traditional music therapy practice has, by and large, managed to ignore the socio-cultural territories surrounding the music therapy sessions and, more critically perhaps, kept these 'outside' music therapy practice. Inside the existing and received canon of music therapy theory and techniques, a culturally neutral stance has preserved a comfortable seal between 'inside' and 'outside'. Within 'neutral' practice, clients are invited to enter the 'therapeutic space' (which is private and confidential) within which the client and therapist enter into a therapeutic relationship. Surrounding this entry are a complex set of social conventions: beginning with the setting (let's say an institution of sorts), the referral system (activated either as a result of the client's request for music therapy, or the carer/professional's suggestion or request), the music therapy room (generally closed, physically and figuratively, after the client enters it), the music therapy technique or approach used by the therapist (which enables the therapist to work, and to understand the work and the client in a particular way), and the duration and frequency of sessions (generally negotiated between therapist and the client/carer according to a set of conventions). Once these conventions are more or less in place, there is 'the music therapy session', in which the roles of client and therapist are activated. The 'session' is followed by another set of conventions, this time to do with reporting, evaluating, assessing, reflecting, and theorizing about the session. In this model, music therapy skills are equally neutral: we can apparently transport ourselves from one working/regional/ socio-cultural/professional context to another, confident that our skills apply everywhere.

> At the beginning and end of each session, the women sing with depth and fervour, often shifting into spontaneous dancing, and the energy in the group and in the room changes palpably as a result. At the beginning of our work together, when we negotiate the group's expectations, and what/how we can provide these, they say that they want to 'sing and dance to de-stress'. I hardly know where to begin and how – there is already so much music in the group, and do they really 'need' music therapy? In the few days that follow our arrival at Thembalethu, I feel increasingly de-skilled and un-useful.

Who am I, here?

Thembalethu appears to operate within the medical model. The care-workers identify with nurses, look after 'patients', who have a medical condition called HIV/AIDS. *Thembalethu* also offers psycho-social support in the form of counselling: the women speak of patients and themselves as 'having problems', and

they have regular 'case conferences'. At the same time, the women make clear
their stance against traditional African healers, whose methods appear to be
unwelcome. All of this prompts conventional work – as part of the therapy team,
I am there to do music therapy, apparently in the culturally neutral sense. This
confusing state of affairs is presented in this chapter, in that I retain *Thembalethu's*
vocabulary – which is, after all, part of the culture of the organization, and
remove the quotation marks for the remainder of the chapter. This symbolizes
the continuing ambiguities and their destabilizing effects on my professional
presence.

My experience of feeling de-skilled lasts the duration of this three-day
workshop. Within my conventional music therapist's mind, there are several
insurmountable issues: the size of the group (now reduced from 70 to 32); the
women's musical energy (why am I needed, they already know how to use music
to shift their own energy); the complicated expectations and needs (we are here
to offer experiences in various modalities, both for the women's own experience, and also as a model for work that they might do with their patients).

I then try to think about this situation not so much as music therapy, but
rather, an experience of cultural induction. In other words, listening to the
care-workers' singing, to their songs, learning the songs, singing and dancing
with them. Here I experience my self and my body in a way that is different from
my more usual sense of self, and gradually realize that the context is beginning
to permeate my music therapist's listening, *musicking* and thinking.

I begin to listen to, and hear, the group's shifts in tension, harmony and
exhaustion in the group's singing and dancing – in which our therapy team
becomes increasingly familiar and comfortable, even though the language
eludes us. The contents of the songs tend to be quasi-gospel, hymn-like, and, as
a team, we find ourselves wondering whether this choosing to sing 'religious'
rather than secular songs, is part of the *Thembalethu* culture, or whether this is for
our benefit, since some of the songs have English refrains. We then learn that
these songs are part of the group's daily repertoire – whether or not anyone else
is present. Although none of us in the team is especially religious (and two are
non-Christian) we find ourselves singing *Jesus is Great, The Lord brings Joy, Halle-
lujah*, and so on. Here is a sense of the *Thembalethu* women presenting their
group music, in which we are included. There is no invitation or request that, as
visitors, we join in. Rather, there is an assumption that we will become part of
this music. The music is, apparently, non-negotiable, i.e. the women will not
especially sing songs for our language or religious, ethnic sensitivities. This feels
a clear statement about the group's identity being comfortable, inclusive, and at
the same time, fixed: you're either part of it or…not. There seems to be no
choice about singing other songs.

The way that the women begin (and end) songs adds to my questioning of my role and my professional skills. As a music therapist, I am not 'needed' for *musicking* to happen. Anyone begins a song – and within microseconds, it is taken up by all. The person who starts the song remains the 'soloist' or leader, responsible for how the song is sung, and when it ends. Also, over the three days, I begin to recognize the beginning of the song's ending – there is a minute shift in intensity, and a gradual winding down. This is not always as obvious as a *decrescendo* or *diminuendo*, but rather, is to do with the beginning of a quietening even if, paradoxically, the song seems to continue at the same dynamic and tempo.

How am I here?

Does my listening, tracking, witnessing, and becoming 'part of' use music therapy skills? Or is it a 'purely musical' experience? My understanding, with hindsight, is that, in fact, my music therapy skills are activated almost automatically, in spite of myself. In the group I listen not just to the music, but to the group as music: in other words, music is the vehicle through which I 'read' the group in terms of coherence, agitation, fluidity and tension. I 'read' the life of the group, its breath, expanding and shrinking, tightening and 'grooving'.

Here, a question emerges – one that is culturally loaded: why 'read' the group at all? Is this not an imposition of conventional music therapy meaning and thinking frameworks onto a context which does not invite – nor seem to want – this reading, while at the same time apparently operating within a frame that sees me as 'the therapist'? Another question is this: if I am to 'read' the group, then how? In other words, what meaning can we – the women and the therapy team – possibly create and share, given the diversity of norms and contexts? My understanding, which is embedded in conventional music therapy culture, is that through singing, the whole group creates itself and shifts itself into a different musical, emotional, and group space. The women themselves say: 'music makes us feel different', in other words, different from how they feel before singing, and possibly closer to how they would like to feel. Also, the women say that they need to sing because it 'de-stresses' them; *musicking* seems to be about more than just singing, and seems to be related to health: 'de-stressing'. They seem self-sufficient, knowing music's time and power. How, then, am I to be with them?

Shall I take them through a group improvisation, using musical instruments, and then invite them to reflect on this event? This feels inappropriate, and in any case, musical instruments are not part of the women's reality; although by being 'in role', so to speak, this might be congruent with the apparent framework of psycho-social support for the women. Intuitively, my decision was to become part of the larger group, not negating my music therapy identity, but extending this to become a listener, musician, thinker, group participant, singer, and to reflect on events as they happen.

> There are other moments in the three days when our more familiar, traditional (and comfortable) therapeutic skills are called for. For example, one morning one person (whom I shall call Lindiwe) says that her patient died overnight, and she remained with the body and the patient's children, who have now become orphans. She has not been home to see her children but has come directly to our workshop. She feels worried because a gang of older children (also orphaned) have been 'hanging around' her home, and, it turns out, no husband/father/adult takes care of her children while she is working. Lindiwe looks distressed and exhausted and we (the therapy team) are on high alert. The entire group listens attentively. The women next to her put an arm around her shoulders, and other members of the group ask her questions, are receptive, supportive and highly empathic.

Again, as therapists, we might have had a sense of not being needed. Except that this is brought into our large group time. It could have been talked about before – and indeed, on some mornings the women have work meetings before we begin working together as a larger group.

Why, we might then ask, is this information shared with us – why is it not dealt with outside our sessions? One of our tasks, which begins to emerge after hours of team discussion and reflection, is to be there in order to listen to, and share what the women live through every day (and night); to receive and to witness their lives. One of our tasks, also, is to 'become part of' the group in their sense of hopelessness and despair as they share their troubled lives with us. At the same time, we represent a bridge, a link with another world: the noisy, cluttered, and possibly glamorous world of the city where HIV/AIDS is invisible, modern supermarkets are well stocked and people well fed.

Lindiwe's distress is shared with us all, and we, the therapists, are not asked for support or advice, neither are we seen as the 'professionals' or experts at this moment. It feels, rather, as though the women find support and empathy within their group, of which we (the team) have become a part. This feels appropriate. So much so that for us to have shifted their 'problems' into our conventional therapeutic territory would have been disrespectful, insensitive culturally, and rather deaf to the capacities of the *Thembalethu* women. Rather, the team seems to have become a part of the whole group, and this means becoming a part of their way of working.

Why boundaries, here?

In traditional music therapy practice, there is outside and inside, before and after the music therapy session. Some things (such as content and nature of conversations, mode of behaviour, mode of address, ways of engaging) belong only to the inside, some to the outside, and some traverse these two spaces. Traditionally, the notions of professional ethics and confidentiality are named 'boundaries': the boundaries between inside and outside, between the therapist and client, and between during and after music therapy sessions. In other words, boundaries of persons, space and time.

These boundaries make no sense whatsoever within the *Thembalethu* work context – and had we insisted on culturally neutral work, we would have lost one another along the way. As therapists, we might have imposed 'neutral' norms and boundaries, seen these constantly ignored by the women (since these norms would in any case be culturally violating), and we might then have interpreted this 'ignoring' as resistance, hostility, anti-group acts and so on.

Similarly, during the three days, our roles with the women shift constantly. We are 'therapists' and 'clients', as per the traditional model; we are group participants; we are also in role as fellow professionals; and we are all women. The opening vignette of this chapter describes us accompanying the *Thembalethu* care-workers on their home visits, and here we walk through villages while they explain the situation of the various villages, families and patients. We are also fellow persons, sharing food: we are invited to share their lunch, prepared in the *Thembalethu* kitchen, and we, in turn, share our lunch with them. This becomes somewhat complicated because the team uses the lunch hour to reflect on the morning's work.

The shifts between various roles feel natural here. Each role has a distinctive task, with distinctive skills, and just because we flow easily from one role to another does not mean that our roles merge into one 'way of being' together. Our learning, as therapists, is to remain alert to the timing and need for activating any one role. Rather confusingly, roles do not always depend on the physical space or time, so that being together as therapist–client, co-professionals and fellow human beings shifts constantly, both within and outside our session times.

> On a home visit, for example, we walk together through the village on the way to visit a patient, and Anna, one of the care-workers, asks about my home life: am I married, do I have children, where do I live? This is a woman-to-woman conversation, and I am expected to reciprocate.

It would be culturally unthinkable to refuse to flow into this exchange together, even though in a few minutes we shall once again be co-professionals, and an hour or so ago, we were therapist and client. Each of the roles is, however, under-pinned by a 'meta-therapeutic' mode of operating within this complicated context. In other words, as a therapy team, we find ourselves constantly listening, thinking, reflecting about everything that happens – not unlike the therapeutic stance within a conventional therapy session.

I now want to consider another conventional therapeutic group norm, to do with creating a boundary between outside and inside the therapy room and therapy time.

> As part of negotiating and setting the (whole) group contract at the beginning of our three days together, we have all agreed that mobile phones are to be switched off during our session time. However, calls keep coming through – and being answered. The team cannot fathom this out, and we re-negotiate this with the women. Still calls come through, and we discuss this all together, once again. It transpires that some care-workers are on call, their patients may be ill, and they need to be at the end of the phone constantly, and keep their phones activated. We then agree that some people have their phones on, and this seems to work – for the day. Also, folk from the outside come into our sessions frequently, usually to call someone out, or to ask a question. Children peer in through the windows (especially when the women are massaging one another when the eyes at the window become rounder – and there are no curtains), and when the group sings, others come into the room and join the group, singing and dancing.

Within the conventional music therapy framework, we think of 'outside' and 'inside' being distinctive spaces. Here at *Thembalethu* we cannot close the door to everyday life, and in any case, the searing heat means that every possible window and door remain open. The outside world is, simply, a part of the work that we are doing and, in fact, it is not outside at all; it is right here, within the room where we work. 'Life' and 'therapy work' are inseparable, in the spacial, temporal or mental sense.

Whose timing, and when?

The opening vignette of this chapter hints at multi-media co-operation: there are four of us on this project working in art, drama, music and counselling. Each of us is experienced in our own modality, and used to working predominantly in that modality. As a music therapist, I sometimes use image-making, stories and movement, but generally, these are nearer the edge of my (dis)comfort zones. The *Thembalethu* experience of working together challenges each of us, con-fronting us with the limitations and configurations of our own modality.

There are times when, as a music therapist, I feel redundant, and instead of relaxing into this, I find myself thinking that I 'ought' to be doing something with music. Until I realize that as a music therapist, there is a listening that is instant: it has become second nature. The second someone speaks or moves, I hear the vitality of their image, the flow of their movement, the colour of their voice. In a drama exercise, I hear the tight anxiety of the giggling group. In the clay modelling session, I listen to the thick deadness of the silence and the heaviness of the women's hands as they mould clay. Clear as a bell.

With hindsight, I realize that music therapy skills are not limited to music-making, but rather, that music therapy sensibilities seem to transfer across professional territories and arts modalities. In fact, just as in conventional practice we hope and anticipate that the shifts and insights experienced by clients in music therapy sessions transfer to their everyday lives, here is an opportunity for core music therapy skills to be useful in broader, and more diluted contexts. These realizations feel immensely liberating: none of us needs to be 'doing' in our modality in order to feel affirmed professionally, either to ourselves or to one another.

This brings me to considering the timing of therapeutic work. Here at *Thembalethu* the notion of time and timing catches me by surprise, and raises the issue of how – and when – we enter into music therapy.

We are seated round four tables that have been brought together. These are piled high with newspaper, bits of fabric, wool, string, scissors, glue, bits of wire, paint, crayons. Each of us is creating a doll, using newspaper to fashion arms and legs, a torso, a head. Pindi, next to me, works noisily, asking me to pass scissors, glue, wire. Next to her, Kirsten stares at the torso of her doll, while next to her Kate and Rose giggle as they wind wool around their dolls' arms and legs. There is a feeling of industry as each of us gets to grips with our doll. Suddenly I remember a song from my Italian childhood, a song about being very small, and the geese being very tall, and there isn't much to be done about this. I tell the women about the song and they ask me to sing it, which I do... And then I ask whether anyone else remembers a song from their childhood: a song their mothers or grandmothers sang to them...there is a long silence, and the level of con-centration on making dolls rises palpably. Someone begins very quietly, humming a beautiful Zulu lullaby. We all know it, and hum the refrain while Thembi sings the next verse. Then at the refrain proper, we harmonize and grow the song together until it fills the room. We are quiet again and hum as Thembi sings, and we begin to clothe our dolls and coax various bits of fabric and string to remain glued.

Remembering a childhood song is one of those random, daydream-type things that happens when we are not 'really' thinking. A song drifts into my mind, out of context, we might think, unless we listen. A song from childhood – my childhood, long ago in another land. Rather like this 'other land' around the table where we sit with strangers, each absorbed in constructing a doll. A child's activity. As I wonder briefly whether I ever did this kind of thing in my own childhood, I quickly realize that this song, or rather its arrival at this moment, is of clinical import. I spontaneously share it with the group, singing it in Italian, and some of the women join in with the refrain 'ma tu sei piccolina, ma tu sei piccolina …' as I sing the song a second time.

As we sing together – more or less – I see that this might be the way that music begins with us, here, at this moment of making dolls. I then invite the women to remember songs of their own childhood, and there is a long silence. I wonder whether this suggestion is appropriate and begin to feel slightly anxious – until I listen, and realize that folk are thinking, recalling. Eventually, someone says something and everyone laughs, and the Zulu lullaby begins. The energy in the group shifts instantly as we join in, humming along and recognizing bits here and there. The song is repeated – several times – and this gives all of us time to become part of it, especially the last bit which has a sudden hand clicking movement where everyone suddenly moves their arms and hands, whilst still holding dolls.

Music has emerged, at first as something that accompanies what we're doing together and individually, with each absorbed in doll-making, and the thoughts that this evokes. There is a concurrence of various roles and tasks: we all remember our personal pasts, we are all professionals learning new skills (doll-making and story-telling) which we hope to use in our professional context, and we are all women singing together.

Unlike in traditional music therapy practice, I am not 'in control' of when to use music, but I also do not abandon my role or my stance as a musician and music therapist. I learn to listen to minutiae both in sounds and in silence, and make sense of these in musical and clinical ways. It is this 'making sense of listening' – as I see it – that is the result of music therapy training and experience. I 'hear' a song in my head approaching, and know to listen to it, in a context that is not music therapy in the conventional sense. I sense how the song might have meaning; I don't have the time to clarify or be conclusive, but have a strong hunch that its timing is significant. I act on this hunch, bringing not just the song, but also its (personal) context out into the open with the group. By doing this, I model how we might all begin to think about, remember, and sing some songs together. Our sharing and participating in past songs collects us all into another way of being together.

Although there are many more aspects to this work at *Thembalethu*, I now conclude this chapter by drawing some themes from this material.

Making sense of Community Music Therapy

The chapter opened with a statement about the fact that the unfamiliar territory in which this work took place felt utterly de-stabilizing on personal, professional, clinical and musical levels. This de-stabilization made me revise almost everything about my accumulated music therapy skills, on the spot. This revision was uncomfortable, and an induction into what, at times, felt like an unkind baptism. After more than 20 years of practice, I felt de-skilled, uncertain of how any of my skills might be useful or appropriate and, even worse, I was uncertain as to how to 'be present' with the *Thembalethu* women.

The paragraph I have just written poses some questions. The first is that in describing the territory as unfamiliar and untraditional, what is left out of this description is: unfamiliar *to whom*? And untraditional *in relation to which tradition(s)*? Here is an issue to do with contexts and cultural relativism that, I suggest, music therapy practice in the twenty-first century needs urgently to address. Of course, from a European or North American perspective, the context for the *Thembalethu* work is exotic, alien, and so very different that we might question its relevance to music therapy work in more conventional contexts, and in the so-called developed world. This would be missing some critical points, and in any case, there are few societies left that are not experiencing the richness – and tensions – of cultural and social diversity.

In the twenty-first century, wherever we practise, we can no longer simply state that music therapy is 'such and such' a practice, described with the help of 'such and such' theories, without addressing a crucial third bit: context. This is my understanding of the distinction between Community Music Therapy and the consensus model. At the same time, I refuse to leave context outside music therapy practice, and I refuse to leave it in third place, after practice and theory. I want to put context right in the middle of music therapy, and not only that, but context needs to define how music therapy happens, and how we think about it. And by context I mean the collective physical, mental and social reality of all *musicking* participants – not just the mental and social and musical reality of the music therapist operating within the consensus model. The latter is arrogant, and no longer viable in these complicated times of acute sensitivities about who and how we – any one of us – constantly define ourselves in terms of cultural and social nuances.

To practise as Community Music Therapists, we first need to understand ourselves as part of the mental, social, physical and musical context in which we work; we need to know directly its meanings and values to do with music and life, and need to re-frame and possible re-shape our skills in response to the immediate reality of the moment.

In *Thembalethu* it was very clear that my usual, conventional music therapy skills were not needed. Luckily for all, I heard this clearly (and at risk of putting myself out of 'work' so to speak). But the risk was worth taking (or this chapter would not have been born) since it became clear that conventional music therapy skills were useful, but in a new way that needed to be negotiated. The first step was to listen (which music therapy training helps us to develop in specific, multi-layered and nuanced ways) to how the women might – or might not – need, want, or request music in a way different from that which they already created as a group. None of the other therapists had this dilemma, since neither art, massage not drama is part of *Thembalethu's* group life, and counselling is a tangible practice and skill, recognized by the women as separate from who they are as persons, and clearly requested. There was no request for music. This was the mental, musical and social context in which this work took place, and which needed to be respected.

I might have ignored this uncomfortable and rather threatening context. I am an experienced music therapist, head of a music therapy training programme: am I not 'supposed to know' what to do? I might have, instead, imposed a persuasive practice of performance. Here, I might quite easily have shifted the group towards making music differently, making different music, or making music more often. This would have made me feel useful, skilful, and would have been splendidly false.

Another revisioning had to do with 'health', 'illness', and with music itself. I have already described aspects of the *Thembalethu* women's singing as generally gospel-style. To my western-trained musical mind, this singing goes on, and on, and on – often with not too much variation in tempo, phrasing, melody or harmony and with slow build-ups of intensity over time. To a musician schooled in European music, this kind of singing quickly becomes repetitive; there is no melodic, rhythmical or harmonic development, and we generally get the gist of the song after about two renderings. By the fifteenth time I cannot help wondering whether all this repetition is really necessary. If I were to be present as an improvisational music therapist who was totally insensitive to the culture and social context, I might begin to muse that by repeating the same thing over and over again the group was avoiding something (e.g. exploring new territory, musical or emotional); or the group was stuck (perhaps as a result of some traumatic memory); the music perseverative and rigid (after all, it seemed to have little flexibility); and finally, the music was not negotiated with the therapist – it was imposed by the group, and was symptomatic of the group 'keeping control' of the session, not allowing a mutuality with the therapist. And so on.

At *Thembalethu* I decided to *not* think just clinically, but also to think culturally and contextually. My thinking became, quite simply, 'What sense can I make of all of this, given that I am a music therapist, and given that I am not pretending *not* to be one? How can what I might be able to offer have meaning in this group situation? How best can I be useful, given what I hear and experience?'

I would like to propose that any of the themes in this chapter have implications for music therapy work anywhere – even in the most established culturally and socially homogenous of places, and in the conventional music therapy contexts of education, health, and urban places. The profession of music therapy is now surrounded by other professions (community musicians, remedial teachers, special music educators, recreational workers), whose skills and territories are not that distant from ours. There have also been changes in state policies to do with care, hospitalization, attitudes to rehabilitation and education. The world is not what it was, or where it was, when music therapy first emerged as a modern discipline. We need to 'read the signs of the times' and re-frame ourselves within contemporary currents, not only to be a relevant and responsible profession, but also to re-gain the creativity and daring that our ancestors possessed abundantly, and used generously.

In this sense, the geographical and cultural setting for this chapter needs to be set aside, so that we can retain the freshness of our questioning as music therapists: who are we, in these contexts, today, and what are we doing here?

CHAPTER 2

From Therapy to Community: Making Music in Neurological Rehabilitation

Stuart Wood, Rachel Verney, Jessica Atkinson

Introduction

This chapter[1] describes a Community Music Therapy project, 'From Therapy to Community', for adults with neurological disabilities in south-east England. It begins by explaining the foundational values of the project, and then illustrates how it worked through three clinical stories: *Donald, The Friday Group,* and *Joy.* The chapter closes with a description of how the project's impact extended from a medical setting into the local arts scene and the wider lives of participants.

A team of three music therapists created and worked on this project: Rachel Verney (project manager and supervisor), Stuart Wood (project therapist), and Jessica Atkinson (project researcher). We had 15 months to run a project which could offer a new kind of music therapy service to 50 people from their time in acute care to intensive rehabilitation, and into their new life in 'the community'.

A need for change?

Perhaps it unnerves music therapists to consider the possibilities for change which exist within the music therapy profession. Traditionally, music therapy in the UK is a confidential activity in which individuals or groups develop a therapeutic music relationship by making music together, usually through improvisation. This work tends to take place within in-patient hospital settings, in specialist services for particular client groups, or, where children are concerned, in

---

1   This chapter draws heavily on *From Therapy to Community*, Jessica Atkinson's (2002) Report to the Speedwell Trust, in which participant and professional feedback from the evaluation are set out in full. We would like to express our gratitude to Professor Scott Glickman, the Speedwell Trust and NIACE.

schools. The music made in sessions is regarded as confidential therapeutic material and is seldom shared with other staff unless it is used in case reviews or presentations.

While in many cases this status quo makes sense, we were dissatisfied with its restrictions. We regretted the lack of opportunity for music therapy clients to pursue their new interest and ability in music once they had left their treatment institution. Often, the outcome of music therapy is as much in musical and social skills as it is in a personal process. We considered it both arbitrary and wasteful for the beneficial effects of music to decline after a conventional course of music therapy.

In neurological rehabilitation, this happens frequently. People living with neurological damage are often vulnerable and marginalised. Their disabilities tend to occur after a stroke, accidental head injury or onset of disease. This sudden loss of normality creates a new orbit of life in which people must adjust to the loss of basic abilities like speech or mobility, cognition, relationships, jobs, hobbies and the many things they enjoyed previously. While the medical profession provides skilled treatment for those in crisis, it lacks funding and infrastructure to address their ongoing needs once discharged back into the community. We had each experienced the frustration of seeing clients benefiting enormously in music therapy, then being cut off from music only because they were being discharged from their medical unit.

'From Therapy To Community': A background

We believed that the beneficial effects of music therapy could be extended past a person's discharge into their long-term recovery. But what form would the changing needs of patients give to our music therapy activities? We began to design a music therapy project which could accommodate these needs. As the needs of participants changed, so would the forms of delivery. A project of this kind would bring us into new music therapy territory, and thus into an interesting dialogue with prevailing music therapy values. Two values were central to the way we conceived and carried out this project. They were our abiding commitment to our music therapy tradition, and a belief in the role of music in creating community.

As music therapists trained in the Nordoff-Robbins approach, our thinking grew directly from the roots of Nordoff-Robbins music therapy in two important ways. First, many clinical stories from Nordoff and Robbins' early writing commented on the relationship between individual music therapy, group music therapy, working groups and performances. These forms would be employed in a variety of ways to enhance a child's therapeutic process. Their original scales of assessment (Nordoff and Robbins 1977) indicated a progression from individual to group work in that the outcome of a successful individual music therapy process was that a child was able to work well as a member of a group. Individual music therapy aimed towards a child attaining 'high levels of musical-social function in group activities, in order to register the successful application of capabilities and skills acquired through individual therapy' (1977, p.179). While the continuum of individual to group therapy was not conceived by Nordoff and Robbins as a rigid model, it seemed to us a natural progression for clients in neurological rehabilitation.

The second connection with our music therapy tradition was through the recognition that gaining skills was one of the natural outcomes of music therapy, and for Nordoff and Robbins formed the basis for each stage of a child's development. Often the skills a child gained in individual music therapy led to participation in a group. For Nordoff and Robbins, working games and performances were part of the music therapeutic process. We also shared a belief in the role of music in creating community, and in the value of what is known in the UK as 'community music'. Atkinson (2002) defines community music as a movement which 'involves specific communities in developing their own music activities and events and often involves performance by the community for the community' (p.7). The term 'community music' includes a diversity of music-making, a rich resource of professionals and an important body of knowledge.

The UK's leading agency for community music, Sound Sense, states in its website (2003):

> Everyone has been moved by music at some point in their lives. It has the ability to communicate, inspire, excite, motivate, and to express a wide range of feelings and experiences. Community music involves musicians working with all types of people to enable them to actively enjoy and participate in music – so this happens with all types of music, anywhere, and with anyone. Making sure that everyone has equal opportunities to participate is important, and so engaging those who can't normally take part whether for social, physical or technical reasons is an important aspect of community music.

There are clear resonances in this literature with the way some music therapists speak. Music therapy and community music each work from the knowledge that music has the power to reach us all. Both disciplines put this knowledge into action by developing specialist skills in order to engage people who perhaps normally cannot participate. Although there is common ground between music therapy and community music, there are differences. While we were excited by the shared belief in universality and by the professional skills involved, we also had to recognise that there are points of tension ideologically between these worlds. Not only is there a level of tacit mistrust, there are challenges from both sides.

Sound Sense write that community music 'happens with all types of music, anywhere, and with anyone'. Community music tends to include rather than exclude, actively searching out both audiences and participants. Its ethos is often to open doors, both to new participants and more literally in concert spaces and workshops. It also responds actively to the changing needs of its groups. Within community music emphasis is placed on participation, with the result that elements of musical practice such as group workshops and performance are highly developed.

Music therapy by contrast has developed a stronger frame, maintaining a higher level of confidentiality and privacy. In music therapy the skills of co-improvisation in an ongoing relationship are more common. It could be argued that music therapy has developed the skills of drawing out responses and developing them into personal growth and change.

While we were aiming to combine the best of music therapy and community music, we were faced with an ideological tension which was more like 'therapy vs community'. Could we build larger workshops and performances into our project without losing the focus on individual change and development so important to our music therapy work? In its diverse forms, we believed that music can be a bridge for patients to reintegrate into the community. Our project would attempt to put these forms into a single programme. In order to acknowledge the values of both music therapy and community music in this process, we named the project 'From Therapy to Community'.

'From Therapy To Community': The three-stage programme

The project followed a three-stage programme of work (Figure 2.1). Participants would start the programme with individual music therapy. When they were ready they would move into small group music therapy sessions, and music workshops. At this stage, local musicians would be invited to run workshops where they would share their particular field of music. In Stage Three, the members of the music therapy group would join a wider community of participants by attending concerts, joining workshops in the local arts venue, or enrolling on college courses. At each stage, participants would feed back on their experiences. If this linear progression was not appropriate, they would be able to join at their own level, and move at their own pace.

With the planning done, the enormity of this plan became clear. In addition to running the project, the setting-up tasks, archiving, evaluation and continual conceptual work seemed mountainous. Throughout the project we held weekly meetings in which we discussed and monitored the work. In these times the tensions and challenges of this new approach were discussed. Whatever our own excitement and curiosity about exploring new territory, the therapeutic path was always paramount. At the centre of our focus remained the individual participant. Three different stories of participants' experiences on the programme will show how our ideas worked in practice. Each is followed by a brief section addressing the main issues raised.

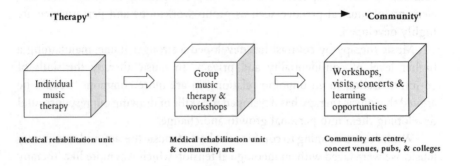

Figure 2.1 The three-stage programme of work

Donald

Donald was 54 when he had his stroke. Formerly a witty, friendly man who had been a keen gardener, he was now unable to speak or use his right side. Even more problematically, the effects of his stroke were complicating relationships with his family. He was dealing with the sudden loss of a social group, and needed to regain his ability to enjoy a life in connection with others. Donald's 'social' needs presented certain challenges. What forms would they take? How would we help Donald piece together a satisfying community again? Would 'From Therapy to Community' live up to its name?

After his music therapy assessment session, it was clear that Donald both needed and preferred to remain in individual music therapy. Through joint improvisation he became able to use his weak right side, organising his body into increasingly strong, steady playing. From his feedback at the end of this stage it was apparent that he had the experience that 'all was not lost' – he did have ability, strength, and the power to create something of his own.

Donald's feedback at this time was given through a profile form which had been designed for the project by his speech therapist. Through picture and gesture he told us how he was finding out more about himself, and about music.

In music therapy he could make something which was his own: 'just for me'. His awareness of music was also expanding, enabling him to make music more confidently, and listen more widely in his own time.

After three sessions he gestured using his communication sheet that he wanted his wife Martha to join the sessions. We thought hard about the implications of this new addition. But we were very aware that Donald was longing to improve relations with his wife. In fact this was a stated rehabilitation aim for him. His multi-disciplinary team felt that there was a chance for Donald to take a step towards his goal of building community by including Martha in his music therapy.

In session four Donald and Martha played music together for the first time in their lives. As they played steady marching music on percussion they smiled at each other. In his first three sessions, Donald had gained enough confidence and skill so that he could support his wife's playing by providing a strong, steady pulse. She was drawn to listen to his contribution, and respond spontaneously in her own way. Their contrasting ways of playing made a complete music when heard together. This sense of belonging, of being complementary, was something they had lost through the effects of Donald's stroke. By gaining command of musical and communication skills Donald was ready to enjoy wider social interaction and group music-making. Martha's feedback revealed her own part in this music therapy process. She said: 'This has made me realise that since the stroke, I have lost my identity. It has made me think about my own needs too.' Martha had not considered herself 'musical' prior to joining the programme. Her participation also allowed her to develop her own identity in music, through the skills of playing and listening.

After eight sessions working as a couple, Donald and Martha chose to go on to the next stage. When they were ready, they joined a music therapy improvisation group. This was made up of participants who had started in individual music therapy, and carers. As they settled into their role in a group, their music-making showed them to be confident, inquisitive musicians. By improvising music, participants offered clear musical portraits of themselves. In a group setting, everyone could hear the individual characters of the group, and respond in their own way. Music was a way into social interaction, and it was the interaction itself. Once the group had found a way of working together, local musicians came in to the rehabilitation unit for workshops in preparation for Stage Three.

Everyone looked forward excitedly to the workshops in Stage Three where they would meet outside the medical setting, in what they considered to be a 'normal' environment. They would be participating in workshops in a local arts centre, where they would be sharing coffee breaks with potters, historians, and actors. Soon, four groups were operating, with a growing presence in the arts centre. We had tailor-made a workshop programme for each group based both on their stated musical preferences, and the new forms of music they had discovered during their earlier work.

For Donald, this phase of work lasted for 14 weeks. In addition to the workshops, the group went out on concert trips. In order for it to be successful, this stage of workshops and trips had to be organised some time in advance. The music therapist therefore had been establishing the participants' preferences and potential from the beginning. We were careful to let the details of the programme be guided by the musical interests, needs and imagination of the participants. The workshops covered are shown in Figure 2.2.

Workshops 1–3	Classical music
Workshops 4–5	Soundbeam
Workshops 6–8	Composing piano music
Workshops 9–11	English folk music
Workshops 12–14	West African music
Workshops 15–16	Samba band
Workshops 17–19	Performing

Figure 2.2 The subjects in Stage Three workshops

Participants created their own pathway through this workshop programme and most attended the entire course.

Through their experiences in individual and group music therapy Donald and Martha were able to participate fully in the workshops and concert trips. This was especially satisfying for them, and they related in their feedback that this was a way in which they could be together socially, in settings which they could contribute to. By now they also had strong musical passions, like jazz drumming, and American folk music, and an ability to pursue these interests. The medical staff who had worked with Donald noticed how he was more outgoing, and said that the inclusion of Martha into the programme had been a vital part of his rehabilitation. They were delighted that music therapy could accommodate his whole life in this way. By participation in the project Donald and Martha took their place as contributors to the music life of their wider community. They had moved from therapy to community.

The way in which Donald's musical community expanded was central to his music therapeutic process. First, he worked solely with the music therapist. Soon this expanded to include his wife, then a small group, then a larger group with workshop leaders and local musicians. Finally, he joined with the local community as an enthusiastic concert-goer and in instrumental tuition. There is no contradiction between the growing social network and the individual rigour of each participant's work. Whatever tensions exist can be overcome by the participant's commitment to musical activity. This commitment is in essence what Nordoff and Robbins (1971) considered the 'central motivating power of music therapy' (p.17).

The Friday Group

Before the Community Music Therapy project started, Fridays were usually quiet. By midway through the project, Friday afternoons were a riot of crashing gongs, booming drums and impromptu gospel singing. For nearly two hours each week the day room would be filled with instruments, and converted from a thoroughfare into a fluid improvisational space where patients, carers, therapy staff and administrators all became participants in the same music. Psychologists could find themselves duetting with stroke patients, managers with care assistants and nurses with visitors.

This group had been set up to provide a time when the diverse people passing through the unit each week could stop and make music together as equals. At the core was a small set of regular members – patients who were involved in other parts of the programme – and staff. Each week this body of musicians would welcome a variety of newcomers to the music-making, whether new inpatients, visitors, students or staff. Our ethos of inclusion invariably attracted new members who were able to tap into the power of music to connect people. Staff members came from across the range of professionals, and included therapists, nursing staff and the chaplain. Initially, their attendance was out of curiosity or support. Many became regular members, valuing the special contact with patients and colleagues that this allowed. The group's music grew into a weekly event, anticipated eagerly. It seemed to embody the shared purpose of the unit, creating a feeling of being a community.

Early on, the group members were: a former GP and a young man with head injuries, an elderly Urdu-speaking gentleman who had suffered a stroke, a lady from Trinidad with MS, the unit's chaplain and a rehabilitation assistant. We learned about each member, including the lives of patients prior to their injuries. Through improvisation they were all able to listen, respond and think as musicians. It was wonderful to observe how the group could accommodate so much – the unexpected outbursts of one, the deep sadness of another, or the occasional awkwardness of staff members. Around the music-making, talk would often turn to how we could improve our shared playing. We developed not only a common style, but also a common set of rules, including how to listen to others, how to 'dive in' to improvising, and when to stop!

The non-staff members of this group were also taking part in other sessions in the week. They brought many of their experiences and ideas from the other groups to enrich and enhance the music we made. Soon participants were deepening their understanding of the improvisations and the concerts or workshops they had attended. Some even brought their compositions from small workshops to the Friday Group for everyone to enjoy.

We were struck by the impact the group made in the unit as a whole. It could hardly be kept secret that this huge body of musicians was meeting in the day room each week. Our sounds permeated, as music does, through walls, out of windows, and down corridors. When therapists came to the group, they could see and hear for themselves how their patients were developing. More importantly, they could share music-making as equal partners with their own patients, with colleagues and strangers.

Staff commented on how the group seemed to bring the 'outside world' into the unit. A senior manager said: 'Music brings a new dimension to the working life of the team by bringing the outside into the unit for the staff – the opposite to what it does for the patients. It loosened the institution up.' This effect of 'loosening' was taken up by others:

> The project allowed people to be around mystery, experienced in music, in
> a way that is not dangerous. This softened a previous brittleness in the unit
> that existed because rehabilitation is about things that are measured, rigid
> and physical, but music is about mystery… Music is a spiritual entity, and
> when you have a musician around, the edges of things get softened.

Crucially, staff members were able to see the therapeutic rigour and effectiveness of music therapy. They trusted the group's structure and format, and celebrated the progress made by their patients. As a part of an accountable music therapy process, the group was in an ideal position to be both clinically effective, and socially uplifting.

As Christmas approached, the group decided to have a party where they could play and sing carols, improvise together, and perform their own compositions. They would invite the whole staff and users of the rehabilitation unit, their own families, and all the participants from the programme. This was to be the final workshop of the programme – performance and celebration as an integral part of therapy. We invited as guests a pair of local musicians who had run our composition and performance workshops. Some members who were having occupational therapy as part of their rehabilitation used their occupational therapy times to make mince pies and decorations for the party. We took time to plan the event as a group, choosing our favourite Christmas songs and practising them, making an order for the party. On the day, people got dressed up, and put effort into being their best, as the final gesture of their time on the programme.

The final Friday Group was, as ever, a riot of sound, colour and movement. We improvised a choral version of *Good King Wenceslas* with solos, harmonies and instruments; a group of participants who had attended a jazz workshop performed their own jazz piece, and our guest musicians performed a beautiful lyrical melody composed by another participant, entitled *Hope for Peace*. The event was an integral part of their therapy experience – a natural conclusion and a time to celebrate their achievements.

While the main focus of the project was to enable individual participants to build communities through their music-making, we could not ignore the need to bring music into the existing community of the rehabilitation unit. This gave rise to the Friday Group. Here music-making could not be secret, nor did it have constant membership. From one perspective we were crossing a number of important boundaries. There were, of course, patients for whom such an open group was not suitable, yet feedback from all sides pointed to its beneficial effects. Patients saw improvement in their rehabilitation, and managers saw improvement in their institution.

Joy

By the end of the 15 months we had learnt that Community Music Therapy had further room to grow. Joy, an elderly vigorous lady recovering from stroke, was to prove that composition, performance and instrumental learning could be important in the Community Music Therapy process.

Joy had joined the programme early on, having begun in individual music therapy. She had two aims: getting movement back into her right hand, and learning the piano. As she progressed, they became one: making good music. This was not without its difficulties, of course. She tended to focus on the physical effects of her stroke, and became frustrated with her body when her hands did not do exactly what she felt she 'had told them'. Would we find a way to let the process of music therapy happen, without worrying about the end product?

At times when she least expected it, Joy would play with such ease of movement that she would laugh out loud with delight. She discovered that when she simply listened to what she was playing, her body was more free. She began to listen to herself less judgementally, enjoying her new musical abilities, and moving on from her obstacles. She described how 'I always feel better after this, even when it's hard for me. I'm amazed that I've become a musician.' Her other therapists noticed that music was becoming a major motivation in her rehabilitation, and a source of hope in her wider life. She took her therapy seriously, and considered it to be central in her adjustment to her new life.

When she moved into a group, Joy was apprehensive about the possible comparisons between her own abilities and those of others. In the emerging structure of group music therapy she realised that it could actually help her join a group of equals again. From a beginning of chaotic, rowdy music, the group started to give all its members a chance to shine, or sometimes take a low profile, and to work together.

Joy could not have imagined that at the Christmas event she would be joining the Friday Group to perform a jazz piano piece she had written herself. Nor could she have predicted that she would recognise and play fluidly a C major or A minor scale with her 'bad hand'. These achievements would have seemed out of reach to her. For most people, notions of practice, composition and performance are inseparable from music. Joy's commitment to her music therapy work took us naturally into some of these areas.

She became able to construct and remember melodies, making great progress in her cognitive skills after her stroke. Her growing abilities to be flexible with her music and co-ordinate her movement gave her enormous confidence. It was natural for her to share these developments with her husband, family and friends. Soon she was playing musical games with her grandchildren, and teaching her friends about the music they heard at concerts. It was with a buzz of nervous delight that Joy completed the programme by performing her jazz piano piece in a room packed with supportive listeners.

From the start, recovery through music had been the impetus behind Joy's involvement in Community Music Therapy. But for the obstacle of funding, we could see no reason why music therapy should not continue to be central in Joy's rehabilitation. Although Joy's time on the programme had ended, it was time for us to start imagining again. By this stage, we had nearly 50 participants on the programme. Some were in small groups and workshops, others were starting on drumming courses, joining choirs, even finding out about 'jamming nights' in local pubs. Joy was keen to carry on with her piano playing, but needed to work without the pressure of an obvious 'end product'. It was clear that one option for someone at this level of personal and musical awareness would be tuition in an instrument. We were keen to nurture the music-making of our participants, but we knew it would be counterproductive to encourage music lessons in complete independence from the specialist support offered by the programme. We needed a Stage Four.

We imagined that in this stage participants would meet tutors for specialist tuition in an instrument, continuing their musical development in association with the main music therapy programme. Tutors would have to be prepared to learn new skills, collaborate with the music therapist and other professionals, and have a good understanding of the needs of people with neurological disability. It was at this point in our thinking that a former concert pianist and piano teacher with a new diagnosis of MS arrived from South America with an offer of assistance. Here was an opportunity for the project to adapt and include the skills of a piano teacher with empathy and insight. Around the same time, a former professional drummer expressed an interest in helping on the programme. Forced into retirement by a stroke, he now had a new chance to teach others to play the drums, from an intimate understanding of the difficulties involved. Stage Four would have to embrace this resource in a way which could safeguard the experience of participants.

In developing a programme of Community Music Therapy which responds to the changing needs of participants, we encountered the great goodwill and common understanding between the related worlds of music learning, composition, performance and therapy. Our meetings, planning and discussions have also brought out the need for a bridge between people who are motivated by a shared love of music and people.

On the surface, there seems to be a need to bridge the 'product' and the 'process' of music-making. In our ongoing weekly discussions we considered this question along with the tension between learning and therapy. The discipline of adult learning does not only focus on the content of what people learn, but also values the changes that happen through the process of learning. Likewise in therapy there is always an end product, whether this is a stated aim or not. It is in the participant's commitment to musical activity that the division between product and process melts.

Conclusion: Towards a Community Music Therapy process

The foundation for this Community Music Therapy project was in our acknowledgement of our own music therapy values, and of the value of music in creating community. It is exciting that in the end, our focus on a progression from individual music therapy into wider spheres of community has in fact bridged these two values with one Community Music Therapy process. What seemed at first to be contradictions between 'therapy' and 'community' are in fact points of tension which are overcome by the continual commitment of participants to their changing musical work.

The impact of Community Music Therapy extends into a number of differing fields, from the medical setting to community arts and learning. Considering this diversity, it was necessary that no confusion existed for participants. We did not wish to create wrong expectations or disappointments for people at a vulnerable time in their lives. In reality, the main feature of the path that participants took in the programme was their commitment to musical activity. Donald's work was in becoming able to be with people on an equal footing again, through playing and listening. The Friday Group accommodated the diversity of the rehabilitation unit, and its many visitors, within the act of improvising music. Joy was able to work past the limiting effects of her stroke to become a composing, performing and learning musician. Like her fellow participants, she did not share our theoretical concerns about learning and therapy. Her pathway was one of music-making.

In order to facilitate a single pathway of music-making we felt it was necessary to use parts of a new music therapy language that could allow the integrity and specialism of music therapy to remain intact, but would also be meaningful to the many other professionals involved. In this project, the people attending music therapy were not 'patients' of a medical institution, 'clients' in a rehabilitation therapy, or 'students' on a further learning course. They in fact moved between these stages, mostly in progression from one to another. We had to acknowledge the fluidity of the client's identity as a music-maker, and as a result thought of our people as 'participants' in a diverse Community Music Therapy programme.

Could we really offer participants common skills through such a wide music therapy service? What was the essence of the process? Perhaps it was the connective power of music. While neurological impairment hampers connections, both within a person and between people, music by contrast makes connections. In individual music therapy we were working to help participants regain control of their bodies, their communicative abilities, and to discover the potential of their new identities. These skills could be used in a wider sense as participants made links not only with the music therapist but with their families, and with new communities.

Musical improvisation puts people in a unique kind of contact with each other, one which does not rely on body language, verbal language or social status. In those moments where such barriers come down, and social roles change, we experience what Ruud (1998) calls *communitas*. Citing anthropologist Victor Turner, he describes communitas as 'an intense comradeship in which …distinctions disappear or become irrelevant'. He suggests that this state is common during music-making, particularly improvisation:

> improvisations in music therapy seek to build a community ('communitas')
> through a temporary leveling-out of all social roles. During improvisation,
> all traditional expectations regarding the role of therapist do not apply:
> music therapists try to build a spontaneous, immediate community...
> (Ruud 1998 pp.131-2)

A concept of communitas was useful for providing a single value for what was an
increasingly diverse programme of work. Our project did not have to prescribe
the forms in which musical community could be experienced. Instead, it could
focus on nurturing the connections which arise when people make music
together and with a music therapist. The power of music to connect people has
an impact which can extend far into a participant's life, like ripples in a pond.
Figure 2.3 shows the widening 'ripple effect' of connection made possible by
Community Music Therapy.

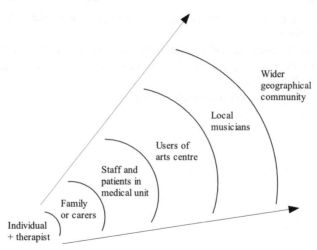

Figure 2.3 The 'ripple effect' of 'From Therapy to Community'

Individual music therapy brought participants out of isolation into relationship
with the music therapist – the starting point for building 'community'. This also
enabled them to gain a new control over physical and cognitive abilities, leading
to a new sense of identity and self-knowledge. As individual participants they
could join with the therapist to practise being with others again. On the introduction of carers or family members into the process they began to widen their
sphere of community. Together, they moved on to use their skills with others
within the medical unit.

Participants were also coming into musical contact with professionals and friends with whom they could share their new-found confidence and skill. In turn this extended beyond the medical treatment setting into the local music venues and arts centres where they attended music workshops, and recitals. At last the participants had reached a stage where they could be contributing members within a community of musicians and concert-goers, in their own town and out into the wider geographical area. Few people come to neurological rehabilitation as islands. They arrive as spouses, parents, children or friends of someone. Their former lives were as communal people. We were proud that music could bring them back into community, and build it into their future.

References

Atkinson, J. (2002) *From Therapy to Community.* Report to the Speedwell Trust. (Unpublished).

Nordoff, P. and Robbins, C. (1971) *Therapy in Music for Handicapped Children.* London: Victor Gollancz.

Nordoff, P. and Robbins, C. (1977) *Creative Music Therapy.* New York: John Day.

Ruud, E. (1998) *Music Therapy: Improvisation, Communication, and Culture.* Gilsum, NH: Barcelona Publishers.

Sound Sense (2003) http://www.soundsense.org

PART II

What has Theory got to do with it?

CHAPTER 3

Rethinking Music and Community: Theoretical Perspectives in Support of Community Music Therapy

Gary Ansdell

Introduction

In support of its traditional focus on cultivating intimate musical companionship, music therapy has utilised two discourses – on *music* and on *therapy*. Community Music Therapy's gentle revolution has been motivated by the realization that a third support is needed – a discourse on *community*, standing also for how music is a social and cultural phenomenon, and how it creates and sustains musical community.

In this chapter I explore this third theoretical 'support' and the possible relationships between music and community. The current elaboration of Community Music Therapy is timely, given the newly available and interconnecting body of thinking (and rethinking) in the areas of music and its relationship to socio-cultural life. This may help support and illuminate what many music therapists are currently doing, thinking and experiencing.

I outline aspects of this newer thinking on music from musicology and related disciplines, and then on 'community', and also review how music therapists are beginning to use these ideas in describing and understanding their work (whether they call it 'Community Music Therapy' or not). I aim to give an overview rather than a comprehensive account – as a guide to further reading and exploration. Not all of this material is new *per se*, though it may be newer to the discourse of music therapy.

Music

Music is not a thing at all but an activity, something that people do.

Christopher Small

Rethinking Music

'Music may be what we think it is; it may not be...' writes Philip Bohlman in a recent book called *Rethinking Music* (Cook and Everist 1999), in which musicologists explore new perspectives on what music is, and how we talk about it. Bohlman continues his chapter 'Ontologies of Music':

> Music may be feeling or sensuality, but it may also have nothing to do with emotion or physical sensation. Music may be that to which some dance and pray and make love; but it's not necessarily the case. In some cultures there are complex categories for thinking about music; in others there seems to be no need whatsoever to contemplate music. What music is remains open to question at all times and in all places. (Bohlman in Cook and Everist 1999)

Within academia this 'rethinking' of music has been variously called 'new musicology', 'critical musicology', 'theoretically informed musicology' or simply 'current musicology' (Cook 1998; Cook and Everist 1999; Williams 2001). Musicology has become a reflexive discipline – conscious of its stance, history, values and methods. It is exploring new practices and repertoires, witnessing new situations and asking new questions.

As musicologists[1] have studied a broader range of 'other' musics and musicians (ethnic, popular, commercial, applied) they have realised that 'music' has to be understood within (and not despite) its cultural context and its use(s). As Alastair Williams writes: 'The study of music as culture is a good description of the recent shifts that have taken place in musicology as a whole' (2001). This shift in traditional musicology has come from musicologists finally rubbing shoulders with ethnomusicologists (who study the musics of others) and with critical theorists from other humanistic disciplines such as cultural studies, anthropology and sociology, who are interested in social uses of music (including music therapy). Another input has come from cutting-edge interfaces between the social and biological sciences. The rethinking of music reflects the

---

1   By 'musicologist' in this chapter I mean anyone reflecting seriously about music – which will include a variety of distinct (but increasingly overlapping) professional identities: musicologists, ethnomusicologists, music psychologists, sociologists of music, social psychologists of music, biologists of music, ethnographers, etc. (see also Ansdell 2001).

culturalist, ethnographic, sociological and anti-essentialist emphases in many other contemporary academic and practical disciplines.

From all of these varied sources, new and different questions have become part of what musicologists think about, such as:

- Is music an object (a text) or an act?

- Is it a process or a product?

- Is it 'autonomous' of people, society and culture, or a product of them?

- What does music mean? Why do we have it?

If I could express this paradigm shift in one statement it would be: music is more than *notes*. The old musicology was constructed around the ideology of 'musical autonomy' ('music itself'), which was supported by a structuralist methodology that understood music's meaning to be somehow contained within its structure. To study music was therefore to analyse in an objective way musical 'text objects' which you took from what Lydia Goehr (1992) calls the 'imaginary museum of musical works'. In contrast to this, the 'new musicology' has shifted its attention from 'music as object' to *musicing*[2] as a social and cultural event: from something abstract, unworldly, to something very worldly. Within this newer thinking the meaning of music is a lived experience happening within social and cultural contexts. You therefore need to study it by being within-and-amongst the 'musicers' and within their social and cultural context.

This new perspective has questioned the very idea that there's something which is the 'music itself'. It suggests that it is as vital to study the discourses and practices that surround and construct music as it is to study the immanent structures and forms of a score (Cook 1998). If you *do* study musical texts then they are seen as much as a recipe (instructions) for a musical event such as a performance, as an abstracted text to be deciphered or hallowed for its formal beauty.

A summary of the shift of thinking between the so-called 'old' and 'new' musicology might involve the following statements:

- 'Music' is not an autonomous object – it is embedded in socio-cultural process.

---

2   The term 'musicing' will be discussed later in this section. It is important to note here that, although 'music as process' is not a new conception, its clinching in the word 'musicing' allows a shift in discourse about music – something new in everyday music-talk.

- Music is not a universal (or natural) phenomenon – it is a cultural phenomenon and lives in and through locally-defined contexts.

- Music's meanings are seldom 'immanent' within it – they are socially and culturally constructed.

- Musicing is not just a mental phenomenon – it happens within and between bodies.

- Music is not just a notated artefact – its basic reality is lived performance.

- Music does not just express emotion and meaning – it enacts and constructs them.

- Music's expressive forms are as crucial as its structures.

- Music is seldom just a private pleasure – it is always already a social participation.

- Musicing can both reproduce the legacy of another and allow the performance of the self.

Music is not found but *made* – in human, social and politically interactive contexts. But this view sometimes feels strange because of the tradition of thinking about music many of us have inherited from music education. As Nicholas Cook explains:

> Music somehow seems to be natural, to exist as something apart – and yet it is suffused with human values, with our sense of what is good or bad, right or wrong. Music doesn't just happen, it is what we make it, and what we make of it. People think through music, decide who they are through it, express themselves through it. (Cook 1998, p.vi)

A new map of music

As Cook's words may suggest, this newer understanding of music adds in useful territory to the conceptual 'map' that music therapists can use when looking at how music functions in their work at social and cultural levels – as well as at the more traditional physiological and psychological ones.

In the following sections I will expand on the statements made in the previous section by reviewing some of the material from the 'new musicology' and other disciplines concerned with:

- *musicality* as a core human capacity to respond to, and to make, music – involving social and cultural implications for individuals and communities

- *musicing* as the deployment of musicality through musicianship-in-action – leading to activities and events which attract participation and create relationships.

Because the rethinking I describe in this chapter is of the whole concept 'music', you will find some ambiguity in the following sections concerning this word. You may also be irritated by the invented terms 'musicing',[3] 'musicers', etc. The point, however, is to challenge conventional thinking. Assume therefore that inverted commas are always implicit around the word 'music'.

Musicality as core human capacity

The notion of there being a 'core musicality' in humans has been standard for some time, both to music therapists and to anthropologists such as John Blacking (1973). There is now, however, a new convergence of specialists bridging the biological, psychological and socio-cultural areas who are interested in what makes humans musical, and how this capacity is formed, works and is used.

Colwyn Trevarthen and colleagues have given empirical demonstration of a basic 'communicative musicality' through studying early interaction between infants and carers (Trevarthen and Malloch 2000; Trevarthen 2002, 2003; Ansdell and Pavlicevic, in press). This body of theory has increasingly emphasised the connections between such core human musicality and social companionship and cultural learning. Music has shown itself to be more than the icing on the evolutionary cake that biological reductionists such as Pinker (1997) have suggested. It appears instead that we are 'primed' for musicing from infants upwards, as Ellen Dissanayake's work (1995, 2001) has confirmed from an ethological perspective. The unique communicative functions of musicing have survival value, and many of its features can be understood in terms of their social and cultural functions (DeNora 2000).

Related to this is the growing literature from cognitive neuro-science on the mechanisms of musical communication. Cognitive scientist and jazz musician William Benzon (2001) suggests that the brain and music have evolved together, and that *musicking*[4] continues to play the role it had in humankind's beginning: 'the forge in which the new forms of social being emerge' (p.238).

---

3   I shall use David Elliott's (1995) term 'musicing' rather than Christopher Small's (1998) rather more archaic-looking 'musicking'. Both of their concepts are outlined below.

4   His term – but acknowledged as being borrowed from Small's (1998) book *Musicking*.

Benzon's neurodynamic model suggests that *musicking* simultaneously creates a favourable coupling of the nervous system within us, and at the same time it creates an interactive coupling between *musicking* people which has a neurological base to it. 'We sing and dance, therefore we are a community,' he writes. What is unusual in Benzon's thinking is that his model includes both a neurobiological and a cultural level – he emphasises the need to think about music both as something happening inside our heads, also between our social selves, and in our complex musical cultures.

This trend for broader thinking is also a feature of the latest thinking within music psychology. Recently, this area has adopted a frame which includes the cultural and contextual aspects of musical behaviour (Clarke 2003; Davidson, Chapter 5 this volume). This 'new' social psychology of music is, like many of the other disciplines mentioned here, seemingly converging on an 'ecological' view – where the meanings, functions and contexts of music and musicing are beginning to be understood together.

Musicing as musicality-in-action

Christopher Small's (1998) now famous definition of *musicking* also arose from his rethinking of some very traditional questions about music: *What is the meaning of music?* and *What is the function of music in human life?* Why, he asked himself, was he unable to get satisfactory answers?

> It is easy to understand why. Those are the wrong questions to ask. There is no such thing as music. Music is not a thing at all but an activity, something that people do. (Small 1998, p.2)

Although hardly a new concept in ethnomusicological or sociological circles, coining the word *musicking* has nevertheless accelerated thinking about music as something more action-oriented, more about process and context. Small's definition of 'musicking' is intentionally provocative:

> To music is to take part, in any capacity, in a musical performance, whether by performing, by listening, by rehearsing or practicing, by providing material for performance (what is called composing), or by dancing. (Small 1998, p.9)

This leads to the equally provocative statement: 'Performance does not exist to present musical works, but rather, musical works exist in order to give performers something to perform' (p.8). Small's concept turns on its head traditional musicological concerns, placing the main emphasis not on 'music' but on the 'musicer': 'What are human beings that they should like to practice musicking?' he asks.

The rest of Small's book gives a 'thick description' of a classical concert, peeling away its layers of contextual, social and cultural meaning. At root, he argues, *musicking is about the creation and performance of relationships* – amongst people and things within contexts. The relationships between the tones 'inside' music are only one part of the story. Musicking allows us to explore, affirm and celebrate our diverse real and symbolic human relationships. 'It is the relationships that it brings into existence in which the meaning of a musical performance lies' (p.193). Musicking is thus a type of ritual situation, enacting ideal relationships which then become the foundation of community:

> Such ideas held in common about how people ought to relate to one another, of course, define a community, so rituals are used both as an act of affirmation of community ('This is who we are'), as an act of exploration (to try on identities to see who we think we are) and as an act of celebration (to rejoice in the knowledge of an identity not only possessed but also shared with others). (Small 1998, p.94)

Another musicologist, David Elliott, independently developed the concept *musicing* in his book *Music Matters* (1995), which presents a critique of music education philosophy based on the assumptions and values of traditional musicology. Elliott outlines instead what he calls a *praxial* philosophy of music based on the idea of musicing as 'musicianship-in-action'. For him musicing is a form of musical knowledge (or 'knowing' – a 'know-how') which helps us develop our self and our society. 'In this praxial view', writes Elliott, 'music-making is inherently valuable...for the doing itself, meaning "for the sake of the self"' (p.121).

Elliott's 'conversion' to this way of thinking about music is interesting. He told me how it was partly motivated by trying to match his own passion and interest in jazz to traditional musicological approaches, and partly through dialogue with his squash partner, the well-known ethnomusicologist Timothy Rice. Like many music therapists, Elliott realised that if thinking and practice felt so badly matched, then something was wrong somewhere!

Musicing in everyday social and cultural life

Anthropology and sociology have influenced this newer thinking in music by showing how music takes on meanings within social and cultural frames. For example, Timothy Rice (2001) suggests, from his experience of musicing with a family of Bulgarian musicians, how music is given contextual meanings by the way we frame it with various metaphors. Indigenous musicers may not explicitly talk about their music in these ways, but an ethnomusicologist can tease them out. Rice suggests the following metaphors, as just a start to the possibilities:

- 'music as text' – where it is an artefact to be preserved and analysed

- 'music as humanly organized sound' – where it is as an activity to be performed and witnessed in a specific context

- 'music as emotional or social expression' – where it is a behaviour that needs to be interpreted and understood.

For Rice a key characteristic of music is its surfeit of meanings, and how such meanings can only be fully understood within their social and cultural contexts.

There is a strong family resemblance between this ethnographic perspective and another important strand of the rethinking of music. This is the sociology of music and the 'new' social psychology of music. What these varying perspectives have in common is an interest in music in relation to social being, where music is seen as a 'sounded way of life' as Peter Martin (1995) puts it. They attempt to link musicality and musicing to social and cultural practices.

The best example of recent work in this area is Tia DeNora's influential book *Music in Everyday Life* (2000).[5] In this she gives a vibrant and convincing sociological reading of musicing, attempting to explore the basic question: How does music get into social life?

In contrast to the 'older' sociology of music such as Adorno's, with its grand theorising about music as a representation of social structures, DeNora explores the 'everyday life' of music and musicing. She examines what is behind the seemingly ubiquitous 'power of music'. DeNora begins from the fact that people use music in a variety of contexts for different reasons. But whilst music is clearly socially and culturally mediated, it also seems to possess certain qualities and 'powers' that allow personal and social things to happen. How?

> Does music make people do things? Is it like a physical force or a drug? Will it affect all its recipients in similar ways? Is it possible, not only to document music's effects, but to begin to explain how music comes to achieve these effects? (DeNora 2000, p.19)

DeNora investigates through ethnographically-oriented case studies the mechanisms through which the cultural material of music gets into social-psychological life. One study explores how Lucy, a middle-aged woman, uses listening to Schubert as part of her 'care of the self'. Another study looks at how people construct a musical environment (and by implication a

---

5   See also DeNora (2001), a shorter paper which concentrates on music and emotion in which she summarises her theory: 'In short, music is a resource for the practical constitution of the entities we know as "selves" and also for emotions and states that we refer to as "intersubjective"' (p.176).

social-psychological one) as a background for 'intimate behaviour'. Then there is a study of a music therapy session with a learning-disabled client, one of music use within neonatal care, a karaoke evening, women using music in an aerobics class, music and shopping behaviour. In all of these DeNora does not stop at observing music use, but develops a theoretical perspective based on sociological theory to ask *why* and *how* this phenomenon, music, actually works in these contexts:

> music has power. It is implicated in every dimension of social agency... In all of these examples music is in dynamic relation to social life, helping to invoke, stabilize and change the parameters of agency, collective and individual [...] Music is a resource – it provides affordances – for world-building. (De Nora 2000, pp.20 and 40)

One of the important theoretical tools built up through the book's examples is a two-fold process of *musical affordances* and *musical appropriations*. Musical affordances are the resources music and its materials provide – of moods, messages, energy levels, actions – which rest on the unique properties of music but which are constituted uniquely within situations of use. The important thing to understand about an 'affordance', however, is that it does not just mean that music has certain abstract qualities – say, slowness and mellowness. Rather, an affordance stands in relation to a possible use by somebody. For example, a flat surface affords standing on, or slow music can be used to calm yourself down. An 'appropriation' then becomes how an affordance is *used*. So musical appropriations are the unique 'takings' and 'usings' of music for 'the constitution of human agency, the being, feeling, moving and doing of social life' (p.45).

For example, in her study of an aerobics class music is neither just a background to the excercising, nor is it just a stimulus that 'makes' the exercisers do things. Rather, the music has to be actively appropriated by the women: 'Music here is a medium of decribing 'how' – how to move, how to think, how to include, how to begin, how to end, how to mingle' (p.92).

DeNora's central suggestion is that music does not have power in and of itself – it offers its power only by virtue of how it is taken and used. Here DeNora is in agreement with Nicholas Cook and the new musicologists in the view that music is a cultural and social, rather than a metaphysical or natural force.[6]

---

6   For a further useful discussion of 'musical affordances' from a psychology of music perspective see Clarke (2003).

The importance of DeNora's work in the rethinking of music is that it gives attention to the nuts and bolts of the mechanisms of *how* music affects people, in a way which also includes social and cultural factors. Music, she argues, is essential to the maintenance of personal and social being: '[it] is much more than a decorative art; it is a powerful medium of social order' (p.163). She also acknowledges that for many people music has an existential domain where there is a 'passing over into music'. Here:

> music's recipients may not become the music *per se*, but they become music filtered through themselves – and it is this that should be meant by the concept of music's powers to mediate and to inform. (p.161)

Music as an ecology

Earlier I talked of a 'new map' of thinking about music. We have looked at three major territories on this new map: a new sensitivity to *musicality* (and to Trevarthen's suggestion of an innately 'communicative musicality') with its bio-psycho-socio-cultural determinants; the concept of *musicing* as musicali-ty-in-action and the creation and performance of relationships; and *musicing-in-context* – where musical affordances and musical appropriations within social and cultural contexts create musical experiences. This map may only be half-drawn as yet – but its landscape is perhaps richer than ever before. A way to perhaps summarise this map would be to characterise music as an *ecology*.

Joseph Kerman, the musicologist who threw down the gauntlet to tradi-tional musicology in the early 1980s, and is seen as the father of the 'new musi-cology', wrote in his book *Contemplating Music*: '…by removing the bare score from its context in order to examine it as an autonomous organism, the analyst removes that organism from the ecology that sustains it' (Kerman 1985, p.43). Several people have subsequently suggested that we should consider music as an ecology. I wrote in an earlier article on the relationship between musicology and music therapy:

> I would like to suggest a change of metaphor for music itself (and hence for music therapy) – one that sees music as an *ecology* rather than a *structure*. An ecology is a balance of interlinking forms and processes in a context that sustains them and guarantees diversity. (Ansdell 1997, p.43)

'Music' in Community Music Therapy

Nicholas Cook (1998), one of the foremost popularisers of the 'new musicol-ogy', links music therapy with the idea of music being a medium for negotiation across cultural barriers. However, in his recent historical analysis of music therapy, Peregrine Horden (2000) comments that in accounts of contemporary music therapy 'the social dimension is relatively neglected'. Some contemporary music therapists agree with Horden. As I have argued elsewhere (Ansdell 1997, 2001) the second generation of music therapy has indeed underused recent theory from musicology and the social psychology of music, which would address this lack.

There have, however, been honourable exceptions to this. Even Ruud (1998) pioneered a socio-cultural orientation to music therapy a generation ago, followed now by Brynjulf Stige's systematic work (2002, 2003). Some key contributions to this active fitting of musicological theory to perspectives of music therapy include the following.[7] The list is not comprehensive but aims to show some main currents:

- Lee (1992, 1996) pioneers the reintroduction of musicological discourse into music therapy theory.

- Pavlicevic (1997) and Robarts (1996) link the psychobiological work on 'core musicality' by Trevarthen and others to music therapy.

- Bunt and Pavlicevic (2002) link protomusicality theory to the question of emotion in music therapy.

- Ruud (1998), Stige (2002), Ansdell and Pavlicevic (forthcoming) question or broaden the psychobiological link from a more socio-cultural perspective.

- Ansdell (1997, 2001), Ruud (1998) and Stige (1999, 2002, 2003) address critical issues to do with rethinking the modelling of music in music therapy, and link aspects of the 'new musicology' and 'new' social psychology of music to music therapy.

- Aigen (2001, 2002) links musicological theory on idiom, communication and cultural identity within music therapy improvisations.

This is not to suggest that the emerging thinking of Community Music Therapy has uncritically absorbed all that the 'new' musicology and 'new' social psychology of music has to offer. What is genuinely new in the music therapy field in the last few years is the arrival of a systematic 'critical' or metatheoretical perspec-

---

7   These references exclude the important contributions of the current volume.

tive on music therapy – exploring and evaluating how theory has been used in the construction of the discipline, profession and traditions of practice.

Music therapy is clearly now ready to appropriate the newer thinking on music and musicing – all of which fits well with the basic agenda of Community Music Therapy: to musicalise the community.

I turn now to recent thinking and rethinking about 'community', and how music therapists are explicitly linking music and community within the emerging discourse of Community Music Therapy.

Community

> Community is where community happens.
>
> *Martin Buber*

Rethinking community

Thinking about *community* leads to an almost immediate sense that you may be talking about something which exists only in people's minds. Unlike the discussion of music in the previous section, *community* is intangible, often more of a hope than a reality, often part of political spin or academic hype. 'One of the most elusive and vague [terms] in sociology, now largely without meaning' is how one reference book puts it (Abercrombie, Hill and Turner 1984).

But the questions remain… Is there any such *thing* as community now? Or is it just a feel-good utopian discourse, the 'warm circle' of a contemporary paradise lost? Is it perhaps no more than the rich person's escape route from what the sociologist Zygmunt Bauman (2001) calls 'liquid modernity'? Or perhaps a euphemistic way of referring to the ghettos of the urban poor? Some say that we have only begun to talk about community as it has actually vanished. *The Guardian* newspaper, June 29 2002, featured 'community' recently in its 'words to be banned' column!

It is necessary to think about community in relation to *individuality* – or, to put it another way, in the relationship between self and society (Bauman 2001, 2003; Boyce-Tillman 2000). They seem to evoke and define each other, perhaps even contain each other.

Consequently, in this section I outline some of the thinking (and rethinking) about community from both 'sides' of this situation, at how individuality and community define and mirror each other. I conclude by asking how current community discourse links to emerging formulations of Community Music Therapy.

Varieties of community

First we need to make a distinction between *community* and *society*. Community is a shared or common life and understanding, 'the locus of ultimate personal fulfilment: communion, fellowship, mutuality and intimacy' (Kirkpatrick 2001). Society is 'the locus for the impersonal distribution of power among large groups of people for attaining political and economic ends according to principles of justice' (Kirkpatrick 2001).

Although identified as a core and founding concept of sociology, the concept of community has resisted standard definition – even though one stalwart sociologist, George Hillery, unsuccessfully analysed 94 examples in the hope of establishing one (Marshall 1998). In *Keywords* (1976) Raymond Williams highlights the associations of immediacy, locality and mutual obligation in the term community. He writes of the 'local, face-to-face' quality of 'certain kinds of direct and directly responsible relationships' characteristic of community. This links to anthropological definitions that characterise community as a social group not exclusively based on kinship, but instead built by co-residence and everyday interaction. 'Communities command an identification and allegiance that is rooted in the shared history and shared experience of its members' (Monaghan and Just 2000).

The varying conceptions of community could be simplified as:

- *communities of place*: self-contained geographical communities of traditional and pre-industrial societies – and later urban religious/ethnic communities of association

- *communities of hope*: utopian communities of spirit or justice (religious, hippy, utopian, etc.) pursuing common ideals

- *communities of interest*: based on identity politics (black/gay/women) or shared craft. Technology has now made 'virtual communities' possible, globally linking people who have things in common.

All three, however, connote some sense of belonging and mutuality. I will add a further to these: communities of circumstance: 'circumstantial communities' occur when people live together in a hospital or institution by force of the circumstance of their illness or socially imposed sanctions.

Community as a value-symbol

The sociologist Zygmunt Bauman has recently written a book entitled *Community*, which emphasises how 'community-talk' functions as a feel-good symbolism in today's society: '…whatever the word "community" may mean, it is good "to have a community", "to be in a community" […] Community, we feel,

is always a good thing' (Bauman 2001, p.1). It has evocative associations; of the
French communes of the 1870s, of communism itself, but also of rural idylls and
1960s/70s community living and community arts movements. All these have
imprinted the community discourse with a positive value system. This could be
summed up in what the German philosopher Martin Heidegger called 'homeli-
ness' (Monaghan and Just 2000, p.101).

In contrast to this utopian trend, however, has come a recent backlash, a
reaction to the way politicians have used a discourse of community in euphemistic ways. In the UK we have had 'community care' for the mentally ill, 'community policing' for 'difficult' urban areas and – most recently – 'community care
orders' to retain psychiatric patients for the 'safety' of 'the community'.
Zygmunt Bauman (2001) refers to the 'paradox of community' – the price paid
in individual freedom for the hoped-for 'warm circle' of community.

It will be clear by now that community has always been more of an idea
than a reality. In the following section I sketch some of the influential theories of
community that continue to influence our way of thinking about it.

Four theories of community

Making a theory of community was a core idea at the root of the discipline of
sociology (Marshall 1998), stemming from late nineteenth century anxieties
about its loss. The four theories which follow show an interesting line of mutual
influence:

TÖNNIES' GEMEINSCHAFT/GESELLSCHAFT

The so-called founder of 'community theory', the German sociologist
Ferdinand Tönnies (1855–1936) made a key distinction between *Gemeinschaft*,
a community of spirit based on authentic ties and *Gesellschaft*, an artificial social
arrangement leading to individualism (Abercrombie *et al.* 1984). Tönnies articulated the loss of community and the rise of individualism characteristic of
much twentieth century theory.

BUBER'S 'COMMUNITY'

Tönnies' formulation is close to the philosopher-theologian and social theorist
Martin Buber's more spiritual social vision of the relationship between individual and community, as set out in *Between Man and Man* (1947). Here, as usual,
Buber's solution to the seeming dilemma is to look for that which is 'between'
the equally undesirable poles of 'individualism' and 'collectivism'. Man is
neither a gorilla nor a termite, he writes. Instead, he must look to the 'life of
dialogue' which is the 'between' of this polarity. Here:

community, growing community (which is all we have known so far) is the being no longer side by side but with one another of a multitude of persons. And this multitude, though it also moves towards one goal, yet experiences everywhere a turning to, a dynamic facing of the other, a flowing from I to Thou. Community is where community happens. (1947, p.37)

TURNER'S COMMUNITAS

Buber's work influenced many, including the anthropologist Victor Turner, who developed the concept of *communitas* to characterise a mode of being that is characteristic of those in liminal or 'outsider' situations – consisting of closeness and mutuality, immediacy and presence (and opposed to conventional social structuring of roles and behaviour): '...communitas [is] a relationship between persons, an I–Thou relationship in Buber's terms or a We, the very essence of which is its immediacy and spontaneity' (Turner 1974).

As with Tönnies' earlier distinction, there is something communitas stands over and against: life as structure. But it is also an achieved state, part of a cultural process, using cultural artefacts. Communitas is a way of being-together that functions to regenerate a group or institution. Turner describes it as an 'oxygenisation' of social structure. It addresses and describes situations of being-inside, being-outside, being-together.

All three of these theories of community emphasise a move in thinking from community as a place or fixed entity, to community as a state, mode or process – to *communing*. They share the belief that, as with Buber's *I–Thou* relation, community cannot be willed, but comes from the grace of the moment. These theories are also unapologetically utopian.

As the shadows of the twentieth century lengthened, however, another (counter)-discourse of community emerges. This critique questions the risks and price of community as seen from the perspective of individualism: 'Identity sprouts on the graveyard of communities' as Bauman (2001, p.16) comments.

DERRIDA'S 'HOSPITALITY'

A combination of resistance to utopian theories and the new thinking of post-modern and post-colonial theorists have offered deconstructive challenges to the romantic politics of community discourse. The philosopher Jacques Derrida dislikes the rhetoric of community and states:

I don't much like the word community, I am not even sure I like the thing. If by community one implies, as is often the case, a harmonious group, consensus, and fundamental agreement beneath the phenomena of discord or war, then I don't believe in it very much and I sense in it as much threat as promise. (Derrida in Caputo 1997, p.107)

Derrida wants us to be on guard against the self-protective closure of community, the exclusion of the other. He pursues an alternative etymology of 'community':

> to have a *communio* is to be fortified on all sides, to build a 'common' (*com*) 'defense' (*munis*), as when a wall is put around the city to keep the stranger or the foreigner out. (Derrida in Caputo 1997, p.108)

Instead of community, Derrida prefers to talk of *hospitality*, the welcoming of the other. 'In hospitality I must welcome the other while retaining mastery of the house; just so, the community must retain its identity, while making the stranger at home' (p.113). Derrida looks for something porous, open-ended, a community without defence; for 'an *open* quasi-community', 'a community without unity'.

Individuality in relation to community

I now want to start from the other side of the situation: looking at thinking which explores the relationship between individuality and community in contemporary society. For, as Jock Young has remarked: 'Just as community collapses, identity is invented' (in Bauman 2001). This takes us into classic sociological questions such as: What comes first: self or society? Are we formed inside to outside, or outside to inside? What role does culture have in who we are? Where do we find our 'self' today?

The sociologist Anthony Giddens (2002) gives a convincing account of the late-modern 'turn to the self'. He explains how we find ourselves (in most of the West, in much of 'the Rest') in what he calls a 'detraditionalising society'. We live in the push-and-pull of two conflicts: between freedom and compulsiveness, and between cosmopolitanism and fundamentalism. The archetype of modernity is the 'reflexive self', the self-in-construction, acting autonomously: 'I did it my way.' At the same time we are also anxiously pursuing 'relationship' and 'community', using addiction as a parody of tradition. Giddens suggests the idea of 'therapy' is a key clue to this contemporary situation:

> As the influence of tradition and custom shrink on a world-wide level, the very basis of our self-identity – our sense of self – changes. In more traditional situations, our sense of self is sustained largely through the stability of the social positions of individuals in the community. Where tradition lapses, and lifestyle choice prevails, the self isn't exempt. Self-identity has to be created and re-created on a more active basis than before. This

explains why therapy has become so popular in Western countries. When he initiated modern psychoanalysis, Freud thought that he was establishing a scientific treatment for neurosis. What he was in effect doing was constructing a method for the renewal of the self-identity, in the early stages of a detraditionalising culture. (Giddens 2002, p.47)

At the same time a constant in twentieth century thinking in the humanities has been to question the idea of the self-contained individual, the autonomous 'core self'. Indeed as Billington, Hockey and Strawbridge (1998) suggest, the Western academic splitting of psychology and sociology itself reflects the 'self/society' split. With this has come an academic (but also an experienced) division between active, creative self-shaping and passive, social determinism (Elliott 2001). Put another way there are two directions for the self: inside>out, where selfhood is seen as 'personally created, interpretively elaborated and interpersonally constructed'; but also outside>in, where this very selfhood/ identity is constructed from social structures and cultural materials – self as *lifestyle*.

Identity – and the self-concern of the reflexive self – become, as Bauman comments, 'a surrogate of community', the 'warm circle' turned into a rather small, individual circle of safe self, concerned with a therapeutic 'care of the self'. The quintessential contemporary pathologies are not the hysterias of Freud's day but 'narcissisistic pathologies' (Lasch in Elliott 2001). We have arrived at a society where, as Zygmunt Bauman comments, we are 'called to seek biographical solutions to systemic contradictions' (2001, p.144).

An alternative to the anxious, self-creating self is to look at the individuality/community relationship in another way. Anthropological and cultural-comparative studies have been highly influential in changing our views about what a self is, and what a self/society relationship is. A well-known passage by the anthropologist Clifford Geertz explains:

> The Western conception of the person as a bounded, unique, more or less integrated motivational and cognitive universe, a dynamic center of awareness, emotion, judgement and action organized into a distinctive whole and set contrastively both against other such wholes and against its social and natural background is, however incorrigible it may seem to us, a rather peculiar idea within the context of the world's cultures. (Geertz 1993, in Billington *et al.* 1998)

This move is a growing attempt to reach a position where the 'I' is not some essential boundaried self, but something more porous, more transactional within context and relationships: a *process*, a capacity for reflexivity, dialogue, community. This is nearer to Buber, Bakhtin, Derrida: to difference and meeting as central to the politics of identity and community. Psychotherapist Maurice Friedman comes back to Buber's 'We':

> We are used to thinking in terms of polarities – the individual versus the community, or inner versus outer. But to see only the polar extremes obscures a great deal of human reality. The prime human reality is the life of dialogue that takes place in family and in community. To view the individual or the community outside the context of the life of dialogue is like trying to draw a map of the world with only the north and south poles as references. For the life of dialogue, the self versus the world is an abstract notion. The self in the world is the basic reality we all share. (Friedman in Frie 2003, p.54)

Despite the complexity of all of this thinking and rethinking of *community*, it still seems possible to use this concept in a hopeful way. As community has become less a real place and more a process and an achieved experience (as *communitas*), so also identity (fashioned by the reflexive self) has become less a core entity, and more a socially constructed mode within culture. The search and the hope (reflected in the charged discourse of community) is to find a balance between belonging and autonomy, between being-yourself, being-part-of and being-together.

How is the emerging discourse of Community Music Therapy using this rethinking of the relationship between individuality and community? How does music fit into this?

'Community and music' in Community Music Therapy

Other chapters in this book (such as Brynjulf Stige's) explore how many of these concepts from socio-cultural disciplines are being used to rethink the agenda of Community Music Therapy. In this section I will stay with how links are being made between thinking about community and music together.

Whilst contemporary music therapy has cultivated a skilful practice and supporting theory for motivating 'communicative musicality' and working for musical relatedness, based within the 'consensus model' (Ansdell 2002), relatively few links have been made between music, society and community. As I've commented previously, a notable exception to this trend has been the Scandinavian tradition, in particular the work of Even Ruud (1998), who has suggested that music therapists 'could see themselves also as cultural workers, taking music therapy values and approaches into the community' (p.3).

We see throughout this current book, however, how Community Music Therapists are rethinking the role of the social, cultural and communal within music therapy, and also using a new range of supporting theoretical work from thinking about music coming from social and social psychological sources (Jane Davidson's cutting-edge chapter in this book being typical of this trend).

In this section I will briefly review some of the literature in which music therapists are explicitly linking thinking about music to thinking about community. This may not always involve 'communal' events as such, but could be any work beyond the traditional therapeutic dyad where the participants are considered to be more than a collection of separate individuals, and where the work is considered from a communal perspective in some way.

I start with Brynjulf Stige's recent reconsideration of his comments on the place of music within music therapy in light of the additional needs of Community Music Therapy. I will then outline two recent studies which put these ideas into a clinical context.

In his book *Culture-Centered Music Therapy* (2002) Brynjulf Stige presents his 'triumvirate' of *protomusicality-musics-musicing*. In his doctoral thesis (2003) he expands this previous schema in order to be adequate to the needs of Community Music Therapy. Here he characterises music as ecology where 'relationships are perceived and performed in context'. Taking a hypothetical example of a music therapy event where the focus in on the communal aspect, Stige comments:

> The communal musicking is the center and shared focus, and each participant contributes with the cultivated capacities and the perceived affordances relative to his or her life history. [This demonstrates] how communal musicking is at once public and private, social and personal, centred and decentred...a unity beyond uniformity. (Stige 2003, p.173)

Ansdell and Pavlicevic (forthcoming) work from a very similar perspective on a clinical example of a music therapy group in a psychiatric hospital which was considered an 'achieved community'. The group starts off as seven individuals with differences of mood, energy, attention and need; the music a collage of monologues. Gradually, musical communication is achieved and 'concerted action' leads to a sense of musical, physical and emotional congruence. Eventually there is *musical communitas*: a common shared world of time, space, gesture and energy, which nevertheless allows diversity *and* unity. Ansdell and Pavlicevic use ideas from a pioneer sociologist and a contemporary cognitive neurologist to think about this work.

Firstly, Alfred Schütz,[8] whose work connects both with the hypothesis of 'communicative musicality' and with Buber's ideas about forms of human relatedness. Schütz theorised that the specific quality of communication in groups of musicers comes from a form of synchronisation which is not in 'clock time' but in the 'inner' subjective time of individual and shared consciousness. This creates intersubjective experience:

> This sharing of the other's flux of experiences in inner time, this living through a vivid present in common, constitutes…the mutual tuning-in relationship, the experience of the 'We', which is at the foundation of all possible communication. (Schütz in Martin 1995, p.200)

Schütz's hypothesis is finding some verification in cognitive neurology. William Benzon's (2001) work on music's role in social experience has many parallels with Schütz's ideas on the intersubjective 'tuning-in relationships' based on players' synchronization. Benzon's view is that musical communication at these points is no less than a coupling between brains through shared activity. As such 'the neurobiology of music and the neurobiology of social attachment appear to be intimately intertwined' (p.113). Benzon suggests how the brain is motivated to attune to the sounds of a musicing group, and then to reorganize the nervous system to form a 'collective neural state space' – a single system which comprises the whole group: 'The individuals are physically separate, but temporally integrated. It is one music, one dance' (p.164).

The case example of Ansdell and Pavlicevic's group shows a clinical situation developing from problem to solution in this regard. What both Schütz's and Benzon's perspectives share is the centrality of *time* and *timing* being at the heart of musical community, of it quite simply being a case of being-in-time-together.

Another example of approaching clinical work from a communal perspective is Kenneth Aigen's (2001, 2002) extended case study[9] called *Playin' in the Band*. In this he describes how a clinical situation evolved from a conventional Nordoff-Robbins context with a learning disabled adolescent client. The traditional client-therapist-co-therapist role structure of Lloyd, Alan Turry and Kenneth Aigen naturally became something different: a 'band of three'. Aigen describes the musical and social experiences of Lloyd and his two therapists as

---

8   Schütz was a sociologist, philosopher and amateur musician. His ideas on group musical communication are in his essay 'Making Music Together' (1971).

9   Aigen's study is accompanied by a DVD with extensive clinical excerpts portraying the shifting relationship between the three men.

they form a popular music combo and utilize a range of idioms which, as Aigen suggests, 'offer different types of communal experiences to musicians' (p.33).

Aigen uses two theoretical concepts from Keil and Feld's book *Music Grooves* (1994) to discuss this case – *groove* and *communitas* – both of these representing the kind of social thinking I have been talking about in this section. For the three men in 'the band' getting into the 'groove' of an idiom is a way of settling into both the relational space of the interaction and the concomitant 'space' of the music (its type of gestures, character, etc.). Aigen quotes Steven Feld:

> A 'groove' refers to an intuitive sense of style as process [...] getting into a groove also describes a feelingful participation, a positive feelingful and emotional attachment... A groove is a comfortable place to be. (Feld in Aigen 2001, p.34)

Establishing the groove means establishing and maintaining musical communication, which in turn creates the reward: the sharing of common meaning through common feeling. Moreover, a groove can only happen within a musical *culture*, because it depends on recognizing and being able to participate in the 'feel' of the music. As Aigen writes:

> The groove of a music embodies the ethics, values, aesthetics and social relationships of a culture... For Lloyd, to create groove with his music therapists is to find the comfort of a cultural home. (Aigen 2001, p.36)

Another way of describing this process using the concepts outlined earlier would be to say that here we have a social situation of musicing which is the mobilised musicianship-in-action working between these three men. Further, the affordances of the musical idioms and their appropriations by the players allow certain very specific social and cultural experiences to happen.

The second concept Aigen uses to model several key aspects of this six-year therapy is *communitas*. As I outlined earlier, this idea suggests how in social activities such as the men playing in the band here, there is a natural levelling of therapists/client roles within the liminality of improvisation. The musicing between the three men both gives this learning-disabled teenager access to a unique form of creative sociality, but importantly, through the pop and rock music used, access to the kind of *cultural* experience common to most people, but sometimes not available to the 'culturally disenfranchised'. Aigen makes the important point that:

> We can then also consider music therapy not as a specialized service or mode or interaction fundamentally different from normal social processes,

but as a medium for providing essential opportunities for personal development sought by all people. (Aigen 2002, p.95)

Here we have a provocative thought, which is entertained by several music therapists working from a Community Music Therapy perspective recently: is music
therapy actually nearer to the 'music of everyday life' than has been previously
suggested?

Conclusion: *Musical Communitas*

Music is our last and best source of participatory consciousness, and it has this
capacity not just to model but maybe to enact some idea communities.

Charles Keil

A possible link between the newer thinking about music and that of community
could be the concept of communitas. This seems a frequent focal point for many
contemporary music therapists moving towards a Community Music Therapy
perspective (including several in the present volume).

I have suggested in this chapter that the concept of 'community' in
Community Music Therapy could be more accurately characterized as
community in context, rather than a utopian search for community as place or
ideal, or even an enduring association. This could be expressed as communitas:
the graceful but prepared happening of mutual experience within a social and
cultural context. Communitas can be both a nourishment and a critique of host
communities (whether these be circumstantial or natural).

Would it be possible to go one stage further and suggest *musical communitas*
as a focal concept for Community Music Therapy? By musical communitas, I
(and many of the writers I have mentioned in this chapter) mean to suggest the
particular possibilities and qualities of social and cultural experience motivated
and sustained through music and musicing. How the 'music of everyday life' can
afford just what clients and communities need.

Even Ruud (1998, p.131) writes that perhaps 'instead of "aesthetic refine-
ment", improvisations in music therapy seek to build a community
("communitas")…'. Kenneth Aigen's study shows vividly how it is probably
only musicing which could provide what Aigen calls the 'comfort of a cultural
home' as well as the ease of social intimacy. It is no surprise that in a later paper
Victor Turner made links between his communitas concept and
Cziksentmihalyi's well-known *flow state*. The 'optimal experience' of flow is
paralled by the graceful quickening of communitas.

Musical Communitas may then be the link-pin between musical companionship and musical community in music therapy, the two poles which have arti-

ficially pulled apart in the last 20 years, and which Community Music Therapy is perhaps attempting to link again. Working musically with individuals and groups and with communal situations needs to be thought of as complementary, part of the natural continuum which musicing offers.

Here we link back also to the useful formulations by Christopher Small and the 'new musicologists', and to the values of musicing they have brought back into serious thinking about music, thinking which can provide again a solid foundation for music therapy:

> If...*musicking* is an activity by means of which we bring into existence a set of relationships that model the relationships of our world, not as they are but as we would wish them to be, and if through musicking we learn about and explore these relationships, we affirm them to ourselves and anyone else who may be paying attention, and we celebrate them, then musicking is in fact a way of knowing our world...and in knowing it, we learn to live well in it. (Small 1998, p.50)

Brynjulf Stige adds a timely cautious warning in case we should get too carried away with the potentially over-Romantic trope of musical communitas. He wants us to guard against regarding communitas in glorious isolation from the macro-effects of *societas* – the social and political context in which social action nests. Musical communitas (in music therapy or not) can be as much a social critique as a celebration. Equally Stige warns against 'essentialist claims that the nature of music is communal' (2003, p.180). Again, this links with a theme emphasised by the 'new musicology'; how, in Bruno Nettl's words, 'the essence of music as a cultural system...is both that it is not a phenomenon of the natural world and also that it is experienced as though it were' (in Cook 1998, p.131).

Stige counsels that although we must avoid essentialism here:

> [music therapists] *can* argue, however, that music as the performance of relationships in communal practices belongs to the range of possibilities in music, and that music therapy theory and practice is therefore incomplete if a notion of music as milieu and ecology of relationships is not included. (Stige 2003, p.180)

One of the continuing areas of dialogue within any discourse on music within Community Music Therapy will doubtless concern whether the anti-essentialism of a fully 'culturalist' discourse of music risks 'losing the phenomenon': the seemingly singular qualities and functions of music. This is also a common question now within a musicology discourse. Music therapists, however, might be especially well placed to see how the basic question 'Why *music?*' is downplayed when music/speech/ritual are often conflated as 'communicative action' or semiotic systems or just the reflection of intra-psychic life.

Perhaps, as has been explored by Cook, DeNora, Small and the other musicologists, a recognition of 'music's powers' is again becoming central to the thinking and rethinking about music. This newly emerging map, which places 'music's powers' within the everyday life context of society and culture, is of great significance for the discipline of music therapy. Community music therapists in particular are in a position also to make important contributions to the rethinking of music and community, situated as they are within the heart of this territory.

References

Abercrombie, N., Hill, S. and Turner, B (1984) *The Penguin Dictionary of Sociology*. London: Penguin Books.

Aigen, K. (2001) 'Popular Music Styles in Nordoff-Robbins Clinical Improvisation.' *Music Therapy Perspectives 19*, 31–44.

Aigen, K. (2002) *Playin' in the Band: A Qualitative Study of Popular Music Styles as Clinical Improvisation*. New York: Nordoff-Robbins Center for Music Therapy.

Ansdell, G. (1995) *Music for Life*. London: Jessica Kingsley Publishers.

Ansdell, G. (1997) 'Musical Elaborations: What has the New Musicology to Say to Music Therapy?' *British Journal of Music Therapy 11*, 2, 36–44.

Ansdell, G. (2001) 'Musicology: Misunderstood Guest at the Music Therapy Feast?' In D. Aldridge, G. DiFranco, E. Ruud and T. Wigram (eds) *Music Therapy in Europe*. Rome: Ismez.

Ansdell, G. (2002) 'Community Music Therapy and the Winds of Change.' *Voices: A World Forum for Music Therapy*. http://www.voices.no/discussions

Ansdell, G. and Pavlicevic, M. (forthcoming) 'Musical Companionship, Musical Community: Music therapy and the process and values of musical communication.' In R. Macdonald, D. Hargreaves and D. Miell (eds) *Musical Communication*. Oxford: Oxford University Press.

Bauman, Z. (2001) *Community: Seeking Safety in an Insecure World*. Cambridge: Polity Press.

Bauman, Z. (2003) *Liquid Love*. Cambridge: Polity Press.

Benzon, W. (2001) *Beethoven's Anvil: Music in Mind and Culture*. New York: Basic Books.

Billington, R., Hockey, J. and Strawbridge, S. (1998) *Exploring Self and Society*. London: Macmillan.

Blacking, J. (1973) *How Musical is Man?* Seattle: University of Washington Press.

Bohlman, P. (1999) 'Ontologies of Music.' In N. Cook and M. Everist (eds) *Rethinking Music*. Oxford: Oxford University Press.

Boyce-Tillman, J. (2000) *Constructing Musical Healing: The Wounds that Sing*. London: Jessica Kingsley Publishers.

Buber, M. (1947/2002) *Between Man and Man*. London: Routledge.

Bunt, L. and Pavlicevic, M. (2002) 'Music and Emotion: Perspectives from Music Therapy.' In P. Juslin and J. Sloboda (eds) *Music and Emotion*. Oxford: Oxford University Press.

Caputo, J. (1997) *Deconstruction in a Nutshell: A Conversation with Jacques Derrida.* New York: Fordham University Press.

Clarke, E. (2003) 'Music and Psychology.' In M. Clayton, T. Herbert and R. Middleton (eds) *The Cultural Study of Music.* London: Routledge.

Cook, N. (1998) *Music: A Very Short Introduction.* Oxford: Oxford University Press.

Cook, N. and Everist, M. (1999) *Rethinking Music.* Oxford: Oxford University Press.

DeNora, T. (2000) *Music in Everyday Life.* Cambridge: Cambridge University Press.

DeNora, T. (2001) 'Aesthetic agency and musical practice: New directions in the sociology of music and emotion.' In P. Juslin and J. Slobada (eds) *Music and Emotion.* Oxford: Oxford University Press.

Derrida, J. (1997) 'Community without Community.' In J. Caputo *Deconstruction in a Nutshell.* New York: Fordham University Press.

Dissanayake, E. (1995) *Homo Aestheticus: Where Art Comes From and Why.* Seattle: University of Washington Press.

Dissanayake, E. (2001) 'An Ethological View of Music and its Relevance to Music Therapy.' *Nordic Journal of Music Therapy 10*, 2, 159–175.

Elliott, A. (2001) *Concepts of the Self.* Cambridge: Polity Press.

Elliott, D. (1995) *Music Matters.* Oxford: Oxford University Press.

Frie, R. (2003) *Understanding Experience: Psychotherapy and Postmodernism.* London: Routledge.

Giddens, A. (2002) *Runaway World: How Globalisation is Reshaping our Lives.* London: Profile Books.

Goehr, L. (1992) *The Imaginary Museum of Musical Works.* Oxford: Clarendon Press.

Horden, P. (2000) *Music as Medicine: The History of Music Therapy since Antiquity.* Aldershot: Ashgate.

Kerman, J. (1985) *Musicology.* London: Fontana.

Keil, C. and Feld, S. (1994) *Music Grooves.* Chicago: University of Chicago Press.

Kirkpatrick, F. (2001) *The Ethics of Community.* Oxford: Blackwell.

Lee, C. (1992) 'The Analysis of Therapeutic Improvisatory Music with People Living with the Virus HIV and AIDS.' Unpublished Ph.D. thesis. City University, London.

Lee, C. (1996) *Music at the Edge.* London: Routledge.

Marshall, G. (1998) *Oxford Dictionary of Sociology.* Oxford: Oxford University Press.

Martin, P. (1995) *Sounds and Society: Themes in the Sociology of Music.* Manchester: Manchester University Press.

Monaghan, J. and Just, P. (2000) *Social and Cultural Anthropology.* Oxford: Oxford University Press.

Pavlicevic, M. (1997) *Music Therapy in Context.* London: Jessica Kingsley Publishers.

Pinker, S. (1997) *How the Mind Works.* London: Penguin Books.

Rice, T. (2001) 'Reflections on Music and Meaning: Metaphor, Signification and Control in the Bulgarian Case.' *British Journal of Ethnomusicology 10*, 1, 19–38.

Robarts, J. (1996) 'Music Therapy for Children with Autism.' In C. Trevarthen, K. Aitken, D, Papoudi and J. Robarts *Children With Autism.* London: Jessica Kingsley Publishers.

Ruud, E. (1998) *Music Therapy: Improvisation, Communication and Culture.* Gilsum, NH: Barcelona Publishers.

Schütz, A. (1964) 'Making Music Together.' In *Collected Papers, Vol. 2.* The Hague: Martinus Nijhoff.

Small, C. (1998) *Musicking.* Hanover, NH: Wesleyan University Press.

Stige, B. (1998) 'Perspectives on Meaning in Music Therapy.' *British Journal of Music Therapy 12*, 1, 20–29.

Stige, B. (2002) *Culture-Centered Music Therapy.* Gilsum, NH: Barcelona Publishers.

Stige, B. (2003) 'Elaborations Towards a Notion of Community Music Therapy.' Unpublished Ph.D. thesis. Department of Music and Theatre, University of Oslo.

Trevarthen, C. (2002) 'Origins of Musical Identity: Evidence from Infancy for Musical Social Awareness.' In R. Macdonald, D. Hargreaves and D. Miell (eds) *Musical Identities.* Oxford: Oxford University Press.

Trevarthen, C. (2003) 'Neuroscience and Intrinsic Psychodynamics: Current Knowledge and Potential for Therapy.' In J. Corrigall and H. Wilkinson (eds) *Revolutionary Connections: Psychotherapy and Neuroscience.* London: Karnac Books.

Trevarthen, C. and Malloch, S. (2000) 'The Dance of Wellbeing: Defining the Musical Therapeutic Effect.' *Nordic Journal of Music Therapy 9*, 2.

Turner, V. (1974) *Dramas, Fields and Metaphors.* Ithaca: Cornell University Press.

Williams, A. (2001) *Constructing Musicology.* Aldershot: Ashgate.

Williams, R. (1976) *Keywords.* London: Collins.

CHAPTER 4

Community Music Therapy: Culture, Care and Welfare

Brynjulf Stige

I cannot tell you what community work is, only what it is for me, and perhaps for some other people, in the hope that this will help you work it out for yourself.

Alan Twelvetrees

The word 'Community' in the English language

In my view the word 'community' has a certain beauty to it. I enjoy its etymology and the breadth of its contemporary meaning, and I even take pleasure from the sound of the word itself. The word is derived from the Latin *communitas* (of common), and the modern word 'community' is linked to a beautiful range of related meanings. When we speak of community we may think of a locality and the people living there, or we may think of a fellowship of interest and experience. If we speak of 'the community' we may even mean 'the public'. This polysemic word therefore invites us to reflect upon the ecology of socio-cultural life; from the microsystem of, say, a family to the place where we live to the larger organisations of society. Also, I appreciate the possibilities for reflection created if we take into consideration other words derived from related origins, such as the words 'communication' and 'communion'. Especially intriguing I find the fact that the word 'community' is in use both for denotation of social *systems* (for instance a locality and its inhabitants) and of *experience* (of togetherness and of having mutual support). The linking of systems and personal experience is a continuous challenge in human life, and in the word 'community' we may at least project a hope that healthy connections are possible to establish.

My own language has different words for the two aspects of social systems and experience outlined above. Some of the beauty is then lost. Each language has its own beauty, however. In the Norwegian language one beautiful word to consider in this context is 'trivsel'. The etymological origin is the Old Norse noun 'triv', which meant something like happiness and progress (Torp, 1918/1992). This word entered the English language when the Vikings started to 'visit' the islands, and in Modern English the derived verb 'thrive' is in use. The derived noun 'trivsel' in New Norwegian has a slightly broader range of meaning than the English sister word, covering well-being, healthy development, growth, and prosperity. In fact, the closest English word would be welfare, but 'trivsel' is different by belonging more to the vernacular and by focusing upon the strength and resources of individuals and groups in a milieu.

Lately I have been working with the notion of 'trivsel' as a starting point for the discussion of Community Music Therapy in the context of a broader community project (Stige, 2002a). While the beauty of this word is not transferable to the English language, the related notion of welfare will be central to the discussion in this chapter. The way I look at Community Music Therapy, the music therapist is a musicking community worker, that is, a person whose job is to promote social welfare in and through a community. It is quite possible that other music therapists may see it differently. Borrowing language from the epigraph of this chapter, I can only tell you what Community Music Therapy is for me, and perhaps for some other people, in the hope that this will help you work it out for yourself.

Community Music Therapy: A movement, field, model, or paradigm?

The term 'Community Music Therapy' was already in use in the literature in the 1970s. Florence Tyson (1973), for instance, discussed practical challenges in the establishment of music therapy as part of community health services. The context of her discussion was the deinstitutionalisation of health services that started to evolve in many industrialised countries in the 1960s and 1970s (and which evolved further in the subsequent decades). While Tyson clearly communicated how new contexts affect the roles and responsibilities of the therapist, her discussion only to a limited degree challenged the conventional conception of modern music therapy. More recently, music therapists have started to use the term Community Music Therapy in ways that more fundamentally suggest a change in the conception and practice of music therapy, community no longer being only a context to work in but also a context to work with.

It may be countered that this is not new at all. Maybe this is the oldest form of music therapy that ever existed. Musical healing in indigenous cultures has always been healing in context, often as public or semi-public events involving not only 'therapist' and 'client' but larger groups of community (Gouk 2000; Horden 2000). The discussion in this chapter will concentrate on the more recent developments in modern professional music therapy, but a basic premise for my discussion is that these developments are related to an increased sensitivity to culture. This then suggests that history and the heterodox non-professional practices of musical healing are important and valuable sources of influence from which music therapists learn, consciously and unconsciously (Stige 2002b, 2003).

In the context of contemporary professional practice, what, then, *is* Community Music Therapy? The editors of the present volume have co-produced an ambitious definition, and in a recent discussion paper Gary Ansdell suggests that 'a "paradigm shift" may be currently underway in the discipline, with the over-arching model which leads, supports and validates practice turning to one best characterised as Community Music Therapy' (Ansdell 2002, p.109). More modest definitions are in use, for instance in Kenneth Bruscia's (1998) discussion of ecological music therapy, where Community Music Therapy is a sub-area of practice only. One is led to ask: is Community Music Therapy a cultural movement, a field of practice, a new model of practice, or a new paradigm and metatheoretical foundation for music therapy?

There may be elements of truth as well as limitations in all these possibilities, and I am not sure that a definite answer to the question would be helpful at this point. A shared focus among many music therapists talking about Community Music Therapy is, however, that community is not only a context to work *in* but also to work *with*. In other words, community music therapists are concerned with social and cultural change. I will briefly examine three basic assumptions that may support such a focus: that *culture* is central to music therapy theory and practice, that health is expressed as *mutual* care, and that mutual care is related to the issue of human and social *welfare*.

The turn to culture

While human life, including music and therapy, is closely linked to culture, there has been a striking neglect of cultural perspectives in much of music therapy theory. Lately, however, there has been a renewed interest towards cultural issues in music therapy (Ruud 1998; Estrella 2001; Kenny and Stige 2002; Stige 2002b).

There are, of course, several precursors to this recent development; what is new is that a broader community of music therapists has started to recognise it.[1] Kenneth Bruscia speaks of a fifth force in music therapy theory, a force that

> reminds us that all of our work, whether it be theory, practice, or research, takes place within very specific and unique contexts – contexts that not only shape the work itself, but also predispose us to attach our own idiographic meanings to it. This will be the force that debunks many of our uncontextualized generalizations about the nature of music, therapy, and music therapy itself. (Bruscia 2002, p.xv)

The current turn to culture is, as I see it, an anthropological turn. It is thus related to an acknowledgement of contextual factors in the practice and study of music therapy. The turn to culture may also be seen as a cultural movement, in other words, there is a self-reflexive move involved; music therapists are seeing themselves and their work in and as cultural contexts. Stige and Kenny (2002) propose that this turn to culture has certain implications for music therapy theory and practice. First, they advocate that culture-centred perspectives could be integrative of species-centred, client-centred, and music-centred perspectives, and, second, that both music and health may be defined as relational phenomena. Third, they propose that music therapy is constituted as situated practice, and, fourth, that cultural identity development and social change are legitimate goals in music therapy practice.

In my view the turn to culture, and the related implications proposed above, support the emergence of Community Music Therapy practices, that is, welfare-related practices where community is a context to work in and with.

Health as mutual care

The view that health is a relational phenomenon deserves special attention here, and could be related to another implication proposed above, namely that culture-centred perspectives could be integrative of species-centred, client-centred, and music-centred perspectives. To make a long and complicated argument extremely short, I advocate that any music therapy theory is based in some metatheoretical assumptions about humankind and music. I also advocate that such assumptions will be less than adequate if they do not take into consideration both the biological, the psychological, the social, and the cultural aspects of human life (Stige 2002b).

---

1   See Stige and Kenny (2002) where this is discussed.

Empirical and theoretical support for this view is, I think, best developed in the tradition of *cultural psychology* (Cole 1996). Indirect support could also be found where one would perhaps least expect it – in the often criticised sociobiology of Edward Wilson. Wilson (1975/2000) suggests that there are four pinnacles of social evolution: the colonial invertebrates, the social insects, the nonhuman mammals, and humans. The sequence given proceeds from primitive to more advanced, biologically speaking, but Wilson comments: 'It seems as though social evolution has slowed as the body plan of the individual became more elaborate' (Wilson 1975/2000, p.379). While the colonial invertebrates have come close to producing 'perfect' societies, there are already more conflicts between the social insects and definitively less co-operation and more aggression among the nonhuman mammals. While aggressiveness and discord is not very alien to human life, it is still a fact that humans have reversed this tendency in some important ways. 'Human societies approach the insect societies in co-operativeness and far exceed them in powers of communication' (Wilson 1975/2000, p.380). There must be an explanation for this, and the most probable is the human capacity for culture.

As cultural psychologist Michael Tomasello (1999) advocates, the human way of being social is linked to the human capacity for culture. In human societies domains of social activity have been transformed to domains of *cultural activity*. Take two examples: object manipulation, enhanced somewhat among some primates through the use of simple tools, has in human societies been developed extensively through the creation of a diversity of tools and artefacts. Communication, possible for many animals through the use of signals, has in human societies been developed to a tool for personal expression through cultural symbols such as music and language (Tomasello 1999, p.210). In short, any understanding of human life runs short if the social and cultural aspects are not included.

This argument is of relevance for an understanding of human health. While biomedicine has traditionally focused upon diseases as separate entities, a cross-disciplinary interest for the *relational* aspects of health is growing. If human life is based in culture and social relatedness, it makes sense that human health is related to this. The Danish philosopher Ole Dreier has developed a definition of health based upon this argument, and proposes that 'Health is neither just my interest for myself or others' interest for me, but the mutual and general interest and care for each person's possibility for participation' (Dreier

1994, p.199).[2] Following Dreier we then may locate health neither in body, person, nor society, but as a quality of the *interaction and activity* that humans engage in. This is not to say that health threats may not be individual, only that relational and communal aspects must be taken into serious consideration. The individual should be seen in relation to the collective, and vice versa. This notion of health, I think, should be of direct relevance for Community Music Therapy.

Local grounds for social welfare

In a few sentences, the view that has been communicated so far is: human existence is co-existence, and culture enables and regulates such co-existence. Music may then be considered a mode of human co-existence, and health a quality of human co-existence. Co-existence exists on many levels, however; there is an ecology from micro- to macrosystems involved. If this is not understood properly, the notion of health as mutual care may be privatised to indicate just the family or other microsystems, and the link to Community Music Therapy would then be questionable. I therefore propose, as my main thesis in this chapter, that the development of Community Music Therapy is linked to the development of a society's welfare services for its inhabitants.

Welfare is usually defined as well-being, health, and prosperity (of a person or community). Most contemporary industrialised and post-industrialised countries are welfare states, that is, the government guarantees a minimum of welfare for all citizens, through the provision or subsidisation of services of health and education, through income support for people that face sickness or job loss, etc. Many developing countries are also taking steps in the direction of becoming welfare states, by providing services of health and education, for instance, for everybody. To varying degrees, then, governments are taking responsibility for the reduction of inequalities, or at least, for the reduction of extreme suffering and injustice. In the context of a capitalist society, the aim of welfare may be said to be 'to counteract the negative effects of the market for people who, for a variety of reasons, find it a struggle to meet their basic needs' (Giddens 2001, p.332).

Of course, states differ greatly concerning the development of welfare models. The Danish sociologist Gøsta Esping-Andersen (1990) has developed a typology of welfare systems by evaluating the degree of decommodification of services, that is, the degree to which they are free from the market. One extreme

---

2   My translation from Danish. See Stige (2002b, 2003) for a more detailed
      argument.

is the social democratic model, which has been typical of the Scandinavian countries, where welfare services are highly decommodified and available to all citizens as universal benefits. Necessary conditions for such a system are high taxes and a high degree of social equality, the latter of course also being a value shaping and supporting the system. Another extreme is the liberal model, typical of the United States, where welfare is highly commodified. Welfare models that are commodified do not contribute to social equality, but in societies based on such models the basic needs of the destitute are usually provided through means-tested services.[3]

In many countries community projects and community work have grown out of what have been considered defects or shortages of modern societies and of the welfare state system. Some communities are 'left behind' as impoverished and neglected, and community work has been initiated in order to counteract these developments. Such starting points have been especially strong in countries with a high degree of social inequality. Also in countries which developed a social democratic welfare state, with universal rights and decommodified services, there have been concerns about the 'crisis of the welfare state', at least since the 1980s. The welfare state has been considered expensive, ineffective, and too bureaucratic (Grund 1982). In these countries too, much community work has been initiated in order to stimulate new developments of welfare services, often with a focus upon welfare pluralism, that is, the notion that a plurality of sources – not just the government – should deliver welfare services (Twelvetrees 1991).

While the informal mutual support of pre-modern communities may be impossible to recreate in contemporary communities of industrialising, industrialised, and post-industrialised countries, community work may aim at the production of the highest level of welfare possible, sometimes through the integration of public, private, and voluntary efforts. To achieve this, inter-agency relations must be developed, as well as relations between volunteers and professionals, and one of the major professional challenges for music therapists in the years to come will be to be part of this in a constructive way. Community work will hardly work, though, through organisation and professional collaboration only. Polarisation in influence and responsibility between agencies and users is part of the problem of contemporary communities, and sound community work therefore involves the *empowerment* of users and ordinary people, for instance

---

3   It is worth noting that the Scandinavian systems have become more commodified in the last two decades, a tendency many view more as a development of capitalism than of welfarism.

through *participation* in the elaboration of strategies or through the development of user-led services (Stige 2002a).

The roots of Community Music Therapy

I have explained that my thesis in this chapter is that Community Music Therapy could best be seen as part of a mobilisation in the defence and promotion of social welfare. This is related to sensitivity to culture and context, and to an understanding of the social aspects of human life. If health is defined as mutual care, and this view is not privatised but seen in relation to community and society, social consciousness and Community Music Therapy is called for. This seems to be a pertinent challenge in late modern societies, whether we are talking about individualised affluent societies or contexts of conflict and war with concurrent traumas and refugee problems.

The emergence of Community Music Therapy, then, is linked to historical and socio-cultural developments. An interesting fact is that related context-based traditions of music therapy have developed in several countries simultaneously, while only lately has an international discourse about Community Music Therapy emerged. In two previous texts I have explored the roots of late modern Community Music Therapy (Stige 2002c, 2003), and I have proposed that the following sources are relevant to consider:

- models of conventional modern music therapy
- community healing rituals of traditional cultures
- traditions and activities of community music
- models of sociotherapy and milieu therapy
- approaches to community work.

These five domains represent the breadth of influence that I can see behind the current interest in Community Music Therapy. Not every practice of Community Music Therapy will claim to have roots in all five domains. Aasgaard (1999), for instance, concentrates on the relationship to milieu therapy, while Ansdell (2002) concentrates on conventional modern music therapy and the British community music tradition. I think, however, that in considering Community Music Therapy as a movement, as a change of culture in contemporary music therapy, all these domains are of relevance. This does not mean that these five domains could be viewed as stable ancestry; on the contrary, I expect new roots to emerge and gain importance as the 'banyan tree' of

Community Music Therapy grows.[4] One such probable future aerial root is the tradition of community psychology (Orford 1992), which may descend from one of the Community Music Therapy branches, push into the ground and form a new trunk.

In the following I will outline characteristics of the proposed five sources and give examples of how they have influenced my own work with Community Music Therapy during the last two decades.

Models of conventional modern music therapy

Community Music Therapy is clearly both a continuation of, and contrast to, conventional modern music therapy. Sometimes practices are so close that one is led to ask: 'Is there anything new under the bonnet?' Other times the contrasts are greater. In any case it makes sense to examine the relationships involved, as community music therapists are usually professional music therapists, and have their identity and training linked to music therapy as it has developed as a modern discipline and profession. There are some general attitudes linked to looking at music therapy as a discipline and profession; there is a concurrent ethos that most music therapists subscribe to. Part of this is the value of working methodically, of using scientific theory, and of doing research. Specific ideas, depending upon which model of music therapy the music therapist is influenced by, are of course also important. Some models stress systematic assessment and evaluation, others the dialogic character of music-making, others the need for verbal processing of experience, etc.

In my own work I have been influenced by the pioneering work of Paul Nordoff and Clive Robbins (1977). Their music-centred approach has coloured my main attitude and approach to musicking in the context of music therapy. Within a music-centred approach, however, I do not primarily think in terms of 'music as therapy'. The dichotomy that is sometimes constructed between music and interpersonal relationships, or between music-making and verbal process-ing, I do not find particularly clarifying.[5] More important, I have valued the interactive and *dialogic* character of Nordoff and Robbins's approach to music-making (see Garred 2002). This has been a guide for my practice, as has

---

4   The banyan tree, found e.g. in Australasia, is known for its capacity to shoot
     new roots from already established branches. As the banyan tree grows, new
     roots descend and form new trunks.

5   The term 'music as therapy' is taken from Bruscia (1987), who contrasts this
     with 'music in therapy'. I appreciate the value of Bruscia's terms as descriptive
     of positions that have been common in music therapy theory. What I am
     saying is that I do not subscribe to a polarised position in this debate.

been Robbins' role as a sensitive facilitator (Robbins and Stige 1998). This could in many respects be seen as a possible role model for community music therapists, where the enabling and empowering of clients is a core value. In addition to these influences I have allowed myself to borrow from a broad range of music therapy approaches. This eclectic search for new ways of working has been supported by the theoretical works of music therapists such as Even Ruud (1987/1990, 1998) and Carolyn Kenny (1982, 1989), who have advocated the importance of the socio-cultural aspects of music therapy.

Community healing rituals of traditional cultures

Music therapy as we know it today in industrialised and post-industrialised countries is usually considered a *modern* enterprise, and relationships to traditional healing rituals have not always been considered relevant to examine. Contemporary music therapy has been seen as a modern breach, by *not* being based upon myth and tradition but upon rational and empirically tested theories. The above mentioned turn to culture in music therapy theory has changed the perspective somewhat, and opens up a new interest in traditional and heterodox healing rituals. In my view, the potential lies not so much in transplanting these rituals into modern music therapy. To decontextualise practices is not necessarily to show respect, and they may be alien to modern therapists and clients. To learn from history and ethnography is not the same as using other times and practices as recipes in one's own context, or as replacement for one's own tradition and judgement.

I assume that music therapists may learn from traditional healing rituals in at least three ways: first, by examining unfamiliar practices one may discover biases and taken for granted assumptions in one's own theory and practice. Second, by comparative investigation of both traditional and modern practices one may discover patterns of similarities which may then suggest some of the shared biological roots of musicking and music therapy.[6] Third, by developing knowledge about healing rituals of different cultural contexts one may develop one's own cultural sensitivity, which will be increasingly important as more and more music therapists are working in multicultural contexts.

In my own work the ngoma tradition of eastern Africa has represented a thought-provoking and stimulating backcloth. I first observed and learnt about the practice when I lived in Tanzania as a teenager, and later as a music therapy student I tried to integrate influences from the tradition into my own music therapy thinking (Stige 1983). When I started working with Community Music

---

6   See for instance Dissanayake (2000, 2001).

Therapy in August 1983, I hardly had the language to label it Community Music Therapy, but the ngoma tradition continuously challenged my work and the Western assumptions that informed it. Why work with music as sound only, why not integrate movement, dance, myths, and narratives? Why work with individuals or groups only, why not involve the broader community of the locality where these people live? Why concentrate on cure and individual learning, why not also focus upon health promotion in a community perspective?[7] Carolyn Kenny's (1982) discussion of the relationship between modern music therapy and traditional healing rituals has nurtured my interest in questions such as these.

Traditions and activities of community music

In a thought-provoking discussion paper Gary Ansdell (2002) advocates that the two main roots of Community Music Therapy are (conventional modern) music therapy and community music. He is then writing from the perspective of the British context, where community music is a separate tradition of music-making that goes back to the nineteenth century, with attempts to link the social and the musical, building upon the rich amateur music-making tradition in this country. In the 1960s and 1970s this tradition defined itself as *community music*, making the link to community building more articulate. In contrast to the parallel development of music therapy in Britain, community musicians did not organise themselves with the ambition of establishing a discipline and profession.

To my knowledge, community music – as a semi-professional sociomusical tradition and movement – is rather unique to the British and Irish contexts. All music therapists moving into the field of Community Music Therapy will have to consider carefully, however, the amateur music-making traditions of the localities and communities they are about to work in and with. These traditions represent the cultural and social capital of the community.

My own work with Community Music Therapy started with an explicit focus upon the amateur music-making traditions of a rural community in relation to groups of handicapped people in need of community empowerment (Kleive and Stige 1988; Stige 1993/2002). In this particular context community music activities such as marching bands, choirs, rock bands, and folk music bands were especially important. Traditions of community music do not only exist in relation to genres and forms of organised activities, however. They also link to values and social practices of a locality and community. In the

---

7   For a recent discussion of the ngoma tradition, see Janzen (2000).

project referred to above, the local tradition of *dugnad* (working bees as voluntary community work) turned out to be important for the process (Stige 2002b).

Models of sociotherapy and milieu therapy

Community Music Therapy obviously also links to models of sociotherapy and milieu therapy, that is, approaches to therapy and social work that focus upon creating healthy environments, social support, and caring networks instead of just focusing upon the function of each individual client. The terms in use for describing this kind of work differ somewhat with time and place, and also from discipline to discipline (while the work is often inter-disciplinary). In the Scandinavian context, one influential articulation of this approach has been the so-called 'network therapy' (Svedheim 1985).

In the music therapy literature two articulations of this perspective are Aasgaard's (1998, 1999) 'environmental music therapy' and Frohne-Hagemann's (2001) discussion of music therapy as psychotherapy and sociotherapy. My own work has been influenced by the ecological approach of Bronfenbrenner (1979) and by the Norwegian literature on health-work through social networks (Dalgard and Sørensen 1988).

Approaches to community work

Community work is different from sociotherapy and milieu therapy in that it is usually more bottom-up (based on people's own aims more than on aims as formulated by professionals) and in that it is more concerned with community development than with the needs of individual clients (or groups of clients).[8] The starting points and the traditions of community work may differ somewhat from country to country. In Britain, for instance, community work may be said to have some of its roots in the colonial period, where the authorities stimulated community development to adjust indigenous communities to the needs of the state (Hydle 1991, p.16).

This British example should illustrate very well one of the dilemmas often encountered in community work: what is the relationship to political authorities, collaboration or confrontation? In the 1960s and 1970s community work was radicalised in many Western countries, while some radical roots also go back, for instance, to Saul Alinsky's work with community organisations in Chicago in the 1930s (Alinsky 1971). The last couple of decades have seen less

---

8   But consider the epigraph to this chapter. The term 'community work' is used in a plethora of ways.

of radicalism and more of professionalism in community work. Contemporary community work therefore includes a broad range of approaches and attitudes, but most of it is based on subscription to values related to social justice (Twelvetrees 1991).

My own work has been informed by practices of community work that build on the traditions of critical theory and participatory action research (see Stige 2002b, Chapter 10). Critical theory (the neo-Marxist Frankfurt School) provides the community worker with theoretical tools for ideological critique, which may need to be balanced by the more practical and people-centred participatory democracy of the tradition of participatory action research.[9]

Principles of practice

The span of sources that has been outlined, and the basic premise that Community Music Therapy is context sensitive practice, does not suggest that Community Music Therapy is a model of practice, at least not in any narrow meaning of that term. Community Music Therapy is not characterised by a pre-defined set of procedures and techniques, rather by a set of values and basic assumptions. The principles of practices to be outlined here are therefore not prescriptions, but broad guidelines as to which factors to consider in developing a practice.

With whom and where?

With whom do community music therapists work? While in the context of practice it is sometimes (not always) important to know the diagnosis of a client (if s/he has one), to list client populations according to the DSM-IV or ICD 10 in this chapter could create bias in the direction of an individualistic focus. In the context of this broad discussion it suffices to state that community music therapists work with the *relatively disadvantaged*. This links back to the notion of welfare. With social justice as a guiding value the *relative* disadvantage is essential. With *whom* to work is then inevitably linked to *where* one works. Community music therapists have, for instance, been working with groups of handicapped people in need of community empowerment (Kleive and Stige 1988; Stige 1993/2002), or they have been working with circumstantial communities, that is, communities that grow out of shared needs and problems (Aasgaard 1998, 1999; Ansdell 2002; Procter 2002).

---

9   For an excellent and recent description of participatory action research in relation to community development, see Banks and Mangan (1999).

A taxonomy of groups and places to work with could possibly be created. I find it just as helpful to outline two dimensions in relation to which the community music therapist must position the work (Figure 4.1): is s/he working in and with a community of interest, or in and with the community of a locality? Is the client an individual or group in context, or is it the whole community as such?

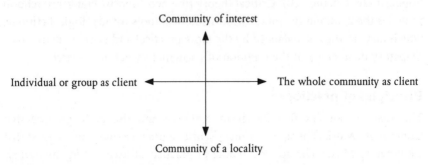

Figure 4.1 Dimensions of practice in Community Music Therapy

Community of interest is a broad notion used to denote communities that are not primarily linked to locality, but to some shared need or interest. This extension of the more conventional notion of community linked to locality illuminates a point of general relevance here: how much must people have in common before we can speak of a community? There is of course no general answer to the question, but it is clear that community is not defined by shared characteristics as defined by an outside observer. The circumstantial communities where community music therapists often find themselves, such as clinics or day care centres, may be considered communities of interest. Communities of interest usually differ from localities in that there is more diversity among members and also weaker social networks. One of the tasks of the community music therapist is then to help build a community and a community feeling.

The community of a locality is how the term community is conventionally used in political theory. It is probably not yet very common that music therapists work with larger localities, such as villages, towns, or streets of a city, but as many societies operate in ways that make certain localities disadvantaged, the relevance of such a focus should be clear.

Some of the sources of Community Music Therapy outlined above indicate that many community music therapists work with individuals or groups as their main clients. I am thinking about sources such as models of conventional modern music therapy, models of sociotherapy and milieu therapy, and certain versions of healing rituals of traditional cultures. In this perspective the community music therapist works in and with a community, in order to help the individual or group, for instance by reducing barriers to their participation within the life of a broader community. Others of the sources listed above – such as traditions and activities of community music, approaches to community work, and many community healing rituals of traditional cultures – suggest that the community itself is a legitimate client for the music therapist. This makes sense if one acknowledges the possibility of a relational concept of health, as outlined earlier in this chapter.

Exactly how?

Exactly how, then, do community music therapists work? This volume gives a broad range of examples of how one could work as a community music therapist. And it may well be that this is the best we can do in describing Community Music Therapy: to give examples of practice. Exactly how one should work is always defined by context. This goes for conventional music therapy too, of course, but the diversity and pertinence of context is probably even higher in Community Music Therapy. What can be outlined, therefore, are some general points only, for the practitioner to take into consideration. At a later stage of the development of Community Music Therapy this could possibly be articulated more systematically in relation to the two dimensions of practice given above.

The above discussion clearly underlines the relevance and importance of *expanding* the focus of the work beyond the triad of client, therapist, and music. The health concern to be worked with may involve relationships with other individuals, groups, and communities, as well as relationships with cultural values, practices, and narrative representations. In relation to authorities, the choice may be between collaborative and confrontational approaches. In relation to clients (individuals, groups, or communities) the choice may be between organising versus enabling approaches, that is, between approaches that are product- or process-oriented.[10]

Community music therapists are working with musicking (Small 1998) in the broadest meaning of this term, that is, with a broad range of activities and relationships. In a discussion of culture-centred music therapy (Stige 2002b), I have outlined some implications for practice that should be of relevance here. Central is the notion of *affordance* – originally outlined in Gibson's

10   An easy-to-read introduction to such dilemmas in relation to community work, with examples that are of relevance for Community Music Therapy, is given by Twelvetrees (1991).

(1979/1986) ecological psychology – which illuminates the *complementarity* of environment and individual that I find essential for Community Music Therapy. Affordance is a relational concept; it describes what someone or something offers in relation to someone or something else. The affordance is therefore in the relationship, not in the 'thing itself', and in my judgement high-quality Community Music Therapy practice is characterised by *careful assessment and application* of the *health affordances* of factors such as *agenda, arena, agents, activities,* and *artefacts*:

AGENDA

The agenda of a therapy process defines what to work with and how. Agendas may be intrapersonal or interpersonal and they may relate to community and culture. Important aspects to consider here are what different agendas afford as well as how the process of negotiating and establishing agendas afford. In Community Music Therapy social change in a community may be part of the agenda, which therefore may need to be publicly negotiated. A balance will often need to be sought between agendas that foster the enabling and empowering of users and clients and agendas that promote more concrete change in the structures, rules, and rituals of a community.

ARENA

Conventional modern music therapy is carried out in a specifically designed setting, a music therapy room in a clinic, for instance. In Community Music Therapy an important element is to assess what different accessible arenas may afford of new possibilities for action, experience, and acknowledgement. One example may be the use of public and semi-public arenas of performance. This has not been so common in conventional modern music therapy, but may often be relevant in Community Music Therapy, especially if inclusive and communicative arenas may be established.

AGENTS

As used here, the term refers to human agents involved in the dynamics of a therapy process. The main agents in therapy are conventionally considered to be the therapist and the client. Community music therapists accept and use positively the possibility of other human agents gaining importance that at points exceeds that of the therapist. Such agents could be local musicians, neighbours, fellow clients of a circumstantial community, etc. The music therapist should, if possible together with the client, assess which agents may be important and how. At times the role of the music therapist changes from that of being a conventional therapist to, for instance, becoming a facilitator, an advocate, a project co-ordinator, a consultant, or simply part of the caring and supportive social network.

ACTIVITIES

Several activities are imaginable in music therapy, such as to *listen*, to *play*, to *create*, to *perform*, to *interpret*, and to *reflect* (Stige 1995). In Community Music Therapy what each activity may afford is assessed not only in relation to the client's needs and resources but in relation to the rituals and rationales of the community to be worked with. Quite often activities will afford differently at different stages of a process. While improvisation (playing and creating) and reflection, for instance, may enable and empower the individual members of a group, later in the process more stress may be put on developing performing activities, as this may lead to community empowerment.

ARTEFACTS

Cultural artefacts, such as musical instruments, technical equipment, songs, and language are important in a person's development of self and identity in relation to a community. How artefacts afford is again relative to both person and community, that is, to biography and to the cultural history of the community.

The five factors discussed above – agenda, arena, agents, activities, and artefacts – all link in various ways and form a complex *web of relationships*. What an arena affords is dependent not only upon the client, therapist, and community in question, but upon how the agenda evolves, upon what other agents become involved, upon what activities are allowed for in the particular cultural space, and upon what artefacts are accessible. The metaphor of *hypertextuality*[11] (Stige 2002b) offers a way of conceptualising the flexible and changing relationships between these components in the music therapy process. There is not a predefined route to follow. Instead there will be a plethora of possible links to explore, with potential for the discovery of new possibilities of meaning and action as well as with concurrent challenges of navigation.

---

11   Hypertext may be defined as a text that does not form a single sequence and that may be read in various orders. The reader can discontinue reading at certain points in order to consult other related material, usually via so-called 'links'.

Musicking as integrative and subversive activity

The practical judgements indicated above relate to the basic principle or value for Community Music Therapy, which I – in relation to the above discussion of social welfare – propose is justice and equity, not charity. Community Music Therapy is therefore about changing the world, if only a bit. To know the difference between what should have been done and what could be done is then essential. What should have been done is defined by one's value system in relation to the needs of the client, what could be done is defined by the tools available, which is relative to context. There is almost by definition a dissonance involved here, and I think music therapists may learn from the following comment made about community work:

> If a community worker can get the balance right, and if she can accept the limitations of the work while continuously striving to overcome them in order to realise her vision, she is likely to find she has a rewarding, though demanding job. And she may be surprised how much she can achieve after all, and how much fun she can have doing it! (Twelvetrees 1991, p.167)

This is also about balancing music's potential as integrative and subversive activity in relation to a community and society (Mattern 1998),[12] and it represents a quest for reflexivity, that is, for reflecting upon one's own position in relation to client, culture, and community (Stige 2002b). Some of my clearest but hardly dearest memories from starting with Community Music Therapy in the early 1980s are situations where people were talking and acting at cross purposes, due to conflicting but often unstated assumptions. The quest for reflexivity therefore also implies the ability and willingness to communicate openly about one's values and priorities. This again requires care and respect for perspectives other than one's own, even when, for instance, one feels that clients do not understand their own interest. If the empowering and enabling of users is a guiding principle for practice, such situations ask for further dialogue and a willingness to revise one's opinions. This is probably one of the main ethical challenges for practitioners of Community Music Therapy.

Assessment and evaluation through ethnography and participatory action research

Before closing this description of how Community Music Therapy could be practised, a note should be made about assessment and evaluation. As Bruscia

---

12	For examples of radical music therapy practices, see Skotheim (1996) and Procter (2002).

(1987) clearly underlines, models and practices of music therapy entail approaches to the assessment of client and evaluation of the music therapy process. If community music therapists neglect these aspects of their work, they may end up as dilettantes and they may run the risk of doing worthless or even harmful work without noticing. While assessment and evaluation is already a challenge for conventional modern music therapy, and much work remains to be done in developing useful approaches, the challenges for the community music therapist are often even higher, since the factors to assess and evaluate multiply. There is need not only for a client profile, but usually also for a community profile. There is no easy solution here, and this will need to be a main area of research and development in the years to come. A preliminary proposal is that the research traditions of ethnography (the study of groups in context) and of participatory action research (user-focused research for social change) are of relevance here (Stige 2002b).

The future: Changing communities

One of the reasons why I think Community Music Therapy is an important thing to discuss – even though we may not agree whether this 'thing' is a movement, field, model, or paradigm – is that it is of high relevance for the development of music therapy in developing countries. In countries struggling with poverty and financial problems, therapy – as conventionally defined and practised in Western countries – is usually for the privileged few. Lately, several authors have voiced concern for a social consciousness in the practice of music therapy: see for example Barcellos' (2002) and Schapira's (2002) reflections from the South American context. Community Music Therapy may be one answer to this challenge, in that it has the potential of being directly targeted to concrete social challenges, as in Sharon Katz's (1993) work with the Peace Train in post-apartheid South Africa or in Pavlicevic's (2003) current concern for communities with people suffering from poverty and disease in the same country.

Community Music Therapy opens up for more economical or distributed practices, as there is focus upon group and community and not exclusively upon individuals. This goes back to my thesis that Community Music Therapy is related to the issue of social welfare. Traditional communities had their own ways of securing mutual aid and of dealing with problems. As a result of processes of modernisation, social mobility increases, social networks change, and the traditional cultures of mutual aid have withered somewhat in most societies today. This is where the welfare state usually comes in, compensating for some of these changes and guaranteeing social stability and justice through at least a minimum of public safety nets. As touched upon above, some countries are in the process of building public welfare systems, others in the process of rebuilding (or even reducing) such systems. In any case, local communities are put to the challenge of contributing to the welfare of their inhabitants, and Community Music Therapy may well be an integrated part of such endeavours.

The initial paragraph of this chapter was a personal note about the beauty of the word 'community'. This beauty could seduce us. The term community is quite special in social and political theory in that it is almost always used in a positive sense. The implied focus upon relationships and contact among people, upon shared responsibilities and efforts, and upon mutual aid and care, appeals to most of us, but is it the whole picture? I would say no. Where communities actually work like this there is usually also another side to the picture, which could be called extensive social control. This is, by the way, the everyday reality of my own private life, in a small town in western Norway. If your child is in any kind of trouble, somebody in town will call you, or maybe the shop assistant will speak to you when you buy your bread and butter. There is no doubt that much care is involved in this system, but there is of course also more control and chatter involved than what one will want at all times. The contrary could possibly be said about some metropolitan contexts of life. Who cares about what happens to your child? Is there any community left at all? Quite often there is. Communities may develop in streets and city blocks, but they are then different from traditional rural communities, for instance by providing more uneven distribution of care and control.

The biologists tell us that humans are social animals, and in some way or another most of us build up social networks that support us and that are essential for the quality of our lives. It is very probable that cultural changes in the future will bring about communities that are quite different from those we are familiar with (Walker 1993), but it is not probable that the relevance and importance of communities will be challenged altogether. The individualisation we see of contemporary culture, for instance, could be described in terms of community altered or liberated rather than in terms of community lost or saved (Orford 1992).

This argument relates to the careful start of this text, where I stated that I cannot tell you what Community Music Therapy is, only what it is for me. The statement relates to the fact that the discourse on Community Music Therapy is still young and unsettled. More significantly, it relates to my judgement that one of the basic premises for Community Music Therapy is that it is context sensitive, and so will change with time and place. I hope Community Music Therapists will be able to develop a notion of community that is open and flexible, that is, a notion which is not nostalgic and utopian and which acknowledges difference, change, and individuality.

References

Aasgaard, T. (1998) 'Musikk-miljøterapi: Uvanlig? Uinteressant? Uutforsket! Kommentarer til Nisima Marie Munk-Madsen.' [Music Milieu Therapy: Uncommon? Uninteresting? Unexplored! Comments to Nisima Marie Munk-Madsen.] *Nordic Journal of Music Therapy 7*, 2, 168–171.

Aasgaard, T. (1999) 'Music Therapy as a Milieu in the Hospice and Pediatric Oncology Ward.' In D. Aldridge *Music Therapy in Palliative Care. New Voices.* London: Jessica Kingsley Publishers.

Alinsky, S.D. (1971) *Rules for Radicals: A Practical Primer for Realistic Radicals.* New York: Vintage Books.

Ansdell, G. (2002) 'Community Music Therapy and The Winds of Change – A Discussion Paper.' In C. Kenny and B. Stige (eds) *Contemporary Voices in Music Therapy: Communication, Culture, and Community.* Oslo: Unipub.

Banks, C.K. and Mangan, J.M. (1999) *The Company of Neighbours. Revitalizing Community through Action-Research.* Toronto: University of Toronto Press.

Barcellos, L.R.M. (2002) 'An Impossible Dream?' In C. Kenny and B. Stige (eds) (2002) *Contemporary Voices in Music Therapy: Communication, Culture, and Community.* Oslo: Unipub.

Bronfenbrenner, U. (1979) *The Ecology of Human Development. Experiments by Nature and Design.* Cambridge, MA: Harvard University Press.

Bruscia, K. (1987) *Improvisational Models of Music Therapy.* Springfield, IL: Charles C. Thomas.

Bruscia, K. (1998) *Defining Music Therapy.* Second edition. Gilsum, NH: Barcelona Publishers.

Bruscia, K. (2002) 'Foreword.' In B. Stige (2002b) *Culture-Centered Music Therapy.* Gilsum, NH: Barcelona Publishers.

Cole, M. (1996) *Cultural Psychology. A Once and Future Discipline.* Cambridge, MA: Belknap Press of Harvard University Press.

Dalgard, O.S. and Sørensen, T. (eds) (1988) *Sosialt Nettverk og Psykisk Helse* [Social Networks and Psychological Health.] Oslo: Tano.

Dissanayake, E. (2000) *Art and Intimacy. How the Arts Began.* Seattle: University of Washington Press.

Dissanayake, E. (2001) 'An Ethological View of Music and its Relevance to Music Therapy.' *Nordic Journal of Music Therapy 10*, 2, 159–175.

Dreier, O. (1994) 'Sundhedsbegreber i Psykososial Praksis.' [Concepts of Health in Psychosocial Practice.] In U.J. Jensen and P. Fuur Andersen (eds) *Sundhedsbegreper i Filosofi og Praksis* [Concepts of Health – Philosophy and Practice]. Århus: Philosophia.

Esping-Andersen, G. (1990) *The Three Worlds of Welfare Capitalism.* Cambridge: Polity Press.

Estrella, K. (2001) 'Multicultural Approaches to Music Therapy Supervision.' In M. Forinash (ed) *Music Therapy Supervision.* Gilsum, NH: Barcelona Publishers.

Frohne-Hagemann, I. (1990/2001) 'Integrative Musiktherapie und ihr Psychotherapeutische Selbstverständnis.' [Integrative Music Therapy and its Psychotherapeutic Self-

Understanding.] In I. Frohne-Hagemann (2001) *Fenster zur Musiktherapie. Musik-therapie-theorie 1976–2001.* [Windows to Music Therapy. Music Therapy Theory 1976–2001.] Wiesbaden: Reichert Verlag.

Garred, R. (2002) 'The Ontology of Music in Music Therapy – A Dialogical View.' In C. Kenny and B. Stige (eds) (2002) *Contemporary Voices in Music Therapy: Communication, Culture, and Community.* Oslo: Unipub.

Gibson, J.J. (1979/1986) *The Ecological Approach to Visual Perception.* Hillsdale, NJ: Erlbaum.

Giddens, A. (2001) *Sociology.* Fourth Edition. Cambridge: Polity Press.

Gouk, P. (2000) *Musical Healing in Cultural Contexts.* Aldershot: Ashgate.

Grund, J. (1982) *Velferdsstaten i Motvind* [The Welfare State under Strain.] Oslo: Universitetsforlaget.

Horden, P. (2000) *Music as Medicine. The History of Music Therapy since Antiquity.* Aldershot: Ashgate.

Hydle, I. (1991) *Kultur og Helse i et Lokalsamfunn* [Culture and Health in a Local Community.] Oslo: Kommuneforlaget.

Janzen, J.M. (2000) 'Theories of Music in African Ngoma Healing.' In P. Gouk (ed) *Musical Healing in Cultural Contexts.* Aldershot: Ashgate.

Katz, S. (1993) 'The Peace Train Tour Souvenir Cassette.' (Audio-tape) Durban: Unity Productions.

Kenny, C. (1982) *The Mythic Artery. The Magic of Music Therapy.* Atascadero, CA: Ridgeview.

Kenny, C. (1989) *The Field of Play. A Guide for the Theory and Practice of Music Therapy.* Atascadero, CA: Ridgeview.

Kenny, C. and Stige, B. (eds) (2002) *Contemporary Voices in Music Therapy: Communication, Culture, and Community.* Oslo: Unipub.

Kleive, M. and Stige, B. (1988) *Med Lengting, Liv og Song* [With Longing, Life, and Song]. Oslo: Samlaget.

Mattern, M. (1998) *Acting in Concert: Music, Community, and Political Action.* New Brunswick, NJ: Rutgers University Press.

Nordoff, P. and Robbins, C. (1977) *Creative Music Therapy.* New York: John Day.

Orford, J. (1992) *Community Psychology. Theory and Practice.* Chichester: Wiley.

Pavlicevic, M. (2003) 'Risk, Indemnity and Social Responsibility in Music Therapy Training.' *Voices: A World Forum for Music Therapy.* http://www.voices.no/mainissues

Procter, S. (2002) 'Empowering and Enabling – Music Therapy in Non-medical Mental Health Provision.' In C. Kenny and B. Stige (eds) *Contemporary Voices in Music Therapy: Communication, Culture, and Community.* Oslo: Unipub.

Robbins, C. and Stige, B. (1998) '– It's so Universal! Clive Robbins interviewed by Brynjulf Stige.' *Nordic Journal of Music Therapy* 7, 1.

Ruud, E. (1987/1990) *Musikk som Kommunikasjon og Samhandling. Teoretiske Perspektiv på Musikkterapien* [Music as Communication and Interaction. Theoretical Perspectives on Music Therapy]. Oslo: Solum.

Ruud, E. (1998) *Music Therapy: Improvisation, Communication, and Culture.* Gilsum, NH: Barcelona Publishers.

Schapira, D. (2002) 'New Sounds in Culture.' In C. Kenny and B. Stige (eds) (2002) *Contemporary Voices in Music Therapy: Communication, Culture, and Community.* Oslo: Unipub.

Skotheim, R. (1996) 'Rockeband som Ramme for å Selvstendiggjøre Beboere på et Psykiatrisk Ettervernshjem.' [The Rock Band as a Context for the Enabling and Empowering of Users of a Psychiatric Community Nursing Facility.] *Nordic Journal of Music Therapy 5*, 1, 43–47.

Small, C. (1998) *Musicking. The Meanings of Performing and Listening.* Hanover, NH: Wesleyan University Press.

Stige, B. (1983) 'Ngoma, Musirør og Anna Rør.' [Ngoma, Music, and Movement.] Unpublished thesis. Oslo: Østlandets musikkonservatorium.

Stige, B. (1993/2002) 'Community Music Therapy as Cultural Engagement.' In B. Stige (2002b) *Culture-Centered Music Therapy.* Gilsum, NH: Barcelona Publishers.

Stige, B. (1995) *Samspel og Relasjon. Perspektiv på ein Inkluderande Musikkpedagogikk* [Interaction and Relationship. Perspectives on Inclusive Music Education.] Oslo: Samlaget.

Stige, B. (ed) (2002a) *Trivselshagen.* [Thrive: Local Grounds for Welfare.] Sandane, Norway: Næringshagen.

Stige, B. (2002b) *Culture-Centered Music Therapy.* Gilsum, NH: Barcelona Publishers.

Stige, B. (2002c) 'The Relentless Roots of Community Music Therapy.' *Voices: A World Forum for Music Therapy.* http://www.voices.no/mainissues

Stige, B. (2003) *Elaborations toward a Notion of Community Music Therapy.* Unpublished Ph.d. dissertation. University of Oslo.

Stige, B. and Kenny, C. (2002) 'Introduction – The Turn to Culture.' In C. Kenny and B. Stige (eds) (2002) *Contemporary Voices in Music Therapy: Communication, Culture, and Community.* Oslo: Unipub.

Svedheim, L. (ed) (1985) *Nätverksterapi. Teori och Praktik.* [Network Therapy. Theory and Practice.] Stockholm: Carlssons.

Tomasello, M. (1999) *The Cultural Origins of Human Cognition.* Cambridge, MA: Harvard University Press.

Torp, A. (1918/1992) *Nynorsk Etymologisk Ordbok* [Etymological Dictionary of the New Norwegian Language.] Oslo: Bjørn Ringstrøms Antikvariat.

Tyson, F. (1973) 'Guidelines toward the Organization of Clinical Music Therapy Programs in the Community.' *Journal of Music Therapy 10*, 3, 113–124.

Twelvetrees, A. (1991) *Community Work.* Second Edition. Hampshire: MacMillan.

Walker, S. (ed) (1993) *Changing Community.* Saint Paul, MN: Graywolf Press.

Wilson, E.O. (1975/2000) *Sociobiology: The New Synthesis* (25th Anniversary Edition). Cambridge, MA: Belknap Press of Harvard University Press.

CHAPTER 5

What can the Social Psychology of Music offer Community Music Therapy?

Jane Davidson

Context

Over the past 20 years, huge strides have been made in the theoretical and empirical work of music psychologists. Initially, the field was largely outlined in terms of its potential to understand human cognitive (mental) processes. In particular, the similarities and differences between thought, spoken language and music were investigated to explore the potential ways in which the mind is organised, and information stored and made sense of both as memories and in its performative acts. This work was important, with several major texts appearing which defined the field. Of note were Sloboda's *The Musical Mind* (1985) and Dowling and Harwood's (1986) *Music Cognition*. But, the scope of the initial research questions and emergent issues tended to remain in the cognitive domain and this meant that the applications of such investigations were often difficult to appreciate by non-psychologists. Since applied studies were scarce, or non-existent, the result was to allow a gulf between theoreticians and practitioners to develop. In terms of music therapy, some small efforts were made for bridges to be built, with Bunt, Clarke, Cross and Hoskyns (1988) exploring what psychology research could offer the therapist.

But, in the mid 1990s, along with a boom interest in psychology in popular culture (self-help manuals, books about lifestyle and so on), researchers with more applied music psychology questions emerged. Trends in the research included studies such as how children acquired musical skills, and how performers presented themselves in the concert context. The researchers began to illustrate that musical thought was not an isolated inner mental process, but more or less dependent on social interaction and socio-cultural conditioning, and thus dependent on behaviour. Though it may seem obvious to any lay person that to hum a tune in your mind is indeed an activity implying a social learning context (you have been taught this tune by others at some point), and that the conditions under which you are humming are in some way social (some particular situation in which you find yourself or perhaps a thought of a social encounter), it is important to highlight the breakthrough nature of these applied social psychology studies at the time.

I was highly involved with applied research during this period and know that many bridges between music psychology and other areas of music research were built, and in my opinion, this has led to a much more interesting view of music, its function and how we understand it. Thus, nowadays, the field of music psychology is a richer research domain, and, specifically relevant to the case of the music therapist, it is a more useful research source. New books of relevance for useful additional reading include: Hargreaves and North's edited collection entitled *The Social Psychology of Music* (1997); MacDonald, Hargreaves and Miell's edited collection *Musical Identities* (2002); Miell, Hargreaves and Macdonald's edited collection *Musical Communication* (forthcoming). Therefore, it is to the field of the social psychology of music that I now turn to discuss the ways in which I believe this research can be of relevance to music therapists working from social and community perspectives. I focus most of the chapter on the practical implications of the music psychology research, but conclude with a number of ways in which I believe the social psychology of music research can help to develop a theoretical perspective on Community Music Therapy.

Applying music psychology studies to therapy practice

A simple review of the literature to have emerged over the past decade would be useful, but I would rather focus the discussion on the elements of social engagement I regard as being particularly relevant to therapy. Hence, I shall define three areas around which my discussion will be focused. First, there is the matter of an individual's isolation from a social context. Indeed, whether living as an owner-occupier or in a special community care facility, there are many people who live extremely solitary lives in all combinations of ways: those with organic illnesses that remove them from an active social (mental and physical) world; those with psychological difficulties (ranging from depression to psychotic episodes) who find social encounter often highly anxiety-provoking and who are regularly shunned by the outside world; and then there are millions of individuals who have no particular ill-health symptoms, but whose social circumstances make them isolated – the elderly, immigrants to a strange language and culture, women with young children, unemployed teenagers. All these individuals seem to be excluded from the well-being promoted by typical everyday human encounters (see research by Myers 1993 and Kaemmer 1993, which suggests that 'equilibrium' is the primary function of social interaction, and music might play an important role in this kind of socialising health equation).

The second area is where individuals come together to form social groups. Again, the context might vary enormously from an everyday setting to a 'special' one. The group, of course, highlights the collective social experience and important impact it has on an individual's sense of being a human.

The third area, as a consequence of research work in domains one and two, explores the social nature of an individual's sense of self. That is, how individuality is highly dependent on all manner of social influences. These influences range from those of a pragmatic type – social etiquette, for instance – to a potentially more psychodynamic type: the influence of a key individual, for example, on someone's disturbed state.

The three areas all feature in this chapter. Discussion will zoom in and out of focus on the individual, the group and the development and emergence of a social self. Prior to embarking upon this exploration, however, it is necessary to point out that in Western culture at least, we have some severe misapprehensions about what music is and who musicians are. Specialist skills involved in playing classical Western instruments have accounted for some myths that only a 'gifted few' can aspire to musical performance success, but therapists know more than other groups of society that music can be with and for all kinds of people. However, some necessary distinctions need to be made. We might define music as a stream of sounds that humans manipulate in terms of pitch, timing, timbre and dynamics for communicative and expressive ends. Whilst the pioneering evolutionary theorist Charles Darwin (1871) could not see the value of music, the archaeologist Sachs (1948) provided evidence from ancient and extremely primitive cultures to show that music was a highly significant part of social behaviour, and thus human communication. More recently, the ethnomusicologist Simha Arom (2000) has stated that music has an intentionality for sharing (rhythms, melodies, harmonies and so on), and so confirms a common cultural identity through its ritualised practices around other forms of community sharing activities such as eating, rites of passage, etc. That is, music exists in categories and repertoires simultaneously reflecting and creating social thought and behaviour.

As for the gifts and talents argument, there is now sufficient research available to demonstrate robustly that with persistence, anyone with average physical and mental faculties can learn to play a Western musical instrument. Of course, there are also individuals such as autistic savants who can develop incredible skills in music, arguably as a result of their 'special' individual profiles.

It is perhaps the lack, for instance, of focus on everyday social activity that seems to leave the savant's mind 'open' and able to concentrate in an extremely concentrated manner on the development of skills in a single domain (Ockelford 2000). Or, alternatively, it is perhaps that most of us cannot open our minds to the richly stimulating and subtle array of information in the world, and it is this which makes our achievements so feeble when compared with the savant's lightning speed in, for example, reproducing musical sounds previously heard.

Allied to the gifts and talents argument is the notion that you have to be a performer in order to be a musician. However, in a recent chapter (see Davidson 2002), I argue that musical playing skills and performance skills are different, and that for some individuals the public forum is not necessary. Therapy can be about one-to-one sharing and have little to do with the spectacle implied in a solo piano recital. There are those, of course, for whom public spectacle might be more important than one-to-one encounters and vice versa. Yet, music is above all things a communicative act, and even if it is simply playing for the self, some external ear is implied. It might be the ear of the composer for whom the sounds have been created, or it might be for a self-reflective player listening to his or her musical output.

Furthermore, individuals might benefit from listening to music as opposed to performing it, and there are many individuals able to develop fine musical recognition skills simply through exposure to musical stimuli. Take, for instance, the case of the teenage boy who has a vast knowledge of a specific pop band, its good and bad live performances and so on. This sort of expertise is self-sustaining and self-taught, and though he is not an instrumentalist, there is a refined musically aware ear in evidence. Bearing these definitions in mind, the types of musicians I wish you to consider in this chapter are: the passive and/or active listener; the performer in an intimate and private context; the performer with a public performance goal; the soloist and the group musician. When there are moments when I do not draw connections between these different people, perhaps it will be informative for you to make connections. Because I am going to cover research which overlaps each one of these categories, I have decided not to sub-divide the chapter based on these different people, but rather to raise discussion points connecting and separating the different research I shall consider.

From isolation to integration: The individual attempting to integrate into a social context

We know that the melodic speech and songs that mothers use to soothe and stimulate their infants may result in some advantage for the baby: typically to promote sleep (Ayers 1973). Owing to the additional proximity of cuddling and bouncing, it appears that the song/play activity may also facilitate the cultivation of reciprocity and communication in one-to-one relationships (Trevarthen 1999/2000). For many infants, this 'motherese' which is both listened to and participated in becomes a key part of both mental and social development. Normal enculturation seems to guarantee that all children will develop using their singing voice, 'learning' in a very natural way the structures of musical language (Sloboda 1985). Gordon's work on standardised musical measures suggests that by nine years of age most of us have acquired a consistent range of listening and recognition skills in music, irrespective of culture, thus suggesting that music is an innate and developmentally affected human ability (Gordon 1987). Taken together, these suggestions indicate that music has adaptive value, helping the infant move from its isolated birth status to a much more integrated social person, interacting first with mother, then playmates and siblings and so on (Papousek and Papousek 1981).

In addition to these, and linking back to the evolutionary evidence for music (Arom and Sachs, for instance), important work by Malloch (1999/2000) has elegantly described the infant behaviours with caregivers as an innate communicative musicality. His compelling video and spectographic analyses of sound and movement interactions strongly support the notion that there is a mutual 'tuning in' achieved in 'motherese' which does indeed promote good adaptation to the social world for the child. Indeed, where mothers are depressed or manic, their infants are not interacted with so 'musically' and so do not – in the short term at least – progress as well in their general development.

This developmental research highlights that we all have the ability to participate in music. It can bring us from isolation to social interaction and it may be a core channel of human communication.

Clearly, these findings can be easily translated to therapist/client interactions. But, of the recent social research I have been involved with, which considers the adult population, one stands out in particular, for it can illustrate the possibility for adaptive behaviour through music in adulthood. This work was carried out by Betty Bailey in Canada, under my supervision (see Bailey 1999). Betty is a psychologist with a strong amateur interest in choral singing and was keen to investigate why and how people engaged in choral singing (for full and published details of this work, see Bailey and Davidson 2002, Bailey and Davidson 2003).

The choristers she selected came from The Homeless Choir in Montreal, Canada. At the time of interview, the choir comprised 20 homeless Francophone Canadian men. Of the whole ensemble, Betty was able to undertake in-depth interviews with the one-third who were absolutely bilingual, so she could speak with them in English. From the interviews she was able to establish several key common circumstances between the interviewees. All had suffered: abusive parents, poverty, failed relationships, several losses of employment. In one case, the man had lost his child in a tragic accident in his home swimming pool. All had suffered from bouts of mental illness with associated self-abuse with drugs and alcohol. Reasons for joining the choir were (in accordance with their own conscious reflections) pragmatic such as: 'to get in off the street'; or accidental 'I was playing chess and someone asked me, so I just went along.' Well, it may seem as if these men would constitute a potential music therapy cohort in terms of being hospitalised and offered therapy. However, these men had never been offered any therapeutic interventions. Rather, a young French priest based in Montreal simply offered to run a choir. The men sang familiar songs and as the choir developed, they began composing simple ones themselves. Many of these pieces were autobiographical in nature.

A brief analysis of the interviews revealed the following effects of the singing on these individuals:

Emotional and personal release

C3:   Singing is magic, I mean you can't touch it, you can't feel it with your hands, but it's somewhere around you...

C5:   When I sing, I am happy...contented with myself, I'm happy with what I did.

C5:   ...when I learned that song, I needed three days, I was crying, that's all, because...I said 'Oh wow, phew, ok I can live now...' You are expressing it.

Music for personal control

C2:   I feel so good you know, it refreshes you... We need that, otherwise we'd go nuts.

Socialising influences

C7:   There are several in the choir...who have succeeded now in this life because of the choir. They have found companionship, a woman...This choir is giving the people hope and happiness.

Betty argued that this 'hope and happiness' was connected very strongly with the fact that the choir permitted the men to have controlled social interactions which involved emotional closeness and proximity to others, whilst also enabling them to vent their anger and frustration.

Self-esteem and communication

Another key point was that the public nature of the performance provided some very significant personal opportunities:

> C6:   I was a homeless person, alone… Then, I could be a group, a force to entertain others. People like us have difficulty socialising amongst themselves outside the choir. When you're with a homeless person communication is seldom good.

So, the musical interactions seem to have short-circuited this difficulty.

Provide mental stimulation

> C5:   I am learning a lot of things. I feel that you create something. We create some harmonies. I develop a good ear. It is a really good thing…I couldn't do that digging a hole somewhere, now could I?

Provide opportunities for free play

> C4:   Sometimes we can be very deep, and uh, sometimes we can, we can make people laugh…

> C1:   I am a clown sometimes…we joke, make movements and dance sometimes.

Fun seemed to be a key element too.

We can use psychological theory to discuss these data. Perhaps the most strikingly relevant theory to apply might be Malloch's communicative musicality. In these data, it seems that the music *per se* offers these men self-concept-enhancing constructs. The inter-relationship of each one of them with the musical materials seems to affect them profoundly. Another outcome appears to be that each individual's participation seems to contribute towards establishing a clearer personal identity, rather like the new-born, having a self-identity co-constructed in its relationship with the primary caregiver.

Thus, both the music and the social interactions are important to the choristers. We know that music has been regarded as being 'meaningful' because of its references to deep bodily knowledge, for instance, basic concepts such as weight, time, space and flow. In recent times, Lidov (1987) and Hatten (1999), and a number of other music theorists have shown how physical gestures not only help us to articulate musical phrases in performance, but that the impact of these gestures is to stimulate physical effects on us. For example, we know in general psychology that if we are watching someone in a state of pain or great joy similar facial muscles will tense in empathy. When listening to music, shivers down the spine, a lump in the throat or other visceral responses occur in empathy with the music itself (Sloboda 1991). This suggests that participation in musical activity itself might, therefore, be akin to two things:

- having an interaction with another human (the music being that person)
- elicitation of powerful physical/affective states.

In the former case, Watt and Ash (1998) have commented that listening to a piece of music is like the action of another person upon us. And, in fact, we tend to ascribe human characteristics to music. In the latter case, it is important to think about those adults in everyday life who use music to regulate mood. Indeed, as Betty's work has developed, she is now investigating why the elderly participate in the local church choir, why Brazilian students choose to sing together, and why Australian school children are so devoted to their band programmes. First and foremost, her respondents comment on the qualities of the music allowing them to express inner emotional states. And, sometimes, the music itself shifts their mood. But, more of this towards the end of the current chapter.

Socially, we know that group interaction can help with personal stress and anxiety. Indeed, according to Cottrell's interpretation of *Social Facilitation Theory* (1972), the mere presence of other people heightens our arousal levels. This can of course help us to feel 'elated' when performing in a group context, and make our individual achievements seem all the greater. Indeed, Cottrell reports that back in 1899 Tripplett was the first to observe this effect when he noted that cyclists could ride much faster together rather than alone. Cottrell speaks of a *learned evaluation hypothesis*, in which the perception of co-actors on an activity affects its performance outcome. If 'non-threatening', they can enhance an individual's performance, but if threatening they can impair matters. Besides co-action there are audiences. Cottrell discovered that if a peformance task was well-learned, performance was normally enhanced by the presence of an audience, the arousal level being induced by the mere presence of the others and working positively to heighten physical capacities such as breath flow, heart-rate, visual acuity and so on. But, if the audience was seen as being highly evaluative and the task was not so well-learned, the individual performers could perceive the arousal as an anxiety state and so become overly aroused and thus perform badly. So, clearly, in such contexts it would be important for choristers to be sufficiently well-trained for them to feel secure performing music. In this way, the group and audience elements can serve to create a very positive individual experience.

One other matter worthy of discussion is that the physical activity of singing itself perhaps adds favourably to the kinds of comments the homeless men were making, for the breath control required creates both a sense of contact with the body's basic life impulse, and also gives some control over the body, which in the case of the homeless men their drug and alcohol abuse had perhaps not permitted.

Social learning in childhood musical experiences

Betty's research is the most obviously therapeutic I shall consider in this chapter. Now I turn to the much more traditional context of research exploring the learning of classical musical instruments. The research I focus on was begun by me in the 1990s along with John Sloboda, Michael Howe and Derek Moore, and was followed up recently by Karen Burland, Derek and myself.[1] In essence, the results of the initial study showed that musical instrument learning in our culture was essentially a socially dependent activity. Indeed, learners who made the most progress were those who worked with their parents as supervisors of practice in the initial stages, and even later as teenagers, the learners were psychologically happier and making more progress if their parents were involved in attending concerts and so on. These were in fact family units in which the parents would often adopt the musical interest of the child, not only attending concerts, but even taking up an instrument themselves. The data convincingly showed the need for this environmental support.

Siblings were other sources of influence, with children initially beginning an instrument in the hope of 'emulating' an elder sibling. But as an independent study by Sophia Borthwick and me showed (Borthwick and Davidson 2002; Davidson and Borthwick 2002), it was essential for a level of niche diversification to be attained if the child was to persist with music. Indeed, inter-sibling rivalry particularly in two-sib families was found to have a profound influence on the music learner's progress. An over competitive relationship between siblings often ended in failure, especially for the younger learner.

Teachers were also found to have a powerful influence. The first teacher needed to be 'nurturing' initially, but then this teacher needed to demonstrate excellent skills and to become a figure of respect and source of inspiration. With

---

1   See the following references for the actual details of the design, participants, etc: Davidson, Howe, Moore and Sloboda 1998; Howe, Davidson, Moore and Sloboda 1995; Howe, Davidson and Sloboda 1998; Moore, Burland and Davidson (in press). The social context of musical success: *British Journal of Developmental Psychology*; Sloboda, Davidson, Howe and Moore 1996.

high achievers, there were very often several teachers involved in their progress, but the parental first teacher was an absolute necessity. Children who did not feel supported by this first teacher more often than not gave up within two years of having started lessons.

These data may not be of direct interest to the music therapist, but a number of themes can be extrapolated:

- music, like any other form of learning, needs to be 'nurtured'
- parent-like support is necessary
- inter-sibling types of rivalries can be damaging
- in terms of leadership for learning, teacher needs to be both soft and assertive, according to the learner's stage of development.

In music, it seems that a feeling of safety and engagement with music as being non-threatening all adds to developing a strong sense of a personal musical identity. The individual's sense of self is positively constructed through music-making and all the social encounters that involves. Of course, this kind of self-construction was seen to some extent in Betty's participants. But here, we see that the whole focus of life is being constructed around musical engagement. It seems important for therapists to consider such research in order to assess how significant a part of someone's life music was, is and may be. Aside from this, it is perhaps useful for a music therapist to consider his/her own musical identity not only to assess how significant music is personally, but equally, how important or unimportant it is or may be for someone else.

The research above focuses again on performance, but we can certainly draw out the significance of its applications for those engaged with all forms of music listening. Indeed, recent therapy work by Magee (2002) has shown how an individual's sense of self is both improved and diminished given the use of music to stimulate reminiscences of the past. But, with Magee's ageing and ill client, music was also used to show physical and mental skills as he attempted to sing an old familiar song, but also, and negatively, he used his ability more or less to engage with the music to monitor his rate of mental and physical decline. So, again, the therapist needs to be vigilant to see in what ways social and personal comparisons are being made in the music. But, it is also important to highlight that listening can be as useful a means of self-monitoring as participation, depending upon the particular case.

Personalities and music

Since Community Music Therapy involves musical performances (See Maratos, Woods, Powell, in this book), this section presents some of the social-psychological complexities involved in musical performance.

The individuals Burland, Moore and I studied seemed to have developed a set of defining 'performing' personality characteristics which were in part connected with the need of giving a public airing to their emotions, and having an 'outer self' presented to the world. This related strongly to some research I had already published on the characteristics of a performing personality. According to my proposition, individuals seemed to be able to manipulate a number of key elements:

- playing with a number of social roles – leader, follower, etc. – and so working as an ensemble to regulate the music as it unfurled

- articulating and presenting their ideas through music in an overt form, through illustrative emotional communication and emblematic behaviour

- working with a musical narrative, so being inside the music, or (as mentioned earlier with reference to Lidov and Hatten), being conversational with the musical language itself

- oppositionally, working outside of the musical narrative, and focusing simply on audience concerns

- being happy to 'show off' and to do this through overt display activities.

My own research (Davidson 2001) focused on singing activities, with the implication that certain individuals develop with more or less the 'correct' behaviours to be performers. There were motivational differences between those who were soloists and those who were ensemble players, with the ensemble performers needing to share and benefiting from the collaborative sense of self – quite like Betty's homeless men. The soloists were much more focused on the challenge of presenting the 'projected self' centre stage. Of course, different people may see themselves more or less as performers. So, on the one hand, it is important that not everyone is 'pushed' to do something that does not fit easily with them. However, the sense of self is far from 'fixed' and it could be that some people enjoy being performers when either exposed for the first time to it, or facilitated to engage in it in a safe environment.

For the therapist, perhaps the most interesting outcome of this research is that it highlighted the subtle non-verbal behaviours essential to creating information about, to perceiving, and then reacting to the performer. These include gaze, in any case important to the establishment of interpersonal relationships (Argyle 1979), as well as facial expressions and musical gestures. Of course, social psychologists have made a specialist study of all kinds of interpersonal communications and have suggested that we present very subtle non-verbal cues to one another, which are easily understandable to most others within the same cultural context. Perhaps the usefulness of some of these outcomes is that the community music therapist engaged in performance practice and even public performances is often working in unusual, spontaneous (and at times difficult) circumstances. Even though different individuals use different types of gestures, the application of this kind of work for the music therapist is that understanding non-verbal cues is important. For the therapist to know whether or not someone is 'showing off' or simply trying to communicate is a necessary and important step. But, of course, keeping with the idea of musical sound and movement often being co-constructed, possessing the same intention, it is also important for the music therapist to be able to 'read' the musical gestures not only in terms of musical grammars, but also for both therapists and clients to 'sensitise' their hearing, to become subtle and open 'listeners', whilst also aware of the body and its expressive potential in defining the individual within a social framework.

So far then we have been able to consider different types of musical contexts, and musical performance for individuals and groups; we have also raised the issue that for some it is more or less necessary to have a performing context.

Conclusions

I hope that the research I have highlighted and the practical implications emphasised will be of use to the music therapist. As I stated in the opening to this chapter, the relationship between individual and group and then the social self are critically important matters for us all to consider. Exploring social theory further, the social self has been emphasised by Doise (1986) who distinguishes between four levels of self. The first two are the socially positioned self and the ideological self. These are in effect the results of group and culture on norms and beliefs. So, for the men in Betty's choir, for instance, the group would have had shared cultural behaviours and practices which would have helped them to feel 'part' of the social collective. The second two levels are concerned with inter-individual and intra-individual. So, small group effects, such as who plays a dominant role and why, are the inter-individual elements. Here, the role of the conductor of Betty's choir may have been significant, or in the case of music therapy, the therapist, leading a group. The intra-individual elements are the individual differences such as the impact of personality and how personality is indeed shaped by the social environment. So, all operate on one another. Considering what a theory of community music therapy might include, there should, in line with this discussion, be some means of articulating the layers of identity and accounting for how the musical socio-cultural world can interact with individuals to create 'selfhood'.

A theory of Community Music Therapy might also need to incorporate the dynamics of the relationship between embodiment, meaning, music and bodily gesture. Whilst analytical devices to de-code musical and inter-/intra-personal interactions in terms of musical and physical gestures certainly help to clarify some of these relationships, therapists need to have their own rationale for investigating the parallels between these different channels of communication. Also, formalising a definition of work that encapsulates all forms of musical engagement and communication would be helpful, ranging from passive to highly active musical performance and/or listening.

Considering the parallels I was making between infancy and developmental work and the work of the therapist, Byng-Hall's (1995) compelling family script theory might also be usefully applied to the theoretical development of Community Music Therapy. According to Byng-Hall, we develop in adulthood according to our childhood models, playing out family scripts 'written' by our parents and handed down across the generations. Therefore, in order to enhance the conditions for music in a community setting, careful monitoring of both the therapist's and individual participant's individual role and behaviour is probably of critical importance. Indeed, any theory of Community Music Therapy should account for the interpersonal roles and quality of the interactions.

Clearly, I am limited in the ground I can cover in a chapter such as this. But I hope that highlighting the critical nature of music as a social act will help music therapists define and refine their practices with music in all manner of community contexts.

References

Arom, S. (2000) 'Prolegomena to a Biomusicology.' In N.L. Wallin, B. Merker and S. Brown (eds) *The Origins of Music*. London: MIT Press.

Argyle, M. (1979) 'New Developments in the Analysis of Social Skills.' In A. Wolfgang (ed) *Non-verbal Behaviour*. New York: Academic Press.

Ayers, B. (1973) 'Effects of Infant Carrying Practices on Rhythm in Music.' *Ethos 1*, 387–404.

Bailey, B.A. (1999) 'The Impact of Choral Singing on a Group of Homeless Men.' Unpublished MA dissertation. University of Sheffield, September 1999.

Bailey, B.A. and Davidson, J.W. (2002) 'Adaptive Characteristics of Group Singing: Perceptions from a Choir of Homeless Men.' *Musicae Scientiae 6*, 221–256.

Bailey, B.A. and Davidson, J.W. (2003) 'Amateur Group Singing as a Therapeutic Instrument.' *Nordic Journal of Music Therapy*, 18–32.

Borthwick, S.J. and Davidson, J.W. (2002) 'Developing a Child's Identity as a Musician: A Family "Script" Perspective.' In R.A.R. Macdonald, D.J. Hargreaves and D. Miell (eds) *Musical Identities*. Oxford: Oxford University Press.

Bunt, L.E., Clarke, E.F., Cross, I. and Hoskyns, S.J. (1988) 'A Discussion on the Relationship between Music Therapy and the Psychology of Music.' *Psychology of Music 16*, 62–71.

Byng-Hall, J. (1995) *Rewriting Family Scripts*. London: Guildford.

Cottrell, N.B. (1972) 'Social Facilitation.' In C.G. McClintock (ed) *Experimental Social Psychology*. New York: Holt, Rinehart, and Winston.

Darwin, C. (1871) *The Descent of Man, and Selection in Relation to Sex*. London: Murray.

Davidson, J.W. (2002) 'The Solo Performer's Identity.' In R.A.R. Macdonald, D.J. Hargreaves and D. Miell (eds) *Musical Identities*. Oxford: Oxford University Press.

Davidson, J.W. (2001) 'The Role of the Body in the Production and Perception of Solo Vocal Performance: A Case Study of Annie Lennox.' *Musicae Scientiae V*, 235–256.

Davidson, J.W. and Borthwick, S.J. (2002) 'Family Dynamics and Family Scripts: A Case Study of Musical Development.' *Psychology of Music 30*, 121–136.

Davidson, J.W., Howe, M.J.A, Moore, D.G. and Sloboda, J.A. (1998) 'The Role of Parental Influences in the Development of Musical Ability.' *British Journal of Developmental Psychology 14*, 399–412.

Doise, W. (1986) *Levels of Explanation in Social Psychology*. Cambridge: Cambridge University Press.

Dowling, J. and Harwood, D. (1986) *Music Cognition*. New York: Academic Press.

Gordon, E. (1987) 'The Nature, Description, Measurement and Evaluation of Music Aptitudes.' Chicago: G.I.A. Publications.

Hargreaves, D.J. and North, A.C. (eds) (1997) *The Social Psychology of Music*. Oxford: Oxford University Press.

Hatten, R.S. (1999) Musical Gesture Course Notes, Lecture 3: Embodying Sound. University of Indiana, Department of Music website.

Howe, M.J.A., Davidson, J.W., Moore, D.M. and Sloboda, J.A. (1995) 'Are There Early Signs of Musical Excellence?' *Psychology of Music 23*, 162–176.

Howe, M.J.A., Davidson, J.W. and Sloboda, J.A. (1998) 'Innate Gifts and Talents: Reality or Myth?' *Behavioural and Brain Sciences 21*, 3, 399–407.

Kaemmer, J.E. (1993) *Music in Human Life: Anthropological Perspectives on Music*. Austin, Texas: University of Texas Press.

Lidov, D. (1987) 'Mind and Body in Music.' *Semiotica 66*, 69–97.

Macdonald, R.A.R, Hargreaves, D.J. and Miell, D. (2002) *Musical Identities*. Oxford: Oxford University Press.

Magee, W.L. (2002) 'Disabilty and Identity in Music Therapy.' In R.A.R. Macdonald, D.J. Hargreaves and D. Miell (eds) *Musical Identities*, 179–198.

Malloch, S.N. (1999/2000) 'Mothers and Infants and Communicative Musicality.' *Musicae Scientiae*, 29–58.

Miell, D., Hargreaves, D.J. and Macdonald, R.A.R (forthcoming) *Musical Communication*. Oxford: Oxford University Press.

Moore, D.G., Burland, K. and Davidson, J.W. (in press) 'The Social Context of Musical Success.' *British Journal of Developmental Psychology*.

Myers, D.G. (1993) *Social Psychology*. Toronto: McGraw Hill.

Ockelford, A. (2000) 'Music in the Education of Children with Severe or Profound Learning Difficulties.' *Psychology of Music*, 197–217.

Papousek, M. and Papousek, H. (1981) 'Musical Elements in the Infant's Vocalisation: Their Significance for Communication, Cognition, and Creativity.' *Advances in Infancy Research 1*, 163–224.

Sachs, C. (1948) *Our Musical Heritage*. New York: Prenctice-Hall.

Sloboda, J.A. (1985) *The Musical Mind*. Oxford: Clarendon Press.

Sloboda, J.A. (1991) 'Music Structure and Emotional Response: Some Empirical Findings.' *Psychology of Music 19*, 110–20.

Sloboda, J. A., Davidson, J. W., Howe, M. J. A. and Moore, D. M. (1996) 'The Role of Practice in the Development of Expert Musical Performance.' *British Journal of Psychology 87*, 287–309.

Trevarthen, C. (1999/2000) 'Musicality and the Intrinsic Motive Pulse: Evidence from a Psychobiology and Infant Communication.' *Musicae Scientiae*. 155–215.

Watt, R.J. and Ash, R.L. (1998) 'A Psychological Investigation of Meaning in Music.' *Musicae Scientiae 2*, 33–54.

Is Community Music Therapy a Challenge to the Consensus Model?

PART III

Is Community Music Therapy a Challenge to the Consensus Model?

CHAPTER 6

Whatever Next? Community Music Therapy for the Institution!

Anna Maratos

At 33, Tony has been living in a psychiatric hospital almost continuously for ten years during which time he has been given a range of diagnoses from schizophrenia to amphetamine psychosis to personality disorder. Over the years, he seems to have soaked up some of the illness surrounding him – this against a background of fallen-through placements at hostels and non-engagement in regular therapy. Tony has, however, been a frequent attendee of open music therapy groups over many years. In one session, the group is talking about a new musical being rehearsed by patients and staff and written by Tony's consultant. He is persuaded to take part.

Initially, Tony hovers on the periphery of the music room during rehearsals, joining in for a few minutes at a time. His speech is very pressurised and he mumbles his lines very quickly under his breath. However, he becomes surprised by his singing voice and eventually chooses to play the key role of Edward Elgar, showing great commitment to rehearsals. By the time we come to do an open rehearsal at a nearby hotel he has requested individual time to practise his solos (which were all improvised). The same day he spends his unemployment benefit (which he regularly spends on amphetamines) on a new pair of shoes.

During rehearsals Tony asks lots of questions about the sort of patients for whom long-stay asylums have been unhelpful or harmful. He begins to talk openly about his fears that the institution may have stopped him developing in some way too. Tony maintains his commitment until the final performance, where his confident strutting about the stage and his spontaneous conducting of the managers are testament to his increased confidence. Tony remarks that the performance has made him lose his fear of mirrors. This appears to be the case metaphorically too – Tony begins to reflect on himself, his feelings and the impact of his experience upon his well-being.

The recent baptism of Community Music Therapy at the World Congress of Music Therapy in Oxford (2002) gave retrospective legitimacy to a unique music therapy project that took place in a mental health unit for adults in inner London last year. The project grew out of an experimental collaboration within a group of staff and patients, motivated by an outward-looking music therapy department which encouraged a musical consultant psychiatrist to write an 'operetta' for the institution. Entitled *The Teaching of Edward*, it was rehearsed over six months, and culminated in two external performances. This required a renegotiation of traditional boundaries on many levels, and a rethinking of some of the basic tenets of music therapy practice. In this chapter, some brief excerpts from the script of the musical run alongside an account of the process of rehearsing and performing it. The principle of building community through music therapy is discussed through a psychoanalytic understanding of institutional dynamics.

The psychiatric institution and music therapy

The acute inpatient unit in the UK

The advent of neuroleptic medication in the 1970s precipitated the transformation of the old asylums into shorter-term acute facilities, with an accompanying change of emphasis away from trying to establish a quality of real life in a removed environment, towards rapid 'engagement with services' and the achievement of 'dischargeability' as soon as possible.

The focus has moved to the community, and substantial resources have been channelled into crisis teams, assertive outreach teams, crisis houses, joint intake services, intensive home treatment teams as newly-created adjuncts to the core community mental health teams (CMHTs). The acute ward has been fairly neglected as a result (Fagin 2001). Staff on wards are poorly paid, work long shifts and are not valued as highly as their community counterparts. In many parts of the country, this has had the effect of draining skilled workers away from the acute wards and into the more satisfying and better paid community jobs.

At a recent annual UK conference of the International Society for the Psychological Treatments of Schizophrenia and Other Psychoses (ISPS), entitled 'Making the Acute Ward a Therapeutic Environment', Jeremy Holmes suggested that frequently, in order to cope with this situation, under-qualified staff resort to defences of cynicism, blame or paranoia, divisiveness, somatisation (high sickness rates), retreat (to the office) and neglect. Empathic responsiveness gives way to coercion and control.

Deikman and Whitaker (1979) observed that

> Remarkably little attention is paid to the unconscious motives of staff in prescribing phenothiazines and similar drugs and the wish of staff to 'disidentify' with such patients to avoid the communication of the psychotic's perspective; to avoid the intensity of psychotic affect and dependency wishes; and to express the unconscious rage that is provoked in them when the patient frustrates their wish to 'help'. (p.212)

These ideas are reinforced by a national survey of recent users of UK acute inpatient services, which reports the following:

> 'More than half (56%) of patients said the ward was an un-therapeutic environment, more than double those who said it was therapeutic (25%)' and, 'more than half (57%) of patients said they didn't have enough contact with staff', and of these 'the vast majority (82%) said that they had 15 minutes or less with staff each day'. (Barker 2000)

At the same (ISPS) conference, Leonard Fagin (2002) discussed this widespread and deep resistance to empathy and empathic relating. A 'them and us' culture between patients and staff frequently results in the chasm allowing projections to go both ways – staff and patients are idealised then demonised by each other; people are seen in two dimensions: as ill, or well.

The local context

Rehearsals for *Edward* took place in a mental health unit with 66 beds located opposite an inner city Accident and Emergency department of a large general hospital. Part of the National Health Service, it serves a culturally diverse population and most people admitted to the wards are suffering an acute relapse of a severe mental illness. The emphasis is largely on 'medicating and monitoring' in order that patients may be discharged back home or to a hostel as soon as possible.

Over recent years, the unit has had the highest staff turnover of any within the Mental Health Trust to which it belongs, although this has improved recently. Job satisfaction amongst ward staff apparently remains low, however, as the vast majority of the ward budget is spent on employing temporary staff, advertising vacant posts and recruiting new staff. Communication and collaborative working between different staff groups as well as between users and staff is difficult, and examples of integrated practice rare.

Therapeutic activities are mainly provided in the day hospital or by day hospital staff on the wards. The day hospital provides a mix of psychosocial and psychotherapeutic groups and individual sessions, including occupational and arts therapies and medical cover by a consultant psychiatrist. Day hospital staff are largely middle class and mostly white Caucasian. In contrast, the wards are primarily staffed by a more ethnically and racially diverse group of nurses and nursing assistants, many of whom come from Mauritius or Nigeria.

These multiple dichotomies within the institution seem to be emphasised by the physical surroundings. The building itself is a poorly lit four-storey 'office block' with labyrinthine corridors. Space for staff and patients is limited and this may contribute to the 'pressure cooker' atmosphere that sometimes prevails.

Music therapy in the institution

As the smallest profession in the building represented by two part-time therapists, it took a long time to build up an identity for music therapy and to raise and maintain awareness of the service. Darnley-Smith writes:

> In my experience, whilst music therapy is recognised at a statutory level and we have organised professional structures alongside other healthcare professionals, promoting it on a day to day level as a serious resource requires an enormous persistence and self-confidence... Like many music therapists, I spend a large portion of my week trying to keep the department on the map... (2002, p.80)

As in many other psychiatric hospitals in the UK, music therapy here has mostly been practised to a 'consensus model' (Ansdell 2002a). Consequently, the music room is at the end of a corridor, outside the perimeter of the day hospital, which itself is on a different floor from the wards. The therapeutic work is mainly carried out with individuals and small groups. There is a strong emphasis on the process and the relationship and not on any final musical product. Therapy is seen as clearly different from teaching and most patients attend on the basis of referral procedures (although this is often a self-referral) rather than simply 'dropping in'. Music therapy is predominantly offered on a medium- to long-term basis for an average of two years. There is also an open group where inpatients can attend without commitment, but this is co-run by two music therapists, wholly excluding therefore other members of the multi-disciplinary team.

Generally, music therapists do not socialise with patients in informal surroundings and avoid performing with or for the patients or facilitating 'sing-songs' or Christmas parties. It has been emphasised that music therapy is a form of psychodynamic therapy, not social therapy, and that patients might therefore be confused by relating to their therapist as a co-performer, and the transference relationship contaminated as a result.

These clear but rigid boundaries based on theoretical principles can perhaps be seen as the result of a number of contextual pressures and fears. First, they represent an attempt by the music therapists to be taken seriously and accorded some status and position within the system. There is a constant (and not entirely unfounded) fear of being regarded as valiant do-gooders who bring in instruments from home to play music to patients for relaxation, and who receive no financial reward. In this climate, music therapists perceive an advantage in being neither seen nor heard, and therefore less judged.

These slightly paranoid and defensive feelings seem likely to be in some measure influenced by the surroundings. The institution at its most uncomfortable can feel chaotic or 'uncontained', intensely competitive, and full of undervalued staff. The 'newcomer' status of music therapy as a profession, and the relative youth of the therapists within it, may have contributed to the readiness of our department to take on the anxieties of the patients and to act them out.

The Teaching of Edward

Background to the project

It was these pressures that made me wish to do something to affect the wider context in which I worked. The opportunity arose when I presented at an academic seminar a case of a patient who had been in individual music therapy for three years. The patient's consultant, a professor of psychiatry, became interested in the benefits of music therapy. He told me he had written numerous songs and asked me to put some of them to music for the launch party of his new outreach team. This was a success, and, having seen how it had galvanised the new team, I suggested he write something for everyone at the institution, not just his staff.

The next week I met him by chance at the station and he pulled the almost completed script of *No Room at the Inn* from his briefcase. This was our first attempt at a musical, a parody on the nativity story which also took into account the imminent move of our mental health unit away from its prestigious location in central London to make way for the creation of a specialist heart hospital. This issue united staff and patients who were thus given a chance to begin to process this change through humour and song. Even patients on the locked ward requested a full rehearsal which we facilitated, despite the fact that none was able to leave the ward to take part in the performance.

This initial foray into staff–patient musical collaboration served as an experimental pilot to *The Teaching of Edward*, which was a new musical, requested this time by the cast of *No Room at the Inn*. We began rehearsals on a weekly basis, facilitated by two music therapists and the professor when he was in the country. This grew to twice-weekly musical rehearsals co-run by a number of interested and supportive colleagues (including an occupational therapist and a nurse from the day hospital) and once-weekly acting rehearsals led by a drama therapist trainee on placement. An average of six patients and five staff attended each rehearsal.

The plot of *The Teaching of Edward* is a fictional account of the English composer, Edward Elgar's 'discovery' of music therapy through being persuaded by the patients at the asylum where he was employed to go beyond his usual musician's role of performing to patients.

The following excerpts illustrate the connections between the plot and our own experience of putting on this production, and also exemplify some of the issues that arose for patients along the way.

The first scene

A warm evening in July 1879. On the lawn at the entrance to the hospital. Edward, the new bandmaster, is practising with the Worcester County Asylum Band. The music is not especially stimulating and he is frustrated that he cannot get people more interested in his musical ideas. He finishes for the day; the band leaves and Edward is packing up the music sheets and stands. As he turns to go, he is confronted by a young woman, a patient, who asks him to play for her. Other patients notice what is going on and come outside to try to persuade Edward to play with them. After some early difficulties they compose a song together, *Take Us where the Music Goes*.

TAKE US WHERE THE MUSIC GOES

> *Lo la lo la lo la la*
> *Let us follow by our nose*
> *Lo la lo la lo la la*
> *Whether high or low or around we go*
> *Reaching deep inside or skirting wide*
> *Every little quaver we will savour...*

Much of the time, our rehearsals were characterised by loud and vigorous singing, with considerable laughter and joking. Staff and patients seemed equally keen to make the most of outrageous final cadences, preferring to sing them up the octave, or changing to the major on the last phrase. This was probably a mildly manic response to the anxiety provoked by such a situation – but these moments were often intense, spontaneous and joyous, and they unified the group. There was a tendency, as with open music therapy groups, for the cast to become less anxious and the music more coherent and grounded as the session progressed.

> A new patient comes to the rehearsal and declares he is going to be the director as he doesn't do 'singalongs', and certain verses should only be whistled. A large proportion of the rehearsal is consequently taken up with whistling, which has an unexpected effect upon the group. Whilst initially a kind of manic silliness results in our being unable to whistle due to our inability to stop laughing, this is soon exchanged for a sudden drop in the volume level and an increased listening atmosphere. I offer an improvisatory whistled opening phrase to the group whilst maintaining on the piano the C minor harmony of the song. The group takes this up tentatively at first, and a flourishing of explorative and interactive musicality emerges. The music ends gradually with a fade-out by the director, who whistles the final phrase very quietly, leading naturally to a stillness. I experience this as a satisfying and serious acknowledgement of our having moved somewhere together.

The structured framework of pre-composed songs led to other new experiences too. One participant had one year previously completed three years of individual music therapy during a very difficult time in hospital. He came to rehearsals as an outpatient and, although he had never sung in individual sessions, began tentatively to sing alongside his community psychiatric nurse in the first rehearsal. His voice grew stronger as we went on and at the end he remarked, 'It brought it out of me. I had – what is it? – resonance. A booming voice came out of me.'

Whatever next?

Before the others can take up the theme again they are interrupted by an angry figure in a white coat who storms from the hospital towards the lawn. It is the senior doctor at the asylum, Dr Aloysius Grumple, who is utterly shocked by these scenes of what he considers to be utter degradation.

> Dr Aloysius Grumple (shouting at Edward): 'WHAT on earth do you think you are doing? Have you taken total leave of your senses? Don't you realise what damage you are doing to these mad people? After years of trying to calm them down you've undone all our work in a single day!'

Edward is asked to appear before the Board of Administrators who, predictably outraged, launch into song:

Whatever next? We can't believe
You've done what you have done
You hardly know this hospital
Is not a place of fun
We're in charge of the treatment here
And music nowhere will appear
Compose at will but act your age
And keep performance for the stage!

Although we are unsure until the last moment whether or not any performances will take place due to the unpredictability of the cast, we manage to hold one open rehearsal with invited guests in a hotel situated near the hospital and, following this, an official performance at the Annual General Meeting of the Royal College of Psychiatrists in Cardiff. Although neither of these performances is open to the general public, I have great misgivings about our motivations for doing them, and discuss our motives at length with the professor and other staff. It is clear, however, that for a minority of patients, the idea of doing a real performance is their motivation for attending rehearsals.

Whilst the performances themselves were very challenging for us as music therapists in practical and theoretical terms, it was clear that they were a particularly exciting and unique experience for some patients. Most impressive was the effect a real audience had upon participants. One woman with chronic schizophrenia who had been quite timid and flat in rehearsals, seemed to come alive in costume, and began embellishing her lines and improvising additional interjections to make conversation flow more naturally.

Another woman inpatient with a diagnosis of psychopathic personality disorder caused the entire cast to howl with laughter at her narration and joined in a spontaneous hug and holding of hands with her neighbour. A patient with hypomania, who had been worryingly overpowering at rehearsal, attuned herself perfectly to the group atmosphere during the performance, causing great laughter and enlivening the other performers.

There were also very touching moments where patients and staff would support one another in their lines or their solos. Tony, whose social worker played the female protagonist, was as considerate of her during nervous moments as she was of him. Tony's ability to conduct in time, deliver his lines loudly and without pressured speech, and improvise his solos confidently and with feeling shocked the doctors in the audience who knew him.

We're very nearly sane...

Act 3.   The Board of Administrators is convinced by a patient to let Edward stay. He continues to take the lead from the patients who persuade him to involve them further in new musical enterprises. Members of the Board then hijack the success and claim to have invented music therapy!

Act 4.   It is now 1882. Edward has come to the end of his time at Worcester County Asylum.

Narrator: 'But the Choir are determined to have the final word. Under
      Ebenezer's direction they have planned to deliver a final chorus
      to Edward and Maria, one so loud it will shake the foundations
      of the Worcester County Asylum and make it take notice of
      their new treatment of music therapy.'

Pa pa pa pa pa pa pa pa paa
It's goodbye Edward Elgar
Papa papa papa pa
You're teacher number one
Pa pa papa pa pa pa pa pa
With music as our therapy
Mad thoughts become a melody
We can make them wax and wane
So we're very nearly sane
Papa papa pa pa pa etc

Is this music therapy?

In the story of *The Teaching of Edward*, the beginnings of music therapy are established through a rebellion against the traditional patriarchal institution, where patients were performed *to* and not included *in* the music. The message is about the importance of listening to each other and of exploring new ways of being together in a spontaneous and playful way. Although this is familiar territory for music therapists, the project was an opportunity for us to take this process beyond the session boundary and attune ourselves to the institution as a whole, in the hope of creating something interesting and fresh with the potential for change for everyone. This seems to fit with Ansdell's formulation:

> Community Music Therapy is an anti-model that encourages therapists to resist one-size-fits-all-anywhere models (of any kind), and instead to follow where the need of clients, contexts and music leads. (Ansdell 2002b)

In some respects this project differs markedly from traditional notions of music therapy, and indeed from most of my own work to date. For example:

- Performance – I would not usually ask my patients to stand up and perform in front of others. This has posed difficulties for some patients.

- Process/product – I would usually consider our work together to be an ongoing process rather than leading to a final product.

- Patient/staff roles – these are not usually interchangeable in music therapy sessions.

- Attitude of the professional team – generally my work is approved of by all my colleagues. In this instance some colleagues disapproved.

In other respects, though, the therapeutic value of this work was eminently demonstrable. For example:

- Performance – the experience of preparing for a performance and the performance itself were valued by some patients, although disapproved of by some staff.

- Process/product – there was a clearly observable process through the rehearsals and the performance itself, characterised by reflection and heightening of awareness.

- Patient/staff roles – we were able through the process to focus on the dynamics of the institution.

- Attitude – some individuals (patients and staff) gained insights into their ways of relating to each other.

I will now examine some of these points in more detail.

'Compose at will but act your age' – the implications of performance

The first direct criticism I received about the *Edward* project was from a therapist colleague who responded despairingly to my enthusing about a patient with whom we both worked, and who had 'come alive' in front of an audience. 'But Anna,' she said, 'these people are forced to perform all the time!' Although this is true in one sense for everyone (and particularly for some patients), these performances brought many benefits to participants, as described above. They provided a focus, inspiring commitment and collaboration, but also transformed some people's perceptions of themselves.

However, some core members of the cast, two of whom had made great commitment to rehearsals, were unable to participate in the performances. This was a great disappointment to the cast as a whole, and made the therapists think carefully about the implications of performance for particular patients who wished desperately to perform but, precisely because of this, were likely to feel crippling anxiety when the time came. No matter how much support had been offered it would have been extremely difficult for these people to perform in front of an audience. Despite this, it is possible that they might have been able to perform if more time had been allocated alongside general rehearsals for individual rehearsal and reflection. It felt extremely difficult to be a part-time member of staff at this time because I was unable to offer extra time to individuals who needed it.

Most importantly, we took the lead from the patients, not the staff, and for this reason were not committed to doing any performance until the last minute. Some people came regularly to rehearsals having stated they were not going to be joining in any performance. Others thought there was little point in rehearsing without it, and were focused on the performance dates and venues from the start.

Process versus product

Although this project resulted in a performance product, the project as a whole was a process. It was important to keep thinking reflectively throughout the sessions and to maintain the principles of music therapy which were at the heart of the project. Time was taken to process events verbally, as in a normal music therapy group.

> During a well-attended rehearsal, a very disturbed young man runs into the room, turns off the lights and begins to hack at the air with an imaginary sword in a rather frightening way. He then seems to plant it in the ground, shouts something and storms out. We all stop mid-song as soon as he enters, and I counter moves to instantly recommence once he has left. I ask whether anybody wants to comment on the sudden intrusion. People begin by speculating on what imaginary implement he has been holding, and where he thought he was. For some he was in the jungle, for others he was fighting the doctors. This imaginative dialogue gives way to an open expression of feeling, as much by staff as by patients. Some were frightened, others disappointed that he had not stayed.

> After this incident, this man is a continuous presence on the edge of rehearsals – sometimes popping in to perform a quick act, at other times

remaining outside the room. He does not repeat his threatening behaviour, and the group continues to function with this semi-permeable boundary.

Nor is the product the end of the process. A week after each event (open rehearsal and performance), the cast gathers to watch the video of it and comment on their experience. This is valued by patients who all attend, though unfortunately most staff are unavailable for this.

The product was also a consequence of an earlier process. A number of patients who participated in the project had known me for many years through dropping in to the open group but had never committed to regular sessions. The relationship they formed with me as part of their participation in the *Edward* project enabled two of them (who did not manage the performances) subsequently to refer themselves for individual music therapy.

Patient and staff roles: Re-institutionalising the patients or de-institutionalising the institution?

In early rehearsals, patients (and to a lesser extent staff) would defer to the professor who readily adopted the role of 'director'.

At one rehearsal a patient asks the professor in a childlike voice if she can play the role of the narrator as well as that of a patient. I am dismayed that such a capable and intelligent woman is asking permission from the doctor to be sane in the play, and presumes that this imitates her relationship with him outside rehearsals, perhaps in ward rounds. The doctor responds by colluding with the role she has given him – 'I'll have to think about it as I had someone in mind for the part.'

This sort of interaction both highlighted, and allowed us to address, the unconscious dynamics which keep people dependent upon the institution. The patient went on to play both parts in the open rehearsal, and became more adult and sane in rehearsals leading up to this. The professor began taking more of a back seat. I asked him if it had changed his thinking about how to be with clients and their perceptions of him. He wrote the following:

I had not realised quite how much consultant psychiatrists (with their powers of compulsory detention) were regarded with a combination of fear and loathing… It also helped me to realise how much of what goes on in formal ward reviews is totally phoney…

There was also a change in the way managers treated patients, with a gradual decrease in the use of the more coercive and controlling remarks (for example, one patient was repeatedly told to 'sit down!') to make way for more adult-to-adult communication. The impact would have been greater if senior staff had been able to attend more frequently, and perhaps also if we had been able to set up a separate reflection session for staff, as most were unable to attend the general debrief after the performances.

'Whatever next?' Staff disapproval

My work as a music therapist in the day hospital takes place in the context of multi-disciplinary teamwork. Members of the professional team share insights into work with patients. This is regarded as not only supportive to staff but also offering safety for patients by ensuring that they are not offered opportunities to split the team. This project, however, led to something of a breakdown in this scheme of professional unity.

As mentioned earlier, some of my colleagues dismissed the whole notion of performance as anti-therapeutic. Others complained that day hospital boundaries were being breached by staff participating alongside patients in groups. We were not, they said, here to keep the staff amused, and certainly not to promote doctors at the patients' expense. The professor who had written the musical was regarded as 'un-psychoanalytic', and my collaboration with him was therefore seen by some therapists as inappropriate.

Even more problematic was the choice made by some patients to attend for themselves. One patient had been coming to rehearsals instead of going to his therapy group. Under normal circumstances, the therapist would have communicated this to me as soon as she became aware of the split. But in this instance, I was only told after the patient had been attending rehearsals for three months. We swiftly changed the time of the rehearsal so that the patient could attend both, and he continued to do so until shortly before the performance when he became hostile to the event. Had our combined input been more solid, he would probably have stood a greater chance of deriving benefit from participating in the performance itself.

The support of therapist colleagues would have been a great bonus. Many of these would have been able to help the patients process their feelings about the performance.

Roles within the institution

Rehearsing together meant that everyone had to question and adapt their usual roles in relation to one another within the institution.

My insistence on the therapeutic framework of a punctual start and rehearsals at the same time each week perplexes the Professor who complains that I seem to be so ruled by the clock. He is accustomed to being late and, although people complain about this, they still wait for him to arrive and drop everything to attend to him. This is not the case in rehearsals, which end on time.

Just as staff were not able to maintain the level of power they would normally wield in a ward round or on the ward, so too patients were given the opportunity to think about ways of relating that compounded their problems. At one rehearsal a patient became extremely angry at my suggestion that we have a mixed Board of Administrators (patients and staff, men and women). I was told I should take this seriously and how dare I make such suggestions when I didn't have a clue what it was like to be incarcerated against my will. I wondered aloud whether it was easier for us to play ourselves so that we did not have to think about what it would be like to be in another person's shoes. This opened up a discussion about familiar and comfortable roles within the mental health system, which seemed particularly relevant for the long-term users who tended to join the rehearsals.

For patients, playing the role of asylum staff and so empathising with hospital staff might have incurred unbearable envy, perhaps even internal envy of the healthy part of themselves which manifested itself at rehearsals. Quite a few patients who stayed with rehearsals were naturally talented singers or actors, and perhaps at the start took refuge in the role of a mad patient, which became a container within which it was safe to be a sane, creative performer.

For staff, empathising with patients meant having to tackle their own insecurities, anxieties and dependency on the institution. For example, some of the staff who became involved had been attached to the service for many years and reminisced about the old days when patients and staff would go on week-long camping holidays together. It also meant having to get close to our own insane parts perhaps – acknowledging that we are not all sane all the time.

Community Music Therapy – extending our range of experience

The in-the-moment experience of performing to, and with, one another required a music therapist's listening and clinical improvisation skills. It was as important in this setting as in the more usual open music therapy group to utilise music supportively for an individual soloist or a nervous group (staff and patients). Equally, it was crucial to engage people by the usual means of meeting the client or group where they were in terms of volume, pitch, tempo, mood, colour, timbre, etc. It was also useful to be able to use suspense or tempo changes to unify the group or to sustain people's involvement at difficult moments, albeit within a loosely pre-composed setting.

Therapeutic boundaries of time, place and patient-centredness, and the therapist's ability to think, remained crucial to the process. Two aspects of insanity affect us all to varying degrees at times of stress: a difficulty in thinking reflectively, and a resort to projective mechanisms of defence. Had it not been co-run by psychodynamically oriented therapists, this project might have become a wholesale collusion with both of these ways of operating. They are inherent in the dynamics of the institution and most of the patients who took part were in an acute phase of their illness.

It was tremendously difficult to keep a space for reflection before and after rehearsals. The performances themselves could have been a mere denial of the inequality, envy and power struggles between patients and staff; the rehearsals a manic defence against feelings of impending collapse which were then projected onto the staff team as manifested in their criticisms and fears.

It is certainly true that paranoid processes prevented us from being as proactive as we could have been in presenting our ideas and feedback regularly to all, and fellow professionals continued to be mistrustful of our intentions and our capacity to be aware of and to work non-collusively with the underlying dynamics.

Yet, despite its limitations, the project enabled some staff from different disciplines to work together like a healthy parental couple, overriding barriers of status, hierarchy and to some extent, differences in approach. For example, we did not have to compete with ward rounds for patients to attend rehearsals as the professor would use his own rounds actively to encourage staff and patients to come with him to rehearsals. The music-making provided a medium for spontaneity and intensity of interaction, which, alongside moments of great humour and joy and equally great despair, extended our range of experience within the institution as a linked, thinking and potentially enlivening community.

Acknowledgements

I would like to thank Orii McDermott, Sumi Paik-Maier, Fay Hughes and Bea Scott for their invaluable co-facilitation of the project and Peter Tyrer for writing *The Teaching of Edward* and allowing me to reprint excerpts from the original script. I would also like to thank Phillipa Maddox, my manager at Central and North West London Mental Health NHS Trust, for allowing me to do this unusual project.

References

Ansdell, G. (2002a) 'Community Music Therapy and the Winds of Change.' In C. Kenny and B. Stige (eds) *Contemporary Voices in Music Therapy: Communication, Culture and Community.* Oslo: Unipub.

Ansdell, G. (2002b) 'Do We Puncture the Balloon or let it Fly?' *Voices: A World Forum for Music Therapy 2*, 2. http://www.voices.no/mainissues

Barker, D. (2000) *Environmentally Friendly? Patients' Views of Conditions on Psychiatric Wards.* London: Mind.

Darnley-Smith, R. (2002) Peer response to Lunt, H. (2002) 'The Journey through a Barren Landscape to Practising Music Therapist.' *British Journal of Music Therapy 16*, 2, 79–80.

Deikman, A.J. and Whitaker, L.C. (1979) 'Humanizing a Psychiatric Ward: Changing from Drugs to Psychotherapy.' *Psychotherapy: Theory, Research, and Practice 16*, 2, 204–214.

Fagin, L. (2001) 'Therapeutic and Counter-Therapeutic Factors in Acute Ward Settings.' *Psychoanalytic Psychotherapy 15*, 2, 99–120.

Holmes, J. (2002) *Improving The Therapeutic Environment –Research, Reflection, Re-invigoration.* Paper given at ISPS Annual UK Conference, Nottingham.

CHAPTER 7

A Pied Piper among White Coats and Infusion Pumps: Community Music Therapy in a Paediatric Hospital Setting

Trygve Aasgaard

The participants are first of all the patients: some in wheelchairs, some in beds, many with infusion pumps. But also relatives, students (of various kinds) and people working in the hospital – altogether 20 or 30 persons – may be present. Sometimes a dozen (young and old) start the event by marching (or rolling) through the corridors playing and singing. In front walks the music therapist in top hat, blowing his trombone or recorder. As a rule, more and more participants join the line of musicians as the procession slowly proceeds from the 8th to the 4th floor of the paediatric department. It is important to have time enough also to 'catch' those who react to this unfamiliar event with timidity or apprehension. Bystanders have associated the processions in the paediatric department with the tale of the Pied Piper from Hamelyn (Stai 1999). Like the original Pied Piper, this man's tools are nothing but music. But *he* only takes, for some minutes, those children and adults who want to follow him, to an easily forgotten world within the hospital community. This world is, however, also a real one – but dominated by play, fantasy and pleasurable social interactions. Here, the music therapist strives at treating everyone as a fellow musician, hopefully challenging the individual just so much that the suggested tasks are within her/his capabilities. For some minutes patients are not primarily patients, participating professional staff are not primarily professionals. We will all soon enough be back in the old 'reality'. During 'the musical hour' people come and go all the time, some because of other business, diagnostic/therapeutic appointments, fatigue/uncomfortable symptoms, or simply because of lack of interest. What seems to be important is that the described processions and musical encounters are regular features in the

hospital community; these inclusive rituals shall remind the world that
music man is still alive and present.

Introduction

This chapter describes and discusses some features of Community Music
Therapy applied in paediatric hospital wards that are built and run with the
primary aim of diagnosing and treating malignant diseases. In these settings, the
essentially medical focus on saving lives risks reducing the patient to, simply, a
diseased body, and reducing carers' tasks to treating illnesses. In counterbalance
to this model is the task of 'humanising the hospital community'. This too is an
inter-disciplinary challenge, and as the music therapist, I am particularly privileged to be able to concentrate more on health than on illness, more on
salutogenesis than on pathogenesis. This means working, through music-related
means, with both 'the quality and quantity' of human networks – where the
patient–therapist dyad is but one of many important relationships, and where
therapeutic aims are expanded towards promoting an ecology of health in the
whole hospital community.

Cancer is still the main cause of death in children above one year who die of
a disease. However, progress in understanding and treating childhood malig-
nancies is one of the success stories in paediatrics. The current treatment of
leukaemia is intense, primitive, barbaric, and often effective (Lie 2001). This
progress has its price: the long-lasting treatment usually produces a number of
unpleasant, and partly dangerous side-effects. These factors, plus the inevitable
periods of isolation and hospitalisation influence many aspects related to the
young patients' health, such as 'social relationships', 'self-concepts' and 'joys'
(von Plessen 1995). Although the patient is at the centre of attention and
her/his relatives are placed at the collateral line, 'the illness' also dominates their
lives. A paediatric oncology ward is characterised by the advanced technology
and bustle of a university hospital where curative treatment takes first priority.
Some of the most common stressors for hospitalised children are related to their
experiences of the hospital environment, separation from parents during
medical procedures, the need to interact with strangers, and separation from
peer group and siblings in routine daily events (Melamed 1992, p.142).
Becoming a paediatric patient means temporarily or more permanently dimin-
ishing one's social networks related to family, school, friends, etc. To various
degrees a seriously ill person always becomes stripped of her or his personal

attributes and strength and assumes the role of the *homo patiens.*[1] Patients (usually accompanied by their parents) suddenly find themselves drawn into new formal or informal networks where their position is reduced to mainly being a *receiver* of treatment and care. Community Music Therapy strives to give these patients a voice and bring people together to perform and enjoy music, not as an alternative to the medical treatment, but as a natural agent of health promotion. My points of departure are the music therapy activities within, and sometimes beyond, the boundaries of two university hospitals. Participants and places for *musicing* vary every day and as the music therapist, I seem to have a number of different roles at (more or less) different times, which raises the following questions: when am I, first of all, an entertainer, and when am I a 'serious' therapist?

This chapter addresses issues related to using a community approach on premises where traditional medical paradigms dominate and where music therapy has no traditions. I begin by describing my music therapy practice in the hospital's 'open spaces' and where the music therapy patient is often accompanied by one or two parents. The chapter concludes with a short discussion of the environmental elements presented throughout this chapter.

Musicing in two hospitals: Arenas and participants

Music therapy never goes on in a contextual vacuum. Different *settings* and *participants* determine which meanings can be related to the activities. Paediatric wards in two metropolitan university hospitals constitute the basic arenas for music therapy described in this chapter. Funding for music therapy comes from the Norwegian Childhood Cancer Parent Organisation, and no child is excluded from music therapy activities if interested. All treatment is free, and both parents are allowed public sick leave pension (based on average income) as long as the child is being treated for cancer. One or more relatives usually accompany the sick child during hospitalisation, occupying another bed in the patient's room or in adjacent family rooms. I see relatives as part of the 'human resources' which may be drawn into the different music therapy interventions.

Children with cancer or other serious diseases (and most often their parents) are brought into a hospital 'landscape' where treatment, care, education, and psychosocial support each has a particular position and significance. Every pro-

---

1   *Patior* (Latin) means e.g. to suffer, undergo, allow. The noun, *patientia* means endurance, resignation. I use *homo patiens* as a metaphor for 'a being who suffers'; not to be confused with *'sick role'*, a concept popularised by Talcott Parsons (1951).

fessional person in the hospital (paediatricians, nurses, etc.) and each activity and event has particular links to other professions and professional activities. One of the paediatric departments, 'Hospital 1', fills an eight-storey building with several research institutes and specialised wards including isolation areas/rooms for some children – used before, during and after bone marrow transplantation. The music therapist has a small office, but most practical work goes on in the patients' rooms (isolation rooms included) or in the 'open spaces' (common rooms, play rooms, corridors, entrance hall) of the hospital.

The other paediatric department, 'Hospital 2', is smaller: a one-storey, barrack-like premises with one ward for children under two years of age, one for older children, and limited facilities for proper isolation treatment. Here is neither an entrance hall nor big common rooms, just a kitchenette for relatives and a little corridor with low cupboards where parents sit for hours waiting, chatting or, simply, observing 'life'. This ward has an easily accessible duty room and a centrally placed play room where the music therapist, at times, also 'keeps house'. I 'follow' patients from this hospital when they are transferred to Hospital 1 for bone marrow transplantation. Many aspects of these patients' lives are marked by uncertainty, changing environments, suffering and pathology; a music therapy accompaniment is meant to serve as a continuous health support to a child (and often the near family). I experience few boundaries as to where to work or what to do together with patients and their close relatives. This practice may, perhaps, be characterised as a 'travelling music therapy service across different hospital spaces/arenas' (Figure 7.1).

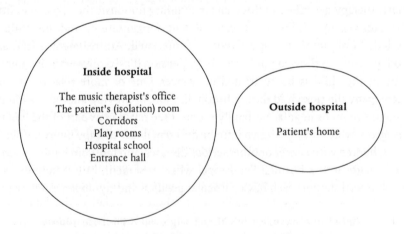

Figure 7.1 Sites for music therapy work

There are several sources for music-listening within the two paediatric wards. Each patient room usually has a TV, video, and often a PC and a cassette/CD player. In one ward, a piano in a corridor can be used by anyone, as can an old grand piano centrally placed in the entrance hall. Sometimes, visiting music or theatre groups are booked for entertainment. The paediatric department of Hospital 1 is proud of its own chamber choir, drawn mainly from members of the medical and nursing staff. The choir has weekly practices in the outpatient ward and performs madrigals, arranged children's songs, carols, etc., three or four times yearly for patients, relatives, and other hospital personnel. I sometimes collaborate with the hospital choir, and have served as accompanist and deputy conductor. The staff choir has also performed songs written by the young patients:

> On one occasion 'Sara', a 14-year-old patient, instructs the 20 choir members to sing her own Spice Girls inspired song (in English): *Dance is Something for All Generations. It's only Limited by your Imagination.* The severely anorexic girl shows the singers how to perform the chorus of the song while she receives her liquid 'supper' through a naso-gastric tube! As a composer she is probably much more advanced than any choir member, and for some minutes this rather shy, 'difficult', critically ill and talented girl makes her therapists and carers sing after her pipe. (After the girl's discharge from hospital, the music therapist continues to be the girl's musical discussion partner. The various musical skills she has developed during hospitalisation are not forgotten and, with the music therapist's rec-ommendation, she commences high school in a class for musically talented and interested youths.)

This kind of musical activity can influence the complex inter-disciplinary and inter-role relationships in the paediatric medical setting. For example, when practising and performing Sara's song, several choir members were rather surprised at experiencing the very sick girl in this completely unusual position.

A quite different form of inter-disciplinary musical expression can often be heard in the paediatric ward of Hospital 2: a ward rock band, *Infusion Complete* (three nurses, one doctor and one pre-school teacher) specialises in making songs about children's experiences and patient–staff relationships. Another 'or-chestra' comes to life every time a child has gone through the approximately two years standard treatment for leukaemia, at children or relatives' birthdays, and indeed on other special occasions. Staff members put on their well-used school band caps, grasp some instrument and walk blowing and banging (often accom-panied by young patients) through the corridor to the play room where the 'guest' is treated like a hero.

Some of these examples of *musicing* are neither the result of my initiative, nor do they depend on my presence. Children sing or play on their own initiative, parents sing with their children, and occasionally nurses sing with or for their patients. I invite all long-term patients who normally play instruments to bring their instruments to the hospital. Many different hospital rooms are used by children or youths for music practice and pleasure! Occasionally, I also visit children in their homes after they have left hospital: to finish our co-operative musical projects or to continue meaningful and enjoyable activities during times of partial isolation in the home environment.

In my study of the life histories of 19 songs by children with cancer, I looked at where, when, and by whom each song had been created, performed and used (Aasgaard 2002).[2] The life histories of these songs went beyond scheduled music therapy sessions in some music room or in the patient's own hospital room, and song participants were not only young patients and a music therapist. Almost all songs had more than one creation/performance site: sometimes 'flying' from one part of the hospital to another, sometimes accompanying a young patient being transferred to a new hospital and sometimes being distributed, in various ways, to the outside world. Some of these songs were developed/performed in several different, even far-away localities, while other songs were only performed in the patient's immediate hospital environment. A song can directly reach audiences far away from the patient's isolated existence, for example as a CD sent by post to classmates. Some patients' songs have even been presented in national TV programmes, reaching audiences of several hundred thousand people. The length of a song's life seems to be related to several things: its aesthetic/artistic qualities, the patient's own involvement and interest, which other persons have taken part in the *musicing*; the more people involved, the more opportunities there are for renewed interest and uses.

---

2   Aasgaard, T. (2003) 'Song Creations by Children with Cancer – Process and Meaning' (Aalborg University). This doctoral thesis is a multiple, instrumental case study of the life histories of 19 songs. Although the songs' lyrics and musical elements have also been considered, the song activities (how, where, when and by whom the songs were created, developed and used) were particularly highlighted to investigate what the songs might have meant to the child in the context of the oncology ward.

The flexible roles of the music therapist in the hospital community

Music is not a standard part of a treatment regime in either of the two hospitals, and is relatively seldom 'prescribed' for a particular patient. This is different from the more formal relationships in paediatric wards/hospitals in, for example, Germany, the United States and Australia. In my practice, individual music therapy agreements are somewhat casual, often with patients or relatives taking the initiative regarding (what I like to call) prospective musical collaboration. Nurses, medical staff or teachers often ask me to see a patient, but further appointments are on a voluntary basis, as a result of the patient's, the family's and my own assessment, and I believe a patient must be allowed to say, 'not interested!' There are so many other therapies and arrangements where these patients have no choices at all...

As the music therapist, I have no self-evident position in this hospital landscape. 'Position' means here both *existence* (simply being there) and administrative or therapeutic *domicile* (i.e. membership of a psychosocial professional team). My professional status, as the representative of a new and unknown discipline like music therapy, is not very high in a university hospital where effective curative treatment is at the forefront. Individually oriented music therapy may 'compete' with more traditional psychotherapeutic and psychosocial approaches (play therapy included). My Community Music Therapy approach may be met with bewilderment and even suspicion: is this hospital (environment) not good enough as it is, and why do we need this Pied Piper amongst us? It is perhaps especially difficult, in a medical hospital, to have the word 'therapy' sanctioned for activities that are not primarily focused on a specific patient or on treating disease.

Because I have spent so much time making music with patients, relatives and 'available and willing' hospital staff in the open spaces (corridors, common rooms, etc.), onlookers often comment on the entertainment qualities of what goes on. It is almost as though music therapy's ability to *divert* the children from boredom and various problems is more appreciated, or noticed, than its ability to *connect* severely ill young patients, and their families, to normal, healthy activities or, simply, to living life.

Planned therapeutic interventions (activities) are bound to be influenced by the position from which I encounter other professionals and the family of the young patient. When I first entered the premises of the two hospitals with music making in 'my bag', there were no other music therapists at any Scandinavian paediatric cancer ward. I experienced myself as being somewhere between a

'Jack-of-no-proper-trades' and a well-meaning entertainer or clown,[3] forming loose administrative and therapeutic links with the cancer advisers, the medical superintendents, nursing officers and with the hospital teachers. It was necessary to state firmly and repeatedly that I did not represent any alternative cancer therapy. I also began to wonder whether a music therapist who works primarily in his office or music room is perhaps more easily considered professional (a true therapist) than one working with, and through, the arts in the hospital community, and expanding his or her focus from one patient to larger environmental relationships. For a music therapist with such interests, the journey from being 'an outsider' to becoming 'an insider' in any hospital team requires humility, optimism, hard work and patience. One medical consultant said, quite frankly, that when he saw me wandering through the corridors with a big top hat, blowing my trombone and conducting regular singsongs with patients/parents/staff, it was difficult to comprehend that this friendly musician was working with relatively clear therapeutic aims, let alone conducting a comprehensive *research* project at the time.

The role of a music therapy practitioner and researcher in paediatrics is clearer when she or he applies accepted and well-known methods, for example, working with individual patients or pre-selected groups in a therapy room, conducting experimental research projects or testing possible 'effects' of music therapy interventions. Instead, my focusing on the whole hospital community and applying longitudinal studies aiming at understanding *social* phenomena related to music therapy seemed to be uncommon in the paediatric oncology ward. An interest in contextual matters – always working with individual patients within a contextually broad perspective – may need some time to receive recognition. There is also the question of the extent to which modern, 'somatic' hospitals want to include cultural and creative therapies in their treatment repertoire.

Musicing in a cancer hospital is probably neither more...nor less... necessary for life than anywhere outside hospital. The importance attached to the music therapist's role and practice in and by the hospital community is surely reflective of a broader social understanding of, and attitude towards, the usefulness of 'art' in human life.

---

3   Two music therapists working in a German hospital, where I once conducted a clinic, said to me that they would not allow themselves to work in the open spaces of the hospital as I did. A therapist arranging noisy processions in the corridors and 'entertaining' people in the common rooms (and even making them laugh) might very easily be considered 'a clown'...seemingly not a very flattering characteristic of a professional, or serious, music therapist.

Working without safety nets: The Musical Hour

My first encounters with children and family members often take place in the Musical Hour (from Norwegian: 'Musikkstund'), a weekly event that grew from the singsongs I arranged together with pre-school teachers in a physiotherapy room at Hospital 1. The Musical Hour became quite a popular weekly event that soon got more spacious premises: the big entrance hall of the paediatric department. In Hospital 2 a similar weekly get-together was held in the play room and corridors. The Musical Hour is conducted with the following aims and activities:

To promote team spirit through meaningful music-related common activities such as singing, acting, playing, etc. (There are many instruments suitable for ensemble use available.) Musical socialisation is believed to be one factor in fostering friendliness and confidence in a milieu where uncertainty and suffering might dominate.

To promote awareness of the individual through presenting each other's names, presenting song-makers and their products, presenting song/instrumental soloists (from the most modest to the most advanced) or simply focusing everyone's attention momentarily on one person, for example, a birthday girl/boy, etc.

To promote meaningful musical/artistic experiences through mini-concerts performed by the music therapist and/or a student, the medical superintendent or any 'guest star' popping up – the musical point of departure may be a medieval dance tune performed on recorder and percussion, just as well as a short Chopin prelude on piano or Sonny Rollin's *St Thomas* performed on trombone and guitar. The distinction between receptive and active, i.e. music therapy, engagement is often not clear. A piece of music may be performed *for* the audience, being occasionally prompted to visualise something, or simply close their eyes for some seconds in relation to the music, and the same piece may also be performed *with* everyone clapping hands, humming or moving along with the rhythm.

To promote fun and laughter through fun and laughter. These distinguished human hallmarks are treated as objectives *per se*. A paediatric hospital does not give many opportunities for such *normal* experiences. The music therapist is also a clown, a fool, an ignoramus: performing funny songs, using puppetry or tales.

As the music therapist, I occasionally talk like a music teacher or, on the contrary, let the music stand on its own. My at times pedagogic attitude is one way of taking the people in attendance seriously: believing I may actually have things to say and do that some will find interesting, believing young and old may be interested to learn or acquire new skills, aiming at never underestimating anyone present.

Often the children themselves, their parents, a nurse or teacher approach me before a session and present a potential soloist, a favourite instrument, or a song that might be included in the programme. Sometimes soloist and I have time for a short rehearsal before the 'show' – but all participants know they may suggest activities or solo elements during the entire Musical Hour. Sometimes a child has made a song text and wants melody and musical arrangement immediately. After the show, a shy child who has been rather passive and 'invisible' during the social activities may now have something to say or to show. Parents approach me to tell me of a child's musical interests or skills or about their own life situation or interests. I often start a little jam session with a child without any preceding formalities, and after the Musical Hour, I visit those who prefer more quiet musical encounters and those who have not been able to leave their rooms – often because of an increased infection risk. Medical staff, nurses or other health care workers spontaneously say that it gives a nice feeling to experience the young and old 'musicians'. When hospital staff participate in the *musicing*, their patients seem highly to appreciate seeing their carers in new roles, if only for a minute or two.

Improvisation is not characteristic of the musical activities, but it does mark the total structure of this weekly event. I may need to skip planned activities and initiate something completely different, if contexts change. Some ideas may not prove successful on one occasion, while other ideas drop dead once and for all. With a group of people who differ so much in age and degree of fitness it is not easy to find activities that suit everybody at the same time. What may be humorous for some may be frightening for others. The same child may appear vigorous and quick-witted one day and fatigued and sullen the next.

Any music therapist who gets involved in sessions like the Musical Hour works without a safety net: not only is the setting rather uncontrollable, but the therapist's incomplete musical skills and (not the least) failures are heard and seen by 'everyone', not least by other members of the hospital staff. It is an understatement to say that I am not always proud of my own therapeutic, musical or dramaturgical 'solutions'.

Working with a sick child always means working with contexts

Because (one or both) parents, as a rule, accompany their sick child during hospitalisation, it is difficult *not* to include these in music therapy activities. In some cases, when the child has no parents 'available', the hospital appoints one staff member to serve as 'near family' during critical periods and times of isolation (Figure 7.2).

Patient

Music therapist

Patient's family (parents, siblings, etc.)

Nursing staff

Medical staff

Hospital school teachers

Hospital pre-school teachers

Physiotherapist

Students (of various kinds)

Other patients and their families

Figure 7.2 Potential participants in music therapy activities

As a rule, I spend one day a week in each ward, and also follow up individual appointments as required. This means that I sometimes visit a child on a Sunday morning or a Saturday evening if this time suits the patient or family. During weekdays, particularly before 4pm, people and activities accumulate in the ward: important diagnostic and treatment procedures are carried out, different specialists are queuing to see the child/family, and children who are ambulant attend school or the teachers visit the sick child. The remaining part of the day/night the family primarily communicates with the nursing staff, and indeed a slower pace marks life in the ward. In my experience, evenings or weekends are often ideal for music therapy work, which can benefit from the relative tranquillity, and sometimes even boredom associated with such times.

I present individual music therapy sessions as a 'project', not least when a child/family is interested in creating a song, learning an instrument, making a recording and the like. The meaning associated with project is different from 'music therapy session'. In the paediatric oncology ward there are so many therapists and therapies, and it is perhaps important for the sick child (and family) also to be engaged in musical activities believed to be both enjoyable and quite 'normal'. I have experienced some older children instantly reacting with disappointment when understanding that I am a music therapist. As one 13-year-old girl once whispered: 'I had hoped we could just make music together.' The musically inventive and talented girl, severely marked by illness, wanted 'time out' from therapies which seemed to focus on her numerous problems. Without trying to hide my professional relationship, I made it clear to her that I was in this special ward simply because I thought music was important for everybody, including those in hospital. Most children understand and accept this common-sense argument. This teenager taught me much about constructing pop tunes – I served primarily as her musical discussion partner and accompanist. One evening I found her and her mother sitting alone in the entrance hall, the girl playing the grand piano with one finger, and the mother writing down a new composition with letters only: C – F – G, etc. (neither of them could read or write music 'properly'). They told me this song was a farewell to the music therapy student who was leaving the paediatric ward the following week.

Improvisational music therapy models such as free improvisation therapy or Creative Music Therapy (Bruscia 1987) may be used when the patient or family member has problems with expressing emotions or is depressed. I might also use similar techniques because the patient seems to get pleasure from this way of *musicing*. The young patient is usually, but not always, the major musical partici-pant, and the co-operative nature of music-making makes it natural for me to adjust my time schedule to that of the family. I try to work fast to make melodies/arrangements/copy cassettes/find required materials. There are so many other reasons for waiting and so many uncertainties in hospital. If I am able to give quick feedback in music-related matters, I may perhaps inspire the child/family to new, creative achievements.

Other family members may have different (and changing) roles in relation to the musical activities. A mother, the patient and the music therapist may play lyres and sing together; a visiting brother or sister may spend a morning as the music therapist's 'assistant'; a whole family may take part in the recording of a new song creation; a nurse or a teacher collaborates with a patient making a text and is joined by the music therapist to accomplish the final musical touch.

> The father of a seven-year-old girl with leukaemia has several individual recorder sessions with the music therapist. Within a period of some few months he becomes a widower, loses his job, and when his youngest child gets seriously ill, he does not have much strength and spirits left (the daughter also sheds many tears at this time). He tells me, after their first *Musical Hour,* that he has a descant recorder at home. We discuss their apparently gloomy life in hospital for a while, and I offer to teach him to play the recorder (even) better, to fill the long hours of waiting and doing nothing. One week later, he has bought himself a treble recorder that we explore together. Within some months he adds tenor and sopranino recorders to his collection. He does not want any lessons, but appreciates small jam sessions and playing well-known tunes with me. One morning his daughter smilingly approaches the music therapist and says that her father has become 'so clever'.

The above example indicates an emphasis on *contextual* and relational matters. Sometimes it is almost as interesting whether it is the relative or the patient who is the major collaborator of the music therapist. Assisting a father to regain energy and do something he thinks is meaningful or enjoyable might well be profitable for the child patient who, most likely, experienced a more lively father.

Another of the contexts for my work emerges when parents, nurses or medical staff notify me about children in hospital who are soon going to die. The day programme for these patients is generally less marked by the busy schedule of those undergoing the many procedures related to diagnostic and curative treatment. It is perhaps an unspoken law that the families in particular are surrounded by love and care, and this becomes my major concern as the music therapist. To promote health is, even at this stage, a relevant objective with these families. The Finnish nurse theorist Katie Eriksson suggests that *love* is the revelation and manifestation of health (Eriksson 1990), and one practical manifestation of this is doing 'good things' to the person being loved. As a rule I collaborate with the parents about what to do, rather than applying predetermined music therapy methods. I may sing together with others present in the sick room or accompany the parents singing a favourite song for their child; once a mother and father asked to sing three- or four-part arrangements at the bedside of their unconscious son (Aasgaard 2000b). Relatives may borrow a pentatonic lyre and sit improvising for long periods in the sick room. Children who are bedridden, weak and fatigued have also, on their own initiative, wanted to take part in improvisations, or even had fun singing 'indecent' songs together with the music therapist.

> On a quiet Sunday afternoon in the play room the two nurses on duty dance the can-can in front of a bedridden nine-year-old girl. 'Clara' has a huge, inoperable abdominal tumour and is not able to sit or stand, but now she is eagerly banging on a keyboard placed slightly lower than the mattress. The music therapist improvises on trombone while the mother watches the show with big eyes. Eventually, mother and daughter laughingly start making dance movements with their hands, accompanied by rather wild trombone choruses and two crazy nurses jumping about in the little play room. A visitor might not easily guess that the young patient, here displaying her love of life, sense of humour and energy, will die peacefully just some few days afterwards.

Events like these may promote collective deep and meaningful moments for all participants. Parents' stories from this period often mention their children's creative acts, appreciation of music or simply humorous events (Aasgaard 2001). I have experienced several times that repeating these stories after the child's death may soothe and support the mourners.

Creating and developing networks of health through *musicing*

In this chapter I have presented some themes related to music therapy in contemporary paediatric hospital wards, focusing on the interplay between the individual and her or his environment – indeed, with a focus on *community*. Context, here, is not just the external frame or background for music therapy interventions, but constitutes tightly interwoven relationships where foreground and background change according to changing perspectives.

The concept *community* primarily refers to people (or rather a body of people associated by some common status or pursuits, etc.), while *environment* directly refers to what is around/surroundings (*Oxford Concise Dictionary of English Etymology* 1996). A community is also influenced by environmental (human and non-human) elements. Kim conceptualises 'environment' through the headings shown in Figure 7.3 (Kim 1983 in Aasgaard 1999).

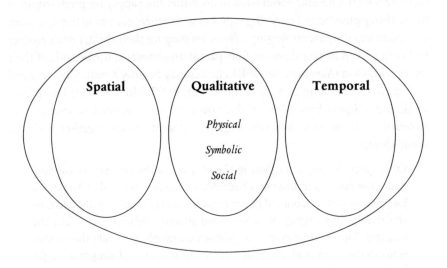

Figure 7.3 Conceptualising 'environment'

Several of the activities mentioned in this chapter can be interpreted as being related to one or more of the characteristics of Figure 7.3. *Musicing*'s spatial, temporal and physical aspects contribute to the formation of some basic threads in a developing web or network of health where symbolic and social 'colours' are particularly conspicuous.

Spatial aspects

Appropriate musical activities in the open spaces may bring more intimacy into big, impersonal rooms or corridors. On the other hand, a music therapist may bring a little of the outside world into the rather small rooms where some patients are isolated for weeks or even months.

Temporal aspects

Regular, music-related events influence the rhythm in the paediatric ward and remind everyone present of other sides of man than sickness and disability. Many patients, as well as their parents, say that they are looking forward to taking part in scheduled musical activities. Some children who are severely marked by fatigue seem temporarily happy with watching the music therapist or other children and adults 'in action'. To expect to do or experience something nice adds pleasurable moments to our lives; the element of expectancy is perhaps an underestimated component of music therapy (Aasgaard 2002). On the other hand, improvised musical 'stunts', like the earlier example of Clara and the can-can dancing nurses, may be welcomed at times where 'nothing happens', providing unexpected time-outs from the trivialities of hospitalisation. Short frequent playful interruptions are perhaps particularly important during extended periods of isolation – when life is at stake – and when the patient's (family's) timetable is marked by scheduled procedures related to treatment and physical care.

Physical aspects

Musicing inevitably influences the soundscape of the hospital, sometimes competing with the sound from electrical devices, trolleys on the move and several other kinds of noise...and sometimes drowning more important conversations or procedures in the vicinity. Some patients are hypersensitive to shrill sounds, and this is probably one reason for the popularity of lyres (pentatonic or diatonic) that are used at the bedside or in small rooms.

Symbolic aspects

The majority of problems related to being sick, receiving treatment, and accompanying or caring for persons with life-threatening diseases can certainly not be eliminated through music or any other artistic activities. Music therapy does not replace any element of, for example, medical or nursing care. But *musicing* (and many modes of 'playing') can inspire any participant – patient or carer – to expand their *role* repertory. Such involvement seemingly leads people into new, social roles for shorter or longer periods. Both the patient and the medical superintendent may be musicians or clowns together, a parent or visiting brother may show others something they are good at. Community Music Therapy in the paediatric wards potentially expands the actual life worlds of the participants. Patients, as well as their accompanying parents, are given 'wings' enabling them to escape, for a short while, from the small and (almost) sterile, isolation rooms: a symbolic re-creation of the environment. This form of music therapy may serve as a significant symbol and hallmark of the overriding therapeutic value: keeping aspects of health in individuals, families and environments – as long as there is life.

Social aspects

Through the described musical activities patients have been assisted to maintain social relations with family, friends and class-mates outside hospital. New 'musical friendships' between patients, relatives and hospital staff occasionally develop during the period of treatment. A Community Music Therapy approach in the paediatric hospital involves working towards creative networks wider than the patient–therapist dyad also when curative treatment has failed and palliative care takes over. The *homo conexus* is a being who is 'part of' (networks). Even very sick patients are often capable of doing more than, simply, suffering and being patient; hospital communities must not make people more helpless than necessary. The momentary musical involvement of a dying child can be understood as a testimony to *health* performance – sometimes the child's last social *participation* in life. Human beings are a social species, and a social being is an active being! The Pied Piper treats his followers with this in mind.

References

Aasgaard, T. (1999) 'Music Therapy as Milieu in the Hospice and Paediatric Oncology Ward.' In D. Aldridge (ed) *Music Therapy in Palliative Care. New Voices*. London: Jessica Kingsley Publishers.

Aasgaard, T. (2000a) 'A Suspiciously Cheerful Lady: A Study of a Song's Life in the Paediatric Oncology Ward, and Beyond...' *British Journal of Music Therapy 14*, 2, 70–82.

Aasgaard, T. (2000b) 'Musical Acts of Love in the Care of Severely Ill and Dying Children and their Families.' *Practice News*, November 2000. www.musictherapyworld.net/pracnews

Aasgaard, T. (2001) 'An Ecology of Love: Aspects of Music Therapy in the Pediatric Oncology Environment.' *Journal of Palliative Care 17*, 3, 177–181.

Aasgaard, T. (2003) 'Song Creations by Children with Cancer – Process and Meaning.' In D. Aldridge (ed) *Case Study Designs in Music Therapy*. London: Jessica Kingsley Publishers.

Bruscia, K. (1987) *Improvisational Models of Music Therapy*. Springfields, IL: Charles C. Thomas.

Eriksson, K. (1990) *Hälsans idé.* Stockholm: Norstedts Förlag.

Kim, H.S. (1983) *The Nature of Theoretical Thinking in Nursing.* Stamford: Appleton.

Lie, S.O. (2001) 'Barn Med Kreft – Store Fremskritt, Mange Gleder og Noen Skuffelser' ('Progress in the Field of Paediatric Oncology'). *Tidsskrift for Den norske lægeforening 121,* 8, 951–955.

Melamed, B. (1992) 'Family Factors Predicting Children's Reactions to Anesthesia Induction.' In La Greca *et al.* (eds) *Stress and Coping in Child Health.* New York: Guilford.

Oxford Concise Dictionary of English Etymology (1996) T.F. Hoad (ed) Oxford: Oxford University Press.

Parsons, T. (1951) *The Social System.* New York: Free Press.

von Plessen, C. (1995) 'Krankheitserfahrungen von krebskranken Kindern und ihren Familien.' Inaugural dissertation. Universität Witten/Herdecke.

Stai, E. (1999) 'Blåser Liv i Syke Barn.' *Verdens Gang.* 17 February, 24–26, Oslo.

PART IV

But is it Music Therapy?

CHAPTER 8

A Dream Wedding: From Community Music to Music Therapy with a Community

Harriet Powell

In a small group music therapy session, three women and a music therapist improvise a kind of song-and-dance routine. The three women have dementia in the early or moderate stages, suffering short-term memory loss, confusion and anxiety. The music therapist supports them by singing with them and playing accordion. It is a playful and creative interaction involving movement, song and much laughter, during which Alice says with delight, 'It's like Top of the Pops!' When we come to a close Doris turns to Alice and says 'There you are – that's right – connection.'

Doris describes lucidly how she has experienced the music-making, and emphatically claps her hands on the word 'connection'. Maybe she refers to a personal feeling of connection in experiencing the flow of the song, in words and motion, as opposed to the fragmentation of her normal speech and movement. She might have responded to a feeling of unity with the other two women and the therapist, with whom verbal communication was difficult, or perhaps both. 'The quality of music as a living pattern' can give 'a sense of mental and physical connection' as well as being 'an experienced shared – the pattern which connects' (Ansdell 1995, pp.213–4).

This chapter is all about making connections, from a personal point of view and an interpersonal perspective. I reflect on my previous work as a community musician connecting and facilitating people in creative process towards performance. I describe my current role as music therapist in the community of a residential home and day centre for older people where connections are made within individual sessions, group sessions and performance. Throughout the chapter, short extracts from one of our performances are interwoven between

descriptions of the process of some individuals and groups towards performance. After reflecting on how this particular performance came about, I discuss
the similarities and differences between my experience of a community music
performance project and this model of Community Music Therapy.

Making connections – Community Music

In the early 1970s, as I was considering applying to the new Music Therapy
course at the Guildhall School of Music in London, a chance meeting took me in
another direction (or possibly a parallel path) into the world of community arts
and an exciting, pioneering organisation called Inter-Action Community Arts
Trust, based in north London. For the next 25 years, in this and other arts
organisations, I was what is now known as a 'community musician' (I don't
think the term had been invented when I started). My work as a community
musician became the basis for my future career as a music therapist.

The community arts movement in Britain is about making the arts relevant
and more accessible to everyone, especially marginalised communities; about
inclusion and empowerment; about giving people a voice; about social interaction and often community action through the arts. As a musician with
Inter-Action's community theatre company, I helped to develop participatory
musical plays with all ages involving structured use of games. These
'game-plays'

> are all of social significance... The social significance lies in the fact that
> they're participatory – with participation on the part of the children and
> follow-up work with them in their own communities. (Itzen, quoting
> Berman, 1980 p.57)

Then throughout the 1980s and 90s, I worked within another theatre organisation, Spare Tyre Theatre Company. Originally a touring theatre, we performed
our own musical plays about health issues. Working alongside a drama specialist, I went on to facilitate creative music-making, again encouraging participation through music-games in music and theatre projects with community
groups. These three-month projects took place with a range of adult groups that
included unemployed young people, some with learning difficulties, some with
emotional or drug-related problems; single mothers; and intergenerational
groups of school age young people with older people.[1]

---

1   Arts Council England, London (formerly London Arts Board), which funds
     Spare Tyre Theatre Company, still refers to it as 'The Heineken of the arts
     world – reaching parts other organisations can't reach.'

With each group, we produced a musical play reflecting aspects of their lives. The plays were devised in group-work where participants improvised scenes and were helped to write songs. These were shaped into the musical play, which they then performed. The process helped develop self-worth, confidence and skills to voice feelings and concerns in a theatrical, musical and often humorous way.

We also ran several projects in residential homes for older people including those with dementia. One project was televised by BBC TV's *Open Space* programme. It involved 20 residents, some with dementia, members of care staff and four unemployed young people from a previous project. Over a period of three months, we shaped themes from their lives into a musical theatre piece. This was then performed to an audience of residents, staff, friends and family. Francesca Turner from *The Guardian* newspaper described the programme as 'a moving and often funny account of what the residents all learned about long dormant talent, new experience and how life in an institution can be enriched' (1993). In making and performing a musical play life was enriched by connecting residents and staff in a creative process and then connecting residents, staff and families during the performance. Our aim was that care staff, whom we trained during the process, might continue to encourage creative activity in the care home. The company had to move on to other projects.[2]

Eventually I felt that the time was right to train as a music therapist in order to work in more long-term music-making relationships, using improvisation rather than pre-planned performance. After completing my music therapy training, I approached the manager of a newly built residential and day care centre about the possibility of providing a music therapy service. Along with some of her staff she had been involved in one of our performance projects at another care home, and had been impressed and moved by the power of music and drama. The manager was keen to try the more ongoing commitment of music therapy.

A Dream Wedding – a musical play by men and women with varying degrees of dementia and their care staff

The performance begins

The dining area of the day centre has been decorated beyond recognition with flowers and a glittering green backdrop. On stage, seated in a semi-circle of two rows are the cast of 32; residents, care staff, the daughter of

---

2   Spare Tyre, ten years later, is developing ongoing project work with a group of older people in the London Borough of Camden.

one of the residents and the music therapist. There is a buzz of excitement as the audience settle into their seats and the average age drops by about 20 years. Friends and relatives, children, grandchildren and great-grandchildren of the performers arrive.

There are some loud shouts as a member of the audience, a resident with dementia, becomes distressed. John slowly gets up from his seat at the centre of the stage area and announces into the microphone: 'Good afternoon, ladies and gentlemen.' There is a hush. 'Thank you for coming. You're all welcome.' Applause. James begins to play *Beautiful Dreamer* on harmonica accompanied by the music therapist on piano. Whatever happens will happen...

The centre where this performance took place is in a deprived, multicultural area of north east London. It is run by the social services department. Within its walls are a residential home, a respite unit, a day care centre and an intermediate care unit. The latter opened recently in partnership with the local NHS Trust. The building is well-designed, light and spacious with outside sitting areas full of flowers and shrubs.

The day care centre caters for 25 people, many with dementia in mild to moderate stages and other difficulties of older age. These service users are still able to live at home with families or in 'supported' accommodation. Thirty-two residents are cared for in four units (one of which is the respite unit). They tend to be older, ages range from 70 to over 100, and many have more advanced dementia. The different areas, staffed by care staff and a small team of occupational, physio and speech therapists, are overseen by a manager and deputy managers.

The service users all come from the local area and the ethnic diversity of the wider community is reflected in the institution. Apart from various forms of dementia, a wide variety of other difficulties of later life include visual and hearing impairment, the effects of a stroke and Parkinson's disease.

To the continuing strains of *Beautiful Dreamer* (played by James on harmonica) Cinderella (played by Gladys who has learning difficulties) enters, sweeping the floor. Cinderella sings *All I Want is a Room Somewhere* and bemoans the fact that she has to do all this work and nobody loves her. What she'd really like is Prince Charming to sweep her off her feet. A Fairy Godmother (Denise, daughter of resident, Louise) appears and says she will take her off to Dreamland where she might meet him. The whole cast sing *Meet Me Tonight in Dreamland* while several couples from the cast come forward and waltz to the music. Cinderella is whisked away by her Fairy Godmother and Jane (who is 95) sings a solo of the Everley Brothers song

Dream, Dream, Dream, performed with a group of six care staff. All but one of them are African Caribbean. Jane has lived in Hackney all her life.

Music therapy is the only arts therapy currently on offer, extended from one to two days in a funding and training partnership with the Nordoff-Robbins Music Therapy Centre. Music therapy sessions generally take place in a small activity room designated for music therapy with an upright piano and a good variety of percussion instruments. There is another piano in a more public place where we have regular open groups.

Over the four years since setting up the post, music therapy has evolved in response to the varied and changing needs of individuals and the institutional community, developing beyond the more conventional therapeutic boundaries of time and space. Sessions do not always happen weekly, individual and group sessions may take place in spaces other than the music therapy room. Also, pre-planned musical/theatrical performances are given by those who have had or are still having music therapy.

> Susan recounts her courting days and sings '*Ma, He's Making Eyes at Me!*' She acknowledges the applause with a bow, a beaming smile and 'Thank you very much' to the audience. More songs, sketches and personal memories about weddings are performed or told by staff and residents. Some songs were chosen with the residents in the planning stage. Some songs start spontaneously and the music therapist accompanies – whatever the key.

Making connections – Community Music and Music Therapy

My approach as a music therapist working in this environment has been influenced both by my career as a community musician, and also by my Nordoff-Robbins training which included an MA research project. Here, I set out to investigate adult music therapy relationships in which clients come to sessions intermittently or suddenly stop coming (whether for practical or personal reasons). The study found that an approach which responds and adapts to the needs of the institution and its clients, particularly in terms of time and physical space, needs to become integral to music therapists, whatever their working contexts. Also essential is a focused approach, which can be summed up in part as 'there is no time like the present' (Powell 1999).

> Wedding memories of the residents are prompted by questions from the staff or music therapist (a 'roving microphone' amplifies their answers). First a member of staff describes her wedding day. Susan says 'Well done!'

Then Myrtle asks Alice if she can remember her wedding day. Alice answers that they went to St Bartholomew's Church, Bethnal Green.

Myrtle asks if she can describe her wedding dress and Alice replies (gesturing with her hands as she does so). 'It was called Jubilee blue – that was the colour of the time – ankle length, long sleeves coming from the shoulder and tied up with satin (she mimes tying a bow at her neck) and a hat.'

Myrtle: So you wore an 'Alice Blue Gown?'

Alice: Yes, right to the last detail.

Myrtle: Alice, will you sing for us?

Alice: I'll make a noise!

Alice sings the song *Alice Blue Gown* which she had sung many times before in a small group music therapy session – a song with significance for her. As she sings it, she notices her son on the front row of the audience and begins to sing to him. (He is the man with white hair on the front row taking out his handkerchief.) At the close of the song, Alice stands and slowly walks towards him. He goes to her and they meet in the space between the performers and audience. They embrace. There is a gentle sigh from the audience. Not a dry eye in the house and a palpable feeling of connection.

Although service users bring with them a diverse cultural heritage, singing, dancing or playing has been a common experience, either in pubs, in social gatherings, choirs, community singing or in church, whether in Britain, the rest of Europe, Africa or the West Indies. Some left Caribbean homes in the 1950s, or more recently, the island of Montserrat after the volcano eruption and now, in later life, long to return. For many, singing solos, performing a particular song or monologue – a 'party piece' – has also been a part of group music-making in their earlier lives. However, many have lost touch with music-making, and have also lost much of their family, social or professional network. Service users may have come from very isolated living situations having lost a spouse, or become disconnected by physical, mental or emotional conditions. They have different difficulties quite apart from different cultural and ethnic backgrounds, and, in addition, may be suffering from Alzheimers, osteoporosis or Parkinson's disease.

The combination of physical and cognitive losses with these other losses may lead to an overwhelming sense of loss: of identity, ability, freedom and capacity to contribute. These can be exacerbated by 'depersonalising tendencies in the care environment and loss of personhood' (Kitwood 1997, p.46).

We should understand dementia as a complex interaction between personality, age, biography, ethnicity, health, gender, neurological impairment and the social psychology and web of relationships that a person has... We need to treat people as unique individuals. (Goldsmith 1996, p.24)

Even though not all can access or enjoy the benefits of large social group music-making as they once did, music therapy may help them to rediscover the world of music in their own personal way and at their own pace and help to recover some of their sense of loss.

Making connections – one-to-one sessions and groups

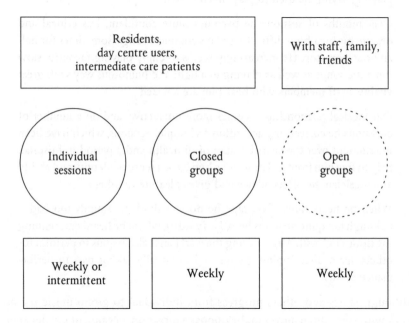

Figure 8.1 Making connections – one-to-one sessions and groups

Residents, day centre users and intermediate care patients have individual sessions weekly or intermittently, since continuity is not always possible. Closed group sessions are generally held at the same time each week with those who can manage a weekly commitment. Open groups also happen weekly and staff or visiting family and friends can also join in.

James, an ex-miner from the north of England, is referred by his key worker on one of the residential units for individual sessions which take place in his room. He is in his eighties, thin and frail with many physical problems

and often in a lot of pain. He suffers some confusion and memory loss associated with heart disease and has a pacemaker. He has no family since his
wife's recent death, and is severely depressed and withdrawn. He rarely
comes out of his room where photographs show a large, fit and smiling
younger man.

In our first session, he sees my accordion and tells me that he used to play
accordion and harmonica in local pub bands years ago. After a while he
asks me to fetch a harmonica from a drawer (where he has several) and
begins to play in short bursts, passages from 1930s songs like *Smoke Gets in
Your Eyes*, *Marta* and *Jealousy*. I accompany him on accordion. He is very
breathless, tends not to finish anything and is discontented with his
playing, saying he used to play much better.

Over months of sessions he becomes more confident, less critical and
despite his breathing difficulties plays complete songs, sometimes for half
an hour non-stop. He increasingly seems to enjoy playing favourite slow
romantic songs as well as playing in a light and humorous way with great
vitality. Staff members who hear him are amazed.

Our musical relationship becomes more interactive, and on a number of
occasions he corrects my accordion technique! Sessions, which have been
intermittent over the years because of ill health and a period in hospital,
help to free him from isolation, give him back a sense of identity and ability
as a musician: he offers advice and gives pleasure to others.

When he hears himself on tape he doesn't think he sounds too bad –
although not quite up to his hero, Larry Adler, whom he heard entertaining
the troops in North Africa during the war! James also begins to perform for
others again, first joining groups and eventually taking part in performance events.

Although James and others progress from individual to group music therapy,
work with some often moves in the opposite direction, because of the degenera-
tive nature of their conditions. Music therapy groups enable older people to
regain a sense of identity, ability, freedom and capacity to contribute, as they do
in individual sessions. They are also further enabled by being offered opportunities for developments in their music-making, whether improvised or
pre-composed, vocal or instrumental.

Small group music therapy in this kind of setting facilitates meaningful
communication and connection between people with different languages and
cultural backgrounds, with different physical and mental difficulties – all can be
enabled and empowered by being listened to and heard in musical terms
(Proctor 2002, pp.101–2), and connected in making music with others. An

'allowing' and inclusive approach gives a group the freedom to 'go with the flow' and to make it an emotionally, socially and musically connecting experience. It encourages equality by accepting whatever anyone brings. The vignettes below illustrate various aspects of group music therapy.

> In a day centre group, four women and one man, who have little musical background in common, are empowered and connected in freely improvised song. Iris and Rose have more advanced dementia and are often anxious and restless. Christopher also has Parkinson's disease, and was extremely depressed and withdrawn when he first attended the day centre. He's had six months of individual therapy before joining the group. On this occasion Iris and Rose leave the room. I start to improvise a song with the words 'They'll be back' (I hope).Christopher joins in, adding very witty rhymes. The song is a funny, running commentary which accepts and reflects what happens, including, as Iris puts on her coat, 'We don't mean to gloat – she's putting on her coat.' Everyone laughs and appreciates his humour. The song evolves in a spontaneous 'spur of the moment' response to what is happening in the session. Fun and laughter connect them emotionally.

> In another group, a reflective, improvised song emerges after a woman who has osteoporosis sees a picture of a bird on the wall, and says 'Let's fly away.' I support this musically and the others identify with her, all singing the phrase. At the end, an African Caribbean woman says 'What we have is what we give – and we give it in the right way.'

> A weekly Thursday morning open group takes place in a public area on the first floor between two residential units. The group assembles slowly. Staff members come with those who need help to walk along the corridor, others hear the music and make their own way. Susan, Gladys and Alice are regulars. Alice used to attend the day centre for years and was a member of a closed music therapy group (remember: 'There you are...connection!'?) Then she had a spell in hospital, became more confused and, no longer able to look after herself at home, became a resident. The continuity of being in a music therapy group has helped her settle into this new home.

> Susan, Gladys and Alice all sing solo songs that have special meaning and significance for them. They also know many of the same songs but often, if some know a song and others don't, we improvise out of a song and then come back to it. Susan has very little short-term memory, and tends to repeat one particular song, even if she has become more flexible over two years in the group. As well as being creative in improvised songs, instrumentally she experiences continuity and satisfaction in her ability. She has

revealed a vast repertoire and variety of songs, which she loves to perform, and often receives spontaneous applause from the group.

Even where there are differences in culture, ethnicity and pathology, there is musical experience in common. There is no right or wrong in music or in behaviour, and connections are made in sharing religious, spiritual or emotional experience and in appreciation of each other's performance.

Staff join in open groups when they can, as do visiting family members (and sometimes they will sing a solo). One resident's daughter, Denise, regularly joins in and tells us that she used to play drums in a band, (she later becomes the drumming Fairy Godmother in *Dream Wedding* and becomes involved in other musical performance events). Care staff, when time permits, also have their own occasional music sessions.

The performance continues

Jane (resident) and Alison (staff) sing a duet 'Why am I always the brides-maid, never the blushing bride?' They sway together in perfect synchrony and Jane waves her bouquet in the air as she acknowledges the applause.

The music therapist, at the piano, starts the introduction to the next song …audience and cast wait…the music therapist starts to improvise out of the song's introduction…we wait…and wait…finally, Sharon (staff), due on stage to act out and lead the others in singing, makes it on stage. She had been having trouble struggling into her old wedding dress to sing 'There was I, waiting at the church!' (I remember the time she said 'You'll never get me singing!')

The deputy manager and another member of staff perform a sketch about married life based on the true story of one of the residents. She is at home with the baby. He comes home drunk having spent the housekeeping money. (The part of the baby is played by the deputy manager's baby son.) After much laughter, Myrtle invites spontaneous comments from the residents. 'What would you do about that husband?' Susan shouts 'Drown him!' – a lot more laughter.

Making connections – spontaneous groups

Like open groups, spontaneous sessions are open to staff and visiting family and friends. They happen all over the place – in corridors, in the lobby areas, outside residents' rooms or out of doors on sunny days. Residents and staff appear from other parts of the building when they hear the music (on one occasion there is dancing in the car park). These groups are visible and audible to others in the building, and are inclusive, linking people in the building. They contribute towards a music therapeutic milieu of the kind described by Trygve Aasgaard. He refers to this as 'music environmental therapy' and writes that 'the individual patient should not be overlooked but the focus for interventions be extended to encompass all present in a defined milieu' (Aasgaard 1999, p.35).

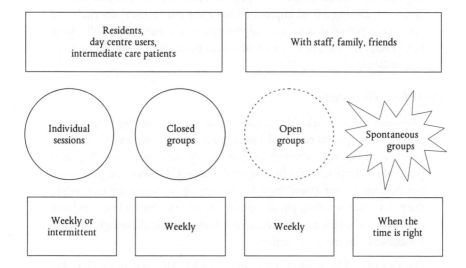

Figure 8.2 Making connections – spontaneous groups

Spontaneous groups range from being very small (perhaps a mother and daughter) to quite large numbers. They may happen in response to the needs of service users, institution or both, when the time is right.

> One 'spontaneous' group happens on an afternoon when many of the staff are having a meeting. About 25 day care service users are sitting in the large activity room with the television on. It seems that a music group which involves them all might be appropriate, rather than a smaller open group in the music room. With their permission I switch the television off and the session starts.
>
> They are seated in a circle around the edge of the room. Halfway through the session, Grace takes centre stage in the middle of the circle. She is from Montserrat, very tall, thin and agile. She starts to sing (and dance) a unique version of the Cole Porter song *Don't Fence Me In*. Someone shouts in encouragement 'Go on girl!' Others around the circle join in or take short solos – some improvised, others know the song. An atmosphere and mood is created in which everyone is involved, whether singing or not, around a

central individual 'performance'. Although Grace is the main 'performer' she allows space for others. I support on accordion and also sing.

At the end of the song, two comments reflect the different cultural backgrounds. A West Indian woman says 'Nice, nice' and a woman in more English tones says 'Jolly dee!' After the song Grace kisses my hand and sings another unique version of a popular song, *Send Me the Pillow that You Dream On*. During a final improvised song she goes around the circle and kisses each person in turn. I am apprehensive as to how some will take it, but all respond warmly. It is a spontaneous performance, with performers and audience.

The performance continues

The music therapist asks Alice a question about her wedding preparations. (Answers are spontaneous and unexpected at times, stories that we have never heard before.) Alice tells us about her grandfather, whom she lived with. 'He had a passion for betting on the horses.' He took the contents of her 'bottom drawer' (the things she was saving for when she married) to the pawn shop and then put the money on a horse! We hadn't heard that one before. She tells it with great comic timing and looks delighted when the audience bursts into laughter.

She also tells of how, when her husband-to-be, Alf, came to the door her grandfather would say 'She's having a sandpaper' meaning 'I was having a wash-down in the back room with a bowl of water and me clean undies!'

When they were married her husband worked in the brewery and she in the laundry. 'So I was in the soap suds and he was in the beer!' Her family on the front row are really laughing.

Susan sings a poignant song *When Your Old Wedding Ring was New* which was pre-planned. Spontaneous melodies come from James on harmonica and songs started by Jane or Susan: it's community singing with an audience who respond with huge appreciation and join in the songs.

Some, like James (described earlier) who begin with individual therapy, have managed to graduate from extreme isolation to a sense of belonging in a group. Thanks to music therapy happenings in the environment, James is able to choose to join a group because he hears it happening. In public performance especially, his playing, like Alice's and Susan's songs and stories, is appreciated by other residents, staff and families.

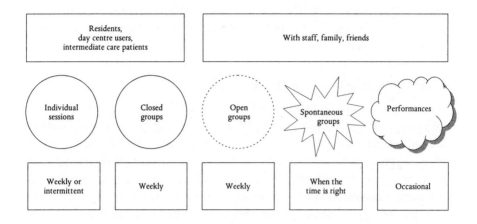

Figure 8.3 Making connections in performance

Making connections – performance

In contrast to spontaneous or regular music therapy groups, musical perfor-mances are planned in advance and happen when the time is right for both the clients and the institution. They involve residents, day centre users, staff, family and friends as participants and audience. Staff or family members who have been involved in open groups or spontaneous groups also become involved in performances. Here, connections are made between people in different types of group work all over the building (see Maratos Chapter 6).

Those who have had or are having music therapy are further empowered, enabled and connected as they contribute to the life of the community. These performances in a large group can be seen as an extension of music therapy and become a part of music therapy with a community. Brynjulf Stige writes that the term 'Community Music Therapy' is now being used in ways that 'suggest a change in conception and practice of music therapy, community in many cases no longer being just a context to work in but also to work with' (Stige 2002, p.28).

New York music therapist Alan Turry, in an analysis of clinical implications for the music therapist of performance writes

> Sharing the results and accomplishments publicly of the music created privately in a music therapy session can be a way of cultivating a sense of achievement within the client. Public sharing can be a way of validating changes the client has made internally…performing with clients is a legiti-mate activity that can bring many potential benefits to the client. (Turry 2001)

Turry emphasises that the therapist determines what the important dynamics and issues are for the client in order to discern what performing (or recording) will mean for them.

Making connections – *A Dream Wedding*

A Dream Wedding was presented in December 2001. Myrtle, a member of the care staff, had the ambition to do a performance having been involved in one of the community music/theatre performance projects described at the beginning of the chapter. She had a lot of ideas but not the confidence to make it happen on her own. I wanted to help but also wondered whether this was part of my role as the music therapist. At first I wasn't sure. Myrtle told me that Gladys, one of the residents who had learning difficulties and had been inappropriately placed here many years earlier, had been talking about the fact that she had never been married and most of the other residents had. Gladys wanted to experience being a bride at a wedding, and Myrtle thought that we could make a musical play about a wedding with Gladys acting out being married. (I was even less sure.)

However, we steered a delicate path in collaboration with staff and residents devising a musical performance with elements of pantomime, concert and cabaret. This would clearly separate fantasy from reality. We planned the framework over about two months (very loosely based on the *Cinderella* story), developing our wedding theme with the residents in Myrtle's 'coffee morning' sessions. Everyone shared memories of their weddings and songs they remembered and *A Dream Wedding* was the result. As already described, the cast, residents and staff related their memories of weddings; they sang, played and danced. The audience of families and friends was amazed, amused and moved. They joined in.

The performance comes to an end

> James plays harmonica as staff and residents dance. Cinderella returns with her prince for the wedding celebrations. The Fairy Godmother says 'Doesn't she look lovely? Must fly – I'm off to play the drums!' She joins three day centre users who are playing percussion. We sing a medley of wedding songs and the Fairy Godmother and music therapist sing *Making Whoopee* as the cake is cut.

> We sing a specially composed song *Oh, What a Dream!* which the cast are now familiar with and staff and residents dance together. From the wider community, the Community Line Dancers perform. They are older people from another day centre. Susan and Jane start up well-known songs and lead us all in singing, including the audience. The manager joins us in the

final song and takes over the lead of a 'Good-bye and thank you' sung to each performer individually and to which some respond. (The song was originally improvised in one of the staff music sessions.) Balloons are let down from the ceiling, food is brought in, the cast and audience eat, drink and dance together for some time after the performance ends.

Other performance events take place at the centre, including more spontaneous ones and concerts with improvised instrumental music. These help create a therapeutic milieu, music environmental therapy (Aasgaard 1999), Community Music Therapy (Ansdell 2002) or music therapy with a community (Stige 2002), enriching lives of individuals and the institution. The staff gains insight in a creative shared experience with those they care for. The performance gives a voice to the service users in terms of their life experience, opinions and feelings, while staff and families see clients in a different light. In fact everyone sees everyone else in a new light.

Connection – Community Music Therapy and community music

There are clear parallels between this music therapy performance project and the community music theatre project I described earlier. Aims of community music and this model of Community Music Therapy may be similar, in enriching an institution by connecting staff, residents and families in a creative process and performance – but how it happens is different. When I was a community musician within arts organisations, the performance, or product, was the driving force during the process. In this residential situation, group performance happens because of the music therapy, but not as the therapeutic goal. Rather, the performance is a by-product or added bonus.

Our production grew out of three main factors: my role as music therapist, developments made by clients within music therapy, and in response to a staff member who had the ambition to do a performance based on the wishes of a resident. A theme then emerged which could be devised with the residents. All the performers, staff and residents, owned the material they performed, the songs they chose to sing and the stories they chose to tell. The music therapist's role in this situation was to value everyone's input and 'allow' in all relationships with staff and clients. I did not take over the direction of the performance – it belonged to us all with equal responsibility for its success. Again, this fits with Trygve Aasgaard's description of environmental music therapy:

The goals will most often be made in collaboration with other staff (or even patients and their relatives). The implementation of the goal is seldom the responsibility of the music therapist. Sometimes the music therapist acts as an inspirer or a 'starter' or simply assists. (Aasgaard 1999, p.35)

Our performance is created from within the community as opposed to expertise being imported into the centre. Also, participants continue to have individual or group music therapy sessions after the performance is over. Turry writes:

Experiencing a sense of being valued and being attended to after the performance by the therapist, clients can feel an internal sense of validation and nurturing that can be more powerful than the public response. (Turry 2001)

Community music
and drama project

Music therapy
with a community

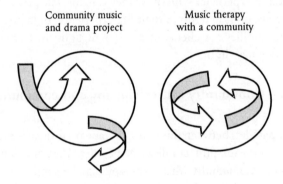

Figure 8.4 Community Music Therapy and community music

Figure 8.4 shows each circle as representing an institutional community. In my community music work, our expertise was available for a finite period, and ended after the musical performance was over. In this Community Music Therapy model, the music therapist has expertise, and facilitates as a member of and within the institutional community. That expertise stays there continuing to help create an all-inclusive 'live' music-making culture. The community and music therapy continue to influence and respond to one another.

My role, as the music therapist in the whole community, mirrors my role in each session and in each performance: listening and responding, empowering, enabling and connecting. Within sessions and performance I try to respond to individual and group needs, to allow and contain within the structure of pre-composed music and the spontaneity of improvisation; within the whole community I respond to the needs of clients and institution, offering the structure of regular sessions and pre-planned performance and the relative flexibility of intermittent sessions and spontaneous groups. As I 'discovered' during my dissertation research:

Whatever and however as music therapists we conceptualise therapeutic boundaries and spaces, it seems to me that these need to be fluid and courageous. Our minds as Music Therapists need to dare to break the rules if we are to come anywhere truly 'being with' the client. (Pavlicevic 1997, p.146)

Final connections

The marriage of this community with music therapy was also a dream wedding: a reciprocal relationship. In Figure 8.5, the arrows indicate the continuity of my role and expertise within the residential home and day care centre, listening and responding, helping to connect and empower people in the building, from individual sessions to small closed, open or spontaneous groups and performance. This is sometimes, but not always, a linear journey by service users. The individual and group sessions in which privacy and confidentiality are paramount coexist within the same building as the more open or spontaneous types of group work and performance work. My music therapist's role may encompass the two (Aasgaard 1999; Ansdell 2002).

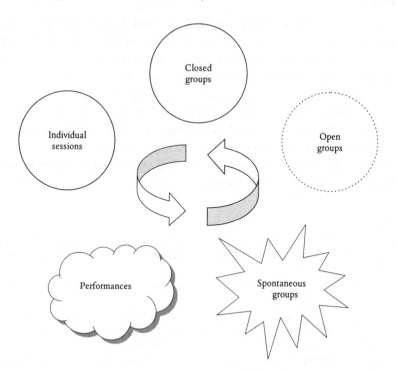

Figure 8.5 Community Music Therapy in a care setting – making connections

In this particular social services provision, it seems appropriate to align theory of music therapy practice (Community Music Therapy) with community arts, as well as the medical profession. As others have suggested (Ansdell 2002; Osborne 2002), in Britain there need to be closer links between community arts and music therapy, so as to give music to everyone. I see various important parts to my role including: helping to unite people in live music-making, encouraging forgotten talent, providing new experiences and also enriching the life of the institution.

Does it matter then if community arts and arts and health initiatives overlap each other's boundaries? Perhaps it is important to acknowledge the music therapist's approaches which, within performance projects, connect the whole community in which they practise. At the last Music Therapy World Congress, Nigel Osborne referred to Community Music Therapy as a potential force for change. The flexibility of a music therapist's role can help provide this force for change by contributing to the quality of life and relationships in the whole institution.

Epilogue

The institution has been undergoing organisational changes causing a certain amount of disruption, difficulty and anxiety for residents and staff. Planned performance projects have not been possible for some time but spontaneous groups, often with elements of performance, are more appropriate and have become more frequent. Music therapy unites people in relationships where communication is difficult, not only within the client group but also within an institution. As I write, the continuity and support, the personal and interpersonal benefits of music therapy seem increasingly important.

I would like to thank the service users and staff for allowing me to write about their Community Music Therapy experience.

References

Aasgaard, T. (1999) 'Music Therapy as a Milieu in the Hospice and Paediatric Oncology ward.' In D. Aldridge (ed) *Music Therapy in Palliative Care – New Voices.* London: Jessica Kingsley Publishers.

Ansdell, G. (1995) *Music for Life. Aspects of Creative Music Therapy with Adult Clients.* London: Jessica Kingsley Publishers.

Ansdell, G. (2002) 'Community Music Therapy and the Winds of Change – A Discussion Paper.' In C.B. Kenny and B. Stige (eds) *Contemporary Voices of Music Therapy: Communication, Culture and Community.* Oslo: Unipub Förlag.

Goldsmith, M. (1996) *Hearing the Voice of People with Dementia: Opportunities and Obstacles.* London: Jessica Kingsley Publishers.

Kitwood, T. (1997) *Dementia Reconsidered – The Person Comes First.* Buckingham: Open University Press.

Itzen, C. (1980) *Stages in the Revolution. Political Theatre in Britain since 1968.* London: Eyre Methuen.

Osborne, N. (2002) World Congress of Music Therapy, Oxford 2002 Keynote Address.

Pavlicevic, M. (1997) *Music Therapy in Context: Music, Meaning and Relationship.* London: Jessica Kingsley Publishers.

Powell, H. (1999) 'Discontinuous Music Therapy: A Contradiction or a Challenge? Interrupted and Short-term Relationships with Adult Clients.' Unpublished MMT dissertation. Nordoff-Robbins Music Therapy Centre/London: City University.

Proctor, S. (2002) 'Empowering and Enabling: Improvisational Music Therapy in Non-medical Mental Health Provision.' In C.B. Kenny and B. Stige (eds) *Contemporary Voices of Music Therapy: Communication, Culture and Community.* Oslo: Unipub Förlag.

Stige, B.(2002) 'The Relentless Roots of Community Music Therapy.' *Voices: A World Forum for Music Therapy.*http://www.voices.no/mainissues

Turner, F. (1993) 'Watching Brief.' *The Guardian,* 27 October 1993.

Turry, A. (2001). Performance and Product. Clinical Implications for the Music Therapist.' musictherapyworld.net

Conversations on Creating Community: Performance as Music Therapy in New York City

Kenneth Aigen

Performance of all kinds is integral to the life of New York City, both in the artistic sense and in the way that its residents take on various roles to negotiate the demands and intensity of daily life. As important is the role of the psychotherapy community. The numbers of psychotherapists and various training institutes are far larger than would be indicated by the proportion of the total United States population that lives in New York City. Mirroring this, the culture of music therapy in this area is one of music psychotherapy. This contrasts with other locales in the United States where the dominant music therapy framework might be educational, rehabilitative, medical, or behavioural.

All these facts are important in the context of the present chapter for two reasons. In the traditional conception of psychotherapy, the process is both confidential and private; it is a matter between therapist and client(s), occurs in a fixed time and place, and usually involves no third parties, either as an audience or in any other fashion. In the music psychotherapy framework, clinical activities that involve performance of any type can be considered reflective of earlier stages of music therapy as a profession as well as better suited to practitioners with undergraduate rather than graduate level training.

Such preconceptions as these are not congruent with the underlying rationale for performance-based therapy processes. While this theme will not be explored extensively in this brief overview, it is important to consider it, both in understanding the performance-based music therapy approaches in the specific culture of New York City, and in applying this model of practice to other music therapy cultures that may be similarly structured.

For music therapists who employ aspects of performance in their work, the evolving theoretical framework of Community Music Therapy is an important development. Performance, by definition, involves a public display of skill, and this public nature necessarily involves moving beyond the walls of the therapy room into the various layers of community that exist beyond those walls. The three examples below illustrate performance-oriented work in a sequence that moves outward from the institutional to the public sphere. David Ramsey's work involves building community within an institution; Peter Jampel's work involves using community-building mechanisms to help link his clients with the world outside of the psychiatric institution; and Alan Turry's joint work with Maria Logis takes place fully in the outside community.

David Ramsey and *The Rejuvenators* at Happy Hour

The Beth Abraham family of health services includes a rehabilitation centre that offers outpatient, short-term, and residential treatment. There is a wide diversity of patients, ranging from young people disabled by traumatic injuries to adults with disabling neurological conditions to elderly people with Alzheimer's disease and other disabling conditions.

An innovative aspect of Beth Abraham's residential program is the 'neighborhood initiative'. The idea is to gather groups of residents into living communities around common interests rather than by disabling condition. Previously, residents with a traumatic brain injury, for example, would be grouped together, even if that meant that people of vastly different ages with nothing in common outside of their disability were expected to function together. The new idea reflects the philosophy that people inside a treatment facility should not be defined by their deficits any more than are people in the outside world. The underlying message seems to be: *You are a person defined by your interests, preferences, and personal goals* and in this way the establishment of communities within the facility is more reflective of how communities in the outside world are formed.

In American culture, the term 'happy hour' is one used by bars to lure in customers. It refers to a time period, usually one or two hours at the end of the work day but prior to dinner, in which drinks are offered at discounts and complimentary snacks are offered. The idea is that people want a place to relax and unwind after work before going home. As part of its overall philosophy of community, Beth Abraham established a Happy Hour on its premises. The music therapy staff were asked to provide live music, doctors and nurses functioned as waiters and waitresses serving the patients and their family members, and patients were allowed a maximum of two alcoholic drinks. In addition to solo and duo performances by music therapists David Ramsey and Tom McClelland,

Happy Hour entertainment also includes the patients, particularly a therapy group called *The Rejuvenators*.

I had an opportunity to speak with David and ask him about the origins of Happy Hour just prior to attending one.

DR: The Happy Hour was one of those things that was started here to facilitate community building. From many perspectives, it had nothing to do with music therapy, except that I'm performing for the community here with, and in front of, a lot of the patients that live here.

KA: Maybe you could tell me what the whole music therapy program consists of and how it all fits together. You have sessions here, you rehearse songs, you have recording sessions, you have the performance...

DR: For this band, and for my pop stuff, we come in and we're working on songs. We have a certain idea about what sounds good, what is pleasing. It's an artistic decision. So when I'm working with Trevor[1] or the band, it's always in the format of working on a song, writing a song, or doing a cover of a song, and we want it to sound a certain way. So we pick the best instruments, the best drumbeats, we spend a lot of time working on that.

KA: ...it's really about creating the most aesthetic object compared to necessarily being self-expressive, or are those two things the same in your mind?

DR: They overlap to some degree. Some people can write an original song that follows conventional song writing dictates and styles and has very little self-expression. Others can do a cover tune, choose sounds that reflect a deep emotional connection, and sing in a way that is more personal than an original piece. This doesn't mean that song writing that is based on cultural notions of what a pop song should sound like is bad. It can help patients feel good about writing songs just like the big boys, something like Frank Sinatra. But it's not particularly self-expressive. They're not really thinking about love situations that they were really in and putting it in a song. They're singing 'Oh baby, baby' because they've heard 'Oh

---

1   Trevor is a client of David's.

baby, baby' a thousand times. There are times when I consciously guide song writing and try to get it into more self-expressive areas. I don't see self-expressive and aesthetic choices as tremendously different. When a person makes a choice that 'I want this sound on a drum,' it really can resonate with something that is very primal and self-expressive.

I have two groups that are rehabilitation groups in a way. I have an aphasic group where people are singing songs and doing vocal exercises and building community based on a shared lack of communication and then an instant restoration of communication. Then I have a MIDI group where physically challenged patients who can't speak use improvisation. They call themselves the *Improvisational Mustangs*. And we do all improvisation. Over time we've learned a few grooves that we really like, we put names to them and then we made a CD. We designed the cover together, we chose the music, we recorded it. In most of the sessions we'd get into a jam, we'd fall into certain grooves and we would later name them to help us remember them. Those grooves became a part of our package and we decided to capture them so to speak. That's when we recorded them. After we recorded them we also thought we would like to perform them. That's how the idea of performance developed. We performed twice.

KA: Was the recording part of the motivation to do the performance? Did hearing that it sounded good lead the group to think that the music deserves to be heard by other people?

DR: I think there was a performance scheduled where the rock band was already performing and I asked the *Mustangs* if they would like to do what we do in session on stage and present that to the community. They wanted to get up in front of people and perform. I think that a public display of one's self is an important part of being a human being, whether it's on stage or it's just in the hallway and saying, 'Let me take command of this situation and tell you something of my thoughts and feelings.' There's not that big of a difference between the gesture of putting your hand up in the middle of a conversation and saying, 'I've got a story for you guys,' and getting up on stage to present yourself.

KA: Performing on a stage is just an exaggeration of what we normally do in our everyday interactions.

DR: It is. It's just that the stage and the lights function like that gesture of holding up your hand and saying, 'Look at me. I want to take the spotlight just for a second.' And even if it's just for a moment, I'm taking the spotlight, I'm saying, 'Look at me. I have something to say. I want to engage you, I want to instruct you, I want to entertain you, I want to do something with this spotlight.'

KA: People think that art is so removed and something in museums but actually we find beauty in our daily life. And you're saying the same thing about performance. Performance isn't this weird thing that only some people do. And yet some people don't have the opportunity to be performers in their daily life.

DR: For a person who doesn't even have the capacity to say 'Ho, wait!' with their voice, or put up their hand and say, 'Stop, look at me,' you have to almost artificially provide it at times. It's almost insane to separate yourself from the culture and say 'Hey, look at me,' and yet on the other hand it's what we do all the time. But, in the process of doing that, you're involved with personal growth as it involves dealing with the personal presentation of self. It's essential to have responsibility for making choices, aesthetic choices, musical choices, in a place where all those choices have been taken away from you.

In a facility like Beth Abraham's, performance builds community in a unique way. This place used to be called the Hospital for the Incurables, the disabled, rejects of society. That became their role. What happens for patients during performances is that the perception of being an invalid is almost instantly changed because you're on stage doing something that's culturally idealized. And so if the person that bathes you is watching you up on stage singing, the next time they bathe you and tend to your personal hygiene, they're going to think of you differently. It instantly and forever changes that relationship.

KA: If the people here are playing a role in society, to be the weak ones, to be the incapable, then you need the contrivance of a performance to allow them to take on a new role and be able to be seen in another light.

DR: Right. If we go back to this conversation about how it happens naturally every day, that's how we assert ourselves as not invalids. Whenever you take control of a conversation, you're taking power. And those little things mount up to where I see that person as somebody in charge, somebody with something to say. And so, again when you've got somebody who can't raise their hand or raise their voice you have to artificially give them the stage to do that. Or else it won't happen. Once the MIDI group was playing and there was one patient in the group who played the drums. He was in a semi-foetal position. He was just curled up in his wheelchair that was more like a bed. He had this one beautiful Michelangelo arm over the side and the rest of him was seemingly lifeless. But this arm was rhythmic, musical, and explorative, and he couldn't talk. He was a mobile DJ before he had this horrible accident. He got out of bed once or twice a week and was put in front of a television. He was really considered a vegetable in many people's eyes. We did that performance and there was this beautiful arm: fluid, musical, and expressive. An artist should have come and drawn that arm. And people lined up after the concert, the staff and patients, just to look over his crib and they were saying, 'Great! I can't believe you. You were great!' And the tears were just running, he couldn't really talk, but the tears were just streaming down his face. And people were seeing him differently. They were saying 'I didn't know you weren't a vegetable.' I mean, they weren't saying that literally. But that was the message. And forever the perception of him on that floor was changed.

KA: He became a person in their eyes. Just the fact that somebody's worthy of being put in front of others is such a strong message in terms of how they feel about themselves and how others will see them.

KA: So what exactly happens at Happy Hour?

DR: Happy Hour is me performing and inviting people up, anybody, patients, staff, family members, anybody. That Happy Hour format is a mixed bag. It's me being a bit of a recreation therapist, God forbid, but it is. It's me playing songs and then trying to break it up a little bit by inviting staff and patients up. So in many regards, it's hard to say that Happy Hour is completely a music therapy event.

KA: Well, let's not even approach that question yet. Let's just describe what it is.

DR: Well, the Happy Hour was constructed with this intent. It was going to be an hour where the patients could come and have a beer and alcohol, which was unusual, and where roles within the community were changed.

KA: Is alcohol otherwise not allowed in the facility?

DR: No, it's not allowed. This one time is the adult hour. So they were allowed to have two drinks and the president of the hospital, the janitor of the hospital, and the social workers were going to be the waiters and the waitresses and it was going to move from one group of people to the next and break barriers and put people into different roles.

KA: Taking out of normal expectations, and also what some people might say is even socially appropriate. You're a social worker, or you're a therapist and you're serving alcohol to your client? Wouldn't that be unheard of?

DR: Exactly. Everything was a bit out of the norm. Serving alcohol to patients may seem inappropriate, serving alcohol to adult persons is not.

KA: In some sense the focus was on you as the performer, but it was more like we need a reason to make this social thing happen where we're dissolving roles. The music was a focus point but it seems like the purpose of it isn't for everyone to come in to hear David play music. It seems like there was a larger social purpose, about introducing some leveling phenomenon into the community.

DR: I was always struggling to find some music therapy in all this. The one thing that I feel good about in these Happy Hours is bringing the patients up, bringing the janitor up, or bringing an administrator up, and in that way breaking down the roles.

KA: It seems like if you think of therapy not just as psychotherapy but as care in a total sense, then you are caring for the community, if you think of a place as a community. What does it mean that they asked you as a member of the community to do the Happy Hour? They didn't hire a lounge singer.

DR: Well, they do have a lounge singer come in every other Thursday.

KA: Do you think it's any different from what happens, when you do it?

DR: Oh, I think it's tremendously different.

KA: Because you are coming in with the consciousness of a therapist?

DR: You know what? Even if I come in with the same lounge singer consciousness, they have another relationship with me. They know me. Because they know me they could almost see me out there struggling. They know I have no problems in the music therapy sessions. But when I get up there and I can't perform so well they're seeing me as a person.

KA: It's that whole role reversal, that leveling. In terms of this whole community, if this helps the nurse see the patient differently, or if it just makes people more comfortable with each other then you're tending to the emotional health of the community.

DR: I think that that's true.

KA: You doing this is the community entertaining itself because you're part of this community. I think that has a certain meaning. There's something about the fact that you're not coming from outside that has an important social function. How are you thinking of Happy Hour now? As part of your music therapy work, as part of your work as a musician in the community, but not part of music therapy or something in-between? Are you struggling to define it or do you have it well-defined for yourself?

DR: I don't have it well-defined, but it certainly is a part of me being a musician in the community. It's me having the role of a music therapist and then providing alternative ways of seeing that role and then, most importantly, bringing in members of the community and giving them a chance to take on another role and to change the community. Change the community's perception of them. And then, on the music therapy level, give the person a chance to experience himself as successful, as competent, as somebody who can captivate and engage others, and express themselves in a way that draws people in to them. I think that's a satisfying human experience.

Sitting in a long auditorium with ten large tables that are spaced widely apart with bright tablecloths I watch patients slowly arrive in wheelchairs. They are primarily of middle age and older. Some are talking, some are immobile, and others are bobbing their heads and tapping their hands to the strong grooves of recorded pop music. On one level, these people are very isolated from one another; on another level, there is a connection made around the strong beats of 2 and 4 of the recorded music and around the lyric hooks of the songs. Most of the eyes stare straight ahead, but they are in the beat of the music.

Two women dance and groove in their wheelchairs.

The room slowly fills up as four o'clock approaches. Snacks and drinks are distributed to the people around the tables. The room lights go down and the stage lights come up and *The Rejuvenators* are on the stage: David is on keyboards, also controlling bass and drum sounds; Horace sings and is at the microphone; Walter plays the drums and Florence sits in her wheelchair and plays the tambourine with her foot, the only part of the body that she has control over.

> *Don't worry, about a thing, 'cause every little thing gonna be alright*
> *Singin' don't worry, about a thing, 'cause every little thing gonna be alright...*
> *Rise up this morning, smiled with the rising sun, three little birds, sit by my doorstep*
> *Singin' sweet songs of melodies pure and true, sayin' 'This is my message to you-u-u.'*

Bob Marley's message of gentle reassurance sounds especially poignant in this setting. Yet the music grooves and it is clear that it is not just the words that soothe but that gentle reggae groove that gets inside the body is part of the message as well: as long as you can groove and connect to others around groove there are still meaningful experiences to be had in life.

The community is entertaining itself and this is an important point. Sometimes one strengthens the community by acting upon the individuals who constitute it. Other times, the locus of intervention is the community itself and one acts on the community to strengthen the individuals. This idea of acting upon the community is important in understanding the nature of Community Music Therapy. Perhaps one of the meanings of this term is to identify a new level of intervention for music therapists, from individual therapy, to group therapy, to Community Music Therapy, and by its very nature, it is one that demands new ethics and values regarding things such as its public nature, public disclosure, and confidentiality. If one strengthens the community, and individuals can be drawn in to identify with that community, then the individual's sense of self is similarly strengthened.

Willie the janitor comes up and sings as well, performing the song *My Girl.* Some of the lyrics are inspirational:

> I've got sunshine on a cloudy day,
> and when it's cold outside I've got the month of May...
> I've got so much honey the bees envy me,
> I've got a sweeter song than the birds in the tree...
> I don't need money, fortune or fame,
> I got all the riches, baby, that one man can claim...

Willie has a great voice and absolutely no sense of timing. His words come in an irregular fashion and David does a heroic job of following the unpredictable sequence of two-, three- and five-beat measures. Nevertheless, Willie's efforts are appreciated and this seems part of the entire 'leveling' function of the Happy Hour. It is not only the patients who are 'imperfect' in a sense, but all of us are. It is our imperfections that make us human.

> We're havin' a party, Everybody's swingin', Dancin' to the music, On the radio...

A cynical person might see a cruel irony in the term 'Happy Hour' applied to a place that deals with so much constant human loss and suffering. However, it strikes me quite differently as I absorb the music of this community. If we are in Happy Hour now, it means that what came before it qualifies as work. It validates all of the difficult rehabilitation therapies that these people undergo each day as their work, thereby recognizing it for what it is, giving more meaning to it and hence more dignity to the individuals undertaking it. It says, in effect, *you do work hard. What you do counts as work as much as anything else that human beings do, and you too, are deserving of a Happy Hour and whatever fun, pleasure, dignity, and camaraderie that can bring to you.*

Peter Jampel and *The Baltic Street Band* at the After Hours Club

The Baltic Street Clinic of South Beach Psychiatric Center includes the Baltic Street Resource and Treatment Center, a program for people with chronic psychiatric problems. Changes in governmental policy during the mid-1990s have had a profound impact on psychiatric facilities, with the focus now on linking the person with the outside world as much as possible. The overriding treatment goal is to have these individuals function at as high a level as possible *in the community*, and consistent with this change of attitude, the recipients of clinical services are referred to as 'consumers' rather than 'patients.'

With the overall goal being entrance to employment, there is much focus on job training, improving literacy, and acquiring computer skills. The music program at Baltic Street reflects this philosophical change. There are a variety of activities within the total music program, some that fit neatly into traditional notions of music therapy, and some that expand this notion. There are music therapy sessions offered in the traditional sense. There is also a band, *The Baltic Street Band*, that affords different opportunities for performance, both inside and outside the Baltic Street facility. In some performances there are opportunities for clients of Baltic Street who are not themselves in music therapy treatment of any type to make music, and there is also an opportunity for *The Baltic Street Band* to perform the material prepared in their music therapy sessions.

Baltic Street is structured not so much as an institution offering different types of therapy groups but as a community with a collection of programs, each with its own dedicated space, staffing, goals, and participants. Each program is a sub-community built on the idea that the best way to move people to the outside world is to do so in increments. In the movement from an individual therapy session, to participating in *The Baltic Street Band*, to participating in the music program in all of its dimensions, to a consideration of the overall Baltic Street community, and then moving beyond this community to the entire South Beach system to the non-clinical community, we can see gradual integration of the person into increasingly larger spheres until he is integrated in the community at large. New music therapy services and structures are being created to accompany individuals on this journey and the various aspects of the music program at Baltic Street meet this need for reintegration. All the clients participating in the music program clearly benefit from the type of rationale provided by a Community Music Therapy model as the forms of musical interaction are increasingly integrated into the public domain.

Because Peter Jampel has been at this institution for such a long time, we began by discussing how this long tenure affects his work.

KA:　You've worked with many of the clients here on a long-term basis so you've had a professional relationship but you also have a musical relationship that parallels the professional relationship. Are they two different things?

PJ:　Not really. They have evolved in parallel ways. And at times they cross over, but in a lot of ways it's hard to sit in an office and talk for 25 years. And it's hard to play the same music together for 25 years. Like any partnership, relationship, if it doesn't evolve you're going to part ways. People come in, they go out. I think there is a very definite connection between the development of long-term psychotherapy relationships and long-term music therapy relationships, and the partnership has stayed alive because we kept moving to the next thing. And to me the next thing was going back to the thing that always felt most joyous about making music, which was, making music. Actually doing it, and enjoying playing music with people who enjoy playing music.

KA: Do you remember when you first began taking music outside of the therapy session?

PJ: It grew out of community sing. Community sing was the traditional send-off to the week, where it was the last group of the week. All of the Baltic Street community got together, all the staff got together, brought together in music. It performed the ceremonial functions of closing the week together, of saying goodbye to people who may be discharged and going on to other programs. Or being able to deal with losses, deaths in the community, staff members leaving, welcoming new people into the communities.

KA: Music is a vehicle for helping people make transitions in life.

PJ: Yeah. I think that you start from a source, you take a journey, and you might have a destination, but the transitional process has always been very important. Ceremony, ritual, the symbolic joining together through music, and the function that music plays in ritual and ceremony, that's what community sing was all about. It was a place where we joined together at the end of a week and both celebrated and commiserated about that week's events and what we were going through together. And it incorporated performance, always. The musicians in the Baltic Street community were my sidemen in the community sing. So if I had a drummer, a guitar player, or I had, sometimes, a keyboard player I would switch to a different role, and sometimes we had a little trio, and sometimes it might be a student of mine, but often they were community musicians from inside Baltic Street.

KA: They weren't taking the music they had worked on in the music therapy session and performing it publicly. They were supporting the community sing and they were an extension of you as the musical leader.

PJ: But they also had an opportunity to do their own performances in community sing and to shine and to be acknowledged as gifted artists within the community. And they would always have opportunities to take a turn to play a song or do whatever they wanted. My method in community sing was to encourage people spontaneously to emerge as artists within the community.

KA: Would you think of that as different from the music therapy work?

PJ: That integration occurred over time. I started to see that a lot of what happened during the week often culminated in this large performance environment in the community sing. There was a lyrical improvisation going on, straight improvisation going on. There was movement music going on because the music-dance group was always part of the community sing and the dance therapist would always facilitate the movement components. The little group of sidemen would facilitate the dancing or the music. If somebody emerged spontaneously from the audience who wanted to sing a song, coming from their heart, we would be the backup group for them. And we would comp lightly and help support it and there was a sense of community musicians supporting the emergence of other artists within the community in the community sing. That built over time where it became clear that these sidemen and these emerging artists were in need of more. Gradually, they started to say, 'Why don't we just get together on our own because this is not enough time.' I started having another music therapist, Rafael Piccorelli, and we collaborated together and feeling the energy we started to work with these folks who wanted to do more intensive music. That evolved into a kind of rehearsal structure. We were rehearsing in the basement and we looked at the auditorium. Nobody ever used the auditorium. And I said, 'God, performance space! Look at this. Well, why aren't we using this place?' And that evolved into this After Hours cabaret structure that took a few years to get going. But we developed an ongoing, monthly, in-house cabaret.

KA: So around 1990 is when your framework of music therapy began changing to accommodate the idea of performance as being a legitimate component of a therapeutic process.

PJ: As a more intentional, formulated method, not just as part of community sing. We felt something new is growing and there is interest and it is coming from people and they want to do it, and there's energy and a new space and a collaboration with a really fine musician that just added to my own sense of musical wonder and excitement. There was this more intentional consideration about performance as another distinct but connected outgrowth of what was going on. And up until then we started to see the other parts of the music therapy program as offering different opportunities and challenges to people who want to make music.

KA: Do you remember when you first came to the idea of *The Baltic Street Band* performing outside of the Baltic Street facility?

PJ: The very first outside performance was at South Beach for the Martin Luther King day event.

KA: But it was in the South Beach system, it was again moving in the next concentric circle.

PJ: We then got a contract as an HAI[2] performing group, and for two years we did concerts for HAI and we performed for a number of different agencies that HAI had contracts with and we got paid really good money, $450 a performance. Ten per cent went to the agency as a cover fee, and the rest was divided up as pay for the individuals. We always did a certain amount of pro bono work just because that's where we were at. There were a lot of gigs where people would want us to play and we also always looked for some paid gigs. So that happened around 1993 to about 1995. That moved us out of Baltic Street and into different spheres. The After Hours Club developed in 1995 and we became the house band for our own cabaret.

---

2 HAI is 'hospital audiences', an organization that provides performers to hospitals.

The community sing died about seven years ago when the day treatment program was deprogrammed. Day treatment died. My staff left, and all the patients left. Community meetings stopped, and milieu treatment ended at Baltic Street around 1996 and we never resurrected the community sing after that. We reprogrammed around 1998 when the administration here realized they committed a big mistake because people stopped coming here because there was nothing to come for any more. What happened was that people retreated into these little tribes. There were the artists in the art community, there was the band and there were the computer skills people. What happened was that it was like a nuclear holocaust had happened. There was total devastation and little tribes survived this real down period, and only the healthiest structures survived. The band survived.

KA: Survival of the fittest.

PJ: Survival of the fittest. The art studio, and the computer skills program. And they stayed tight because they had their own internal cultures, territories, identifications, staffing; everything else died. The community sing died. There was no community. And when it was resurrected again, those little tribal bands came back together and new tribal bands came back and groups were added, staff was added so that I had a staff to work with again. What started to happen is life emerged again, like after Mount Saint Helens [a volcano] wiped the landscape out, or Yellowstone had a big fire. Life started to re-emerge, and the music therapy program that re-emerged had a much more interesting and tougher life.

And the groups that developed came out of a sense of there being real interest coming from it. The performance work that evolved after that was not just a band playing for a hospital audience but grew from a more of a grassroots level of people who saw that performance was something that had touched them, interested them, inspired them, challenged them, and that performers were now popping up from unexpected places, just like someone getting up and feeling moved to start to sing.

I come to Baltic Street to see the After Hours Club which, today, is being integrated into a holiday luncheon. I take the elevator down to the basement auditorium where I find a room with tables and chairs set up for about 70–80 people, being prepared for a Thanksgiving lunch. In stark contrast to the outside, it is warm and humid in the room from the many trays of hot water being used to keep the food warm. There is a mosaic of mismatched tiles on the floor and there is a unpretentious randomness to the look of the room.

People begin slowly filtering in to the sounds of a band setting up with instruments being tuned, heavy electrical cords being dropped and the random banging of drums being tightened. An out-of-tune banjo is being tuned to an out-of-tune piano.

'Diabetics first!' The call goes out through the room and is echoed by others as the food service priority is established. There's a sudden delay however. 'I'll be right back. There's some macaroni and cheese waiting for me on Flatbush Avenue,' says my host, Peter Jampel. The music will come after the food instead of before it, as is the custom. 'A hungry crowd is not a happy crowd,' observes Peter.

As the auditorium fills up with people, they serve themselves, buffet style. The set up of instruments continues and musical sounds begin filling the environment as the stage is occupied by therapists, music therapy students, volunteers, and of course, in the parlance of Baltic Street, consumers. Voices sing random lyrics, and there are the sounds of an electric bass, electric guitars and piano in the PA system. These sounds are much louder than the sounds in the room of people talking and food being served. In their own way, the electrically amplified sounds seem to announce: the musicians are here and they have something powerful at their disposal.

The music emerges gradually out of the set-up sounds without any special announcement or fanfare. There is a warm-up song, a poem about the holiday of Thanksgiving is read, the songs *Feelings* and *Nights in White Satin* ensue, and then a brief period of jamming follows. Then a man named River sings two songs, *Amazing Grace* and *Bill Bailey*. As he sings *Amazing Grace* – a song of spiritual pain, longing, and fulfilment – the audience is sombre, introspective and focuses on him. Heads nod along with his voice and guitar with a sweet, bluesy harmonica accompaniment. *Yeah, I've been there, I know from what he sings,* the audience's response seems to be saying. This is followed by the song *Won't You Come Home, Bill Bailey,* a song from the early twentieth century, an unusual choice given the relative youth of the performer. After a brief introductory section, the singer moves into the more familiar chorus and the audience members clap along and become enlivened.

This is followed by Avrah, a woman who sings *Girl From Ipanema* and *Strangers in the Night,* a song made famous by Frank Sinatra. This latter song is done in a rap style and the audience becomes very engaged and rocks out with the performers. This establishes a pattern of unusual musical combinations that continues throughout the afternoon. Another old song, *You Are My Sunshine* is done with a funk groove in the style of James Brown, and later the song standard *Night and Day* is done in a Bo Diddley rock and roll beat, based on the well known five-beat clave pattern.

This combination of opposites indicates that normal musical conventions are not so important; what is more important is giving opportunities for individual expression and creativity through the choice of songs and how they are rendered. Moreover, this pattern of using older material and giving it more contemporary readings seems to help integrate the audience. Older people who relate to the song and younger people who relate to the rhythmic realization are brought together in a common experience this way.

As the afternoon winds down, the audience gradually diminishes. The feel of the After Hours Club started as a performance, but as we get to the last few performers it feels more like a bunch of musicians sitting around in a jam session playing for each other. There is a strong sense of this being the essential core of *The Baltic Street Band*. Paul, an older man, walks up in an unsteady manner. There are tremors in his arms and he looks as if he could fall over at any moment. He performs a Ladino song, *Adio Kerida*. Harmonica tones waft over the music with sounds related to the tonality of the song. Paul stares down at the floor, seemingly looking at nothing in particular.

The music ends and he looks up making eye contact with the remaining audience members. Yes, there is a person there, you can see it in his eyes! He just smiles at the recognition with the audience that something of significance has been shared and that through music the community members can experience themselves as unified in something and as part of something larger than themselves. On the surface level, certain members of the community performed music for others. Yet if we consider the community as an organism, we can see how the community musiced for itself as an expression of its strength, unity and continued survival.

Alan Turry and Maria Logis Singing Her Way Through It

Of the three music therapists whose work is described in the present chapter, the work with music therapist Alan Turry and Maria Logis is the only one that is undertaken within a specific music therapy approach, in this case Nordoff-Robbins music therapy. In many ways, the extension of therapeutic activities into the public sphere is congruent with the origins of the Nordoff-Robbins approach. Paul Nordoff was a composer and pianist who came to music therapy via the world of musical performance. Moreover, it was common for the original Nordoff-Robbins team to do public and private performances of works specially composed for therapy. Additionally, the Nordoff-Robbins approach is a music-centered one in the sense that the client's desire to create music is the prime motivational force drawn upon by the therapist. And the desire to create music calls for a public performance as its natural consummation.

As embodied in both the compositional and improvizational aspects of Nordoff-Robbins work, musical creation and performance is a particularly potent way of providing access to the transformative powers of myth, magic, and a connection to the eternal. The need for these things can become more pronounced when one is faced with a life crisis such as confronted Maria Logis. In 1994 she was diagnosed with a form of cancer, non-Hodgkins lymphoma. She describes how she 'turned to God for help' and the answer she received was in the form of a desire to sing. So she began the search for a singing teacher, asking people that she knew if they had any ideas for her. Through these inquiries she met music therapist Alan Turry and began a course of music therapy that continues to the present (April 2003).

The form of their sessions together emerged in a way that Maria would begin vocalizing about a variety of topics and Alan would accompany her on piano. At times these improvised compositions would begin by describing the weather – they also covered the most personal and difficult of issues concerning Maria's fears regarding her illness, her struggles with food, and any and all therapeutic issues that might be expected to come up in a course of psychotherapy.

Maria has been sharing her personal story and the songs created in her therapy sessions, together with Alan, through a variety of public venues since 1996. She has appeared on radio and television programs; she has performed the material from her sessions at private gatherings, concerts, music therapy conferences, support groups for cancer patients, and mental health facilities; she has recorded a CD of these songs singing with Alan on piano and additional musicians on violin and cello; she has allowed her story to be told through newspaper articles and music therapy books; and most recently, she created a one-hour performance piece with a professional set design and an ensemble of four musicians on piano, violin, percussion and woodwinds, that ran for a week in April 2002. Maria's therapy is not only being shared publicly in the community, it is *taking place* in the community. I sat with Maria and Alan together to talk about their process.

KA: What motivated you to want to share aspects of your therapy process in very different public venues, to take what is traditionally considered to be a confidential realm and share that with the outside community?

ML: This was not my idea. At some point I realized that what Alan and I were doing was not singing lessons. So I met Janet Savage [a vocal instructor] and she listened to the session tapes and said, 'There are songs in here.' I didn't identify them as songs, we didn't identify them as songs. We're just doing our work. We were making music. I didn't really define what it was (chuckles). She suggested we listen to the tapes and find the songs. Then she said, 'You should learn them and sing them for your friends. Have a concert in your house.' That was her idea. To Janet, there were songs in our work. She pushed me to share them with people. I think the only reason I agreed was because I was walking on eggs with the oncologists. Every two months I was going back and they were saying, 'You're going to need chemotherapy very soon. The lymphoma will become active, we don't know exactly when.' I felt so threatened. I thought, 'Well, I could be dead in six months. Maybe I should do this.'

KA: And so, the uncertainty of your life at that point pushes you to say, 'Why not do this? What have I got to lose?'

ML: Right.

KA: You're not just sharing songs. You were sharing some of the very personal details of your life. Was that challenging for you?

ML: It is very hard. It turned out to be a way of standing up to the critic inside me that says, 'You are nobody. You can't sing. And this is really ridiculous!'

KA: It seems like something about your particular therapy process required public performance.

ML: Yes, that's right. But I didn't know that performing would be so healing. Now I know it. Three things happened: 1) There were no mistakes possible when I was working with Alan, this was a healing experience; 2) I faced the inner critic and won the contest each time we performed. I learned there was no magic bullet, music gave me the courage to stand up each time the critic knocked me down; 3) My life has changed, I'm becoming a performance artist. The title *Singing My Way Through It* is apt. I sing my way through my fears and sadness.

AT: When Maria performs, it's an affirmation of the changes she's making. I had no plan for it either. When we first started, my idea about the tape was for her to listen to how she's expressing, reflect on her experience, get a sense of control over very scary, painful feelings of anguish. And that was the first kernel of the possibility of it going outside of the therapy room. She did start to share the process with her others, her sister first. I felt Maria was so frozen emotionally, and that the singing experience was so freeing that it would be good for her to listen to it outside of the session. It was a way for her to have the distance of not actually doing it but listening to it. I thought that would give her a little bit of control and distance over potentially overwhelming feelings. She could reflect on her experience.

KA: What's the very first outside sharing you did? Can you recreate the chronology so that we get a sense of how it's grown?

ML: First was doing it for friends at my home. And the second was doing it for my church family. It was at my church for a much bigger audience, more than 60 people. The third time, Janet felt that I had to do it for strangers. Because the first two groups were my friends they were cheering for me because I was still alive. The third time was at New York University for staff and students of music therapy. And Alan arranged that. After that came the music therapy conferences. And after the music therapy conferences there were some other community sharings like at the New School, the training institute for mental health. And people heard about what we were doing and invited us. At all of them we sang live songs and played recordings because we wanted to give people an under-standing of what our process was. But which songs we did, and which recordings we played, changed because we had more material every time we did a conference. The next type of public sharing came on the radio. Then we worked on a CD. And after that I performed, I created a theater piece.

AT: I think that was the first one that I was not involved with.

ML: Right. The first show was at the Creative Center for Women with Cancer. It was as a one-woman show with four musicians and Alan was not part of that. Then the following year I did the same show but somewhat different at the Blue Heron Theater and we had four performances. And we were also interviewed on television and written about in newspapers.

KA: What is it like for you to have your therapist integrated into your life outside therapy and doing things in public with you?

ML: I guess the most important thing I could say is it's been comfortable from the very first moment. The first public sharing at my home, a year after I was diagnosed, was a very important moment. Alan was very supportive in the rehearsals and that day.

KA: I see the fact that you started doing things without Alan as a very positive step. You started to internalize whatever strength he provided for you and find that within yourself. What was it like the first time you did something without him there?

ML: Janet said, 'You need to start working with jazz musicians to really learn these songs.' I started to share this music. These jazz musicians transcribed the music that began to open up this world to other professional musicians. And they were quite interested in this process.

KA: There's a lot of mutual influences going on and different communities opening up to you. The music community is being impacted by the music therapy community and vice versa.

ML: To perform with these musicians was really a tiny step because I'd worked with them for a couple of years. They had transcribed the material. So it was easy for me to make the next step, saying, 'Okay Jon, what instruments do we need for the show? Let's get a violin, let's do this.' It was a small step because I'd been sharing my process. I was not learning my songs in isolation. I was sharing my process with these guys.

KA: You're not sharing just your music. You're sharing your life, the essence of what you're going through. You're not leaping into a new community, but this community moves to you and integrates itself into what you are already doing, and then you move with it. How does what you've shared affect the different communities you move in?

ML: Let me start with my work community. I was in a senior manager's position at Con Edison, and I made a decision mutually with my employer that I want to work part-time. Now that community knows that somebody who is at a pretty high level is leaving that work, which they know well, to do music. That community was affected and my relationship with them changed. Now I'm doing the CD. It's an encouraging role model for people.

KA: You found something you loved and had to do. And someone who lives life that way could be an inspiration for other people.

ML: Right. My church community and my priest were quite supportive right from day one. People there are always interested in what's going on. And since people are praying for other people's health and I was still chemo free, that has a big impact on people. Something in me was getting healthier. So that had an impact on my church community. The musician community is a brand new community, and I am in the kindergarten with the musicians. My life changed because in my work life I was at the top of my game. I am very competent in my work. Now with the musicians I'm a beginner.

KA: But just like you were a role model for the Con Ed community, I'm wondering if you are in a similar way for the musician community, because you're demonstrating where artists can draw inspiration from. Musicians are always dealing with the question of 'Where does my inspiration to create come from?' And you're out there dealing with everything in your life and using it as a source for your artistic expression.

AT: I was just thinking about the idea about crisis being opportunity and I feel like the cancer really shook something and opened you to a kind of willingness to take a risk and change and do this public sharing.

ML: When I look back now, I had a choice to just go into a massive depression once I got diagnosed with cancer, turn myself over to the doctors and just fold up my tent, or go this other way where I said, 'I'm not turning myself over to the doctors, I'm turning myself over to God.' Then God did all this stuff. I didn't have to do anything. All I had to do was to say, 'Yes.'

KA: Except get up on that stage!

ML: Listen, many times when I had to get up on stage, I said, 'You know, God, you got me into this, now you better get me out of it! (Laughter) Please get me through this because I'm shitting bricks!'

KA: Alan, did you want to talk about how all this has changed the sessions?

AT: I don't worry as much if we come in and just sing about the weather or if we're just concentrating on a song. We know the potency of creating an aesthetic form. There's something about that. I mean sometimes Maria will come in and say, 'Look, I want to work on the "B" section of this song today.' We did that last week. To me, the music has therapeutic value in and of itself. When we first started I might have felt, 'Well, wait a second. Is this beneficial? I'm not sure.' But knowing what we've been through, I can see the value in that, just in and of itself.

KA: Something very similar came up with David Ramsey. I asked him, 'Do you see it as contradictory that you're either working on songs or you're working on musical self-expression?' And he said making an aesthetic choice is a form of self-expression because it's expressing your preferences, what's pleasing to you. An aesthetic choice isn't just an aesthetic choice.

AT: It's a personal choice. Yes.

KA: So, is there some level of the aesthetic in the self-expressive?

AT: They're not mutually exclusive. They're artificial distinctions because we have to talk about them. I mean, how can you separate the aesthetic from the psychological, the personal from the artistic? It's all related. If we look at the songs, we've both created more complex things, things with a wider range, things with different kinds of music. I think that those aesthetic qualities that we can look at reflect personal changes, psychological changes. I would say that I'm more accepting when Maria says, 'Look. I really want to create a melody today.' I think, 'Fine, let's do it.' There's something of value to that. You know, 'Let's rehearse this song.' I see it within what we're doing. It's almost like the boundaries between what is therapy and isn't therapy is…when you say 'outside of therapy', well, that performance was so much a part of the therapy process.

The process of reflecting on what songs to choose and not to choose, and how does it feel to consider one and not the other. All those things are part of the therapy process.

KA: So your notion of what is a legitimate part of music therapy sessions has expanded to include things that previously you might have thought, 'Oh, this is working on music. This isn't therapy.' But now your conception of music therapy includes those things.

AT: I think so. I also think Maria has become her own music therapist. She's got a body of understanding on a very experiential level so that she's leading me much more. I think there's been a process of taking in that intuitive knowledge about what music can do for you. The planning for the performances has a real psychological benefit. We've talked about integrating the changes and reflecting on where you've been and where you want to go and I see that as a very important part of the therapy.

KA: Preparing for the performance doesn't just happen outside the therapy room. It's actually a way of working on the things you came to therapy to do. It seems like your personal process necessitates the public performances because it's the best way of addressing the things that you came to therapy for.

AT: Right.

KA: Is there anything else you want to tell me about?

ML: The reaction of audiences. From the feedback we've gotten over and over again, people are very moved by the journey we've been on. The music resonates deeply with them. People are touched, people are changed. Some people might want to even engage in the process themselves. That has definitely happened in at least one case. People want to talk about it afterwards.

KA: Just like this challenges conventional notions of therapy, it challenges conventional notions of performance. After the typical play you rarely interact with the performer outside the contrivance of the performance.

ML: Right. And the audience has a need to share. As a matter of fact. They want to say something.

KA: It is about creating community between performers and audiences, amongst audience members.

ML: There are many artists out there working on what I would call community type theater. At the Creative Center I was part of a project where a team helped a group of us who were all cancer survivors to put together a theatrical piece that was really community theater. It was not about us as professional performers. I don't ever see myself as a professional performer, but a person who's doing community theater. And as I meet more people doing community theater, I say 'Yes, there is something here.'

On the hottest, most humid night that I can remember in New York City, I approach the ticket table for the theatre at the Westbeth Community Center. I am 45 minutes early to see Maria perform *And You Gave Me Music* in the New York International Fringe Festival at 5.30pm. 'The box office opens at 5.10. We do have a moderately full house but there are tickets,' I am told. I feel relief that there will be people in the audience as much as I feel happiness for Maria. She is in a bona fide performance festival and people are coming to see her. Great!

Not only are there people here but the show sells out in the small community theatre room. But this isn't just Maria sitting on a stool telling her story and singing her songs. It is a dramatization of her life with a cast of four in addition to Maria. A four-piece band rounds out the production, which has professional, if simple, lighting, sound, and set design. Maria's story is alternately narrated and dramatized by the cast, which combines the role of a Greek chorus with that of actors in a play.

A scene comes where she meets her music therapist for the first time: 'There are no mistakes when you improvise,' 'Alan' tells her. Interspersed with narration of her story are a variety of songs, such as *Scared and Paralyzed*, *Rats in the Cellar*, and *Sailing South*. Some are songs of fear and desperation while others manifest more hopeful feelings. A white-masked character voices Maria's internal fears, self-criticisms, and most negative emotions. In speaking to this figure Maria says, 'I have a choice. I can walk out of the dark cellar.'

What is especially striking is the degree to which this show embodies what it expresses. Maria sings about her desire to sing! The show dramatizes how, when given her diagnosis of cancer, Maria's prayers were answered by her muses who told her to sing! And that is just what she is doing. The fact of the show's existence, and Maria's participation in it, is a testament to what the show is about.

Maria sings about her life and her battle with cancer. She sings about how the cancer cells can't hide from her immune system and they 'sneak out the back, Jack'. Her continued survival makes the show possible, indeed is the theme of the show. Each event in Maria's life during the years 1995–2002 and in her evolution into a performing artist is mentioned until we reach the night of 22 August 2003, the very night of this performance. Through attending this show, we have become part of the story that Maria is weaving and that will be shared with future audiences.

At the show's conclusion, Maria says: 'Oh my God. You gave me all this music so that I would not be left alone!' She is then enveloped by the warmth, acceptance, and good wishes of an enthusiastic and appreciative audience. She concludes with these words: 'Music takes us places where words could never go.'

At the outset of the show I wondered about my own role. Should I be like a critic, evaluating the show as work of art. But this was not an example of an artist creating an aesthetic form; it was a human being telling her story. I wondered if just by virtue of telling the story through a theater piece she was asking to be judged as an artist? Come to think of it, is any artist inviting judgement just by the fact of creating something? True artists don't self-consciously create 'art'; they just do what they are compelled to do, just as Maria is. Judgement, evaluation, and criticism are creations of audiences, not artists. And aren't these the very things Maria sang about as being things she has had to overcome in her life, just like the cancer. Perhaps performance as Community Music Therapy can forge a new type of art, one that creates meaning and invites participation rather than creating a commodity that invites judgement.

Conclusion

Working in the community outside of the traditional therapeutic frame offers new possibilities for client development and poses new challenges for music therapists. The possibilities exist in the realm of helping clients achieve musical, artistic, and personal growth not possible when the work is confined to the privacy of a therapy room. The professional challenges are in a myriad of realms and, in closing, I would like to briefly touch on these.

The conceptual challenge exists in creating theoretical frameworks to encompass new musical and social processes that simply do not arise in traditional forms of psychotherapy. Intra-personally based theory will not be adequate to the task of providing explanation and guides to action once a therapist engages with a client in the social world external to the therapy session. The publications of Ansdell (2002), Stige (2002), and the present collection are important steps in this direction.

There are also personal challenges to the therapist. New skills are demanded of clinicians who do this work. Therapists who may not be performers have to find a way not only to be comfortable and capable in front of audiences, but to manage the process and dynamics of a performance so that it functions in a way congruent with clinical goals.

All performance has an element of risk involved. How far should therapists go to ensure a successful experience for clients, especially when the possibility for failure is one of the elements that gives the performance its clinical value? When therapists appear in performances with clients there is the risk that they may do more than is necessary because of their own need to appear musically competent. Turry (1998) deals with these and related questions such as the following: When does the desire to create a musically pleasing product obscure the therapist's clinical goals for a client? What about the situation where the creation of a musically pleasing product *is* the clinical focus? How do therapists separate their own personal musical and aesthetic gratification from what is best for the client?

And this leads to one additional area of concern: the realm of ethics. It is clear that music therapists are developing their practice in new ways, both because the culture is changing and because new ways of interacting with clients are being identified that are helpful to these clients. The present chapter discussed examples of therapists and clients engaging in activities outside of the therapy sessions that involve the public dissemination of material originating in therapy sessions, ranging from public performance of songs written and improvised in therapy sessions, to public discussions of these materials. Because these practices can be beneficial to clients, it is necessary to supplement existing ethical guidelines to accommodate these beneficial practices.

How music therapy is publicly portrayed is one concern here. It is essential that music therapists are clear about when they are engaged in the practice of music therapy and when they are engaged in alternate uses of music. This is needed as a protection for clients so that they know what they can expect when receiving music therapy services, and as a protection for the profession of music therapy. Ethical professional practice requires that therapists engage in those practices for which they are trained and that others not engage in professional music therapy activities for which they may not be qualified.

Ethical guidelines for music therapists often preclude the possibility of dual relationships where conflicts of interest may be present. None of the activities portrayed in the present article are necessarily examples of dual relationships, but they do bring up interesting questions that are important to consider, particularly when activities undertaken for the sake of the client produce incidental benefits for the therapist.

One potential difficulty arises when what is good for the client, such as assisting the music therapist in a musical performance, also facilitates the music therapist's ability to carry out his employment responsibilities. In the first two sections of the present article, clients are participating in performances with their music therapists in a way that could be seen as an extension of the music therapist's professional responsibilities. Similarly, in presenting at conferences with a client, a therapist is receiving assistance from a client in carrying out what can be considered part of the therapist's professional responsibilities.

It is also possible that clinical activities may bring other types of benefits to therapists not particularly related to their employment responsibilities. Consider when a therapist engages in public performance with a client, or records a CD with a client that is offered for public sale, and receives financial remuneration for such activities. Such situations can create the appearance of a conflict of interest, although it may not be significantly different from the general situation in therapy in which the longer a client remains in treatment, the more financial benefit accrues to the therapist.

The point is not that any of these activities should necessarily be avoided. Instead, it is that the sphere of professional music therapy practice is changing in a way that demands new ethical, self-reflexive, and conceptual signposts. It is essential to formulate guidelines in these areas, especially the ethical domain, so that these new forms of practice can continue to develop and flourish and provide the profession of music therapy with an important bridge to the community at large.

References

Ansdell, G. (2002) 'Community Music Therapy and the Winds of Change.' *Voices: A World Forum for Music Therapy 2*, 2, 2002. http://www.voices.no/mainissues

Stige, B. (2002) *Culture-Centered Music Therapy*. Gilsum, NH: Barcelona Publishers.

Turry, A. (1998) 'Transference and Countertransference in Nordoff-Robbins Music Therapy.' In K.E. Bruscia (ed) *The Dynamics Of Music Psychotherapy*. Gilsum, NH: Barcelona Publishers.

CHAPTER 10

Playing Politics: Community Music Therapy and the Therapeutic Redistribution of Musical Capital for Mental Health

Simon Procter

All musicking is ultimately a political act.

Christopher Small

This chapter describes my work within Way Ahead, a non-medical community resource centre for people with experience of mental illness in London. As a music therapist who has also worked in psychiatric hospitals, I am intrigued by the contrasting opportunities that Way Ahead offers music therapy and also by the ways in which I find myself responding to those opportunities. My work here will be viewed by some as at best non-mainstream, at worst subversive. But this sits well with the tradition of user-led services and I will argue that music therapy, wherever it may be, has a duty to reflect its host culture in this way. Music therapy – like all other forms of musicking – is a political act. To deny this is simply to side with the powerful.

Commodification and the decline of 'community' in music and mental health provision

The twentieth century was one of unprecedented change, accelerated by the pace of technological and scientific development. This touched both fields that concern me in my work: the provision of services for people with experience of mental illness, and people's relationship with, and involvement in, music. In both cases, the technological and scientific advances made are indisputable. However, the changes they have wrought in people's lives invite analysis.

A century ago, people who were considered mentally ill ended up in large institutions where they would stay for lengthy periods – often for the rest of their lives. These institutions, whilst restrictive and abusive in many ways, nevertheless became their homes. There was no expectation of a 'cure', so instead the focus was on quality of life, as understood by the Victorians: this often included specific encouragement of music and art within the institutions.

Now the situation is quite different. Most people who find themselves in psychiatric institutions are there for short periods. They are discouraged from thinking of any institution as homelike, and discharged as quickly as possible. The primary purpose of being in hospital is not to participate in communal activity, but to have drug dosages adjusted until they are regarded as 'stable'. The development in recent years of atypical antipsychotic and anxiolytic drugs has offered the prospect of doctors actually being able to do something about people's mental distress. These drugs have significant side-effects which can seriously reduce people's quality of life. But there is another, more systemic, side-effect.

The psychiatric system prescribes drugs developed, produced and marketed by a small group of multinational corporations. Even non-pharmaceutical interventions for mental health (such as music therapy) are now required to demonstrate their ability to produce drug-comparable results in drug-comparable terms. In essence, the notion of health has been changed away from one focusing on how people *are* within a social *context*, in relation to other people, towards one which sees people as discrete bundles of physiological and psychological functions which can be assessed and treated *in isolation*. This seems particularly absurd in mental health, where so much of the pathology is described diagnostically in terms of the difficulties people encounter in relating to others. The consequence is that little room (or money) is left for non-prescribing practice which has to do with the well-being of community, or of individuals within community. Thus the role of community in health and well-being – and the empowerment of the individual – is forced out.

And something similar is observable in people's involvement with music. A century ago music was something that people *did* together. It was a way of *being* together – of forming, reiterating and maintaining social contexts. People sang at church or in the pub, played in works bands or participated in organised dancing. Even people who identified themselves with 'higher culture', unless they were of the tiny metropolitan elite, had to play music, or at least attend occasions when music was performed, if they were to hear it.

But with broadcasting and recording, all this has changed radically. In one sense, we live in an age with unparalleled access to music. We can turn on the radio or television, play CDs or download music from the Internet with almost limitless variety. We can 'acquire' music without active involvement in it. At the same time, active music-making seems to be on the wane. Music is no longer a way of people being together: it is a product we consume. In economic terms:

> the whole technology of consumer supply…as well as the matrix of obligations and supports which constrained consumer ambitions, has changed from interlocking concentric circles to radiating lines. The linear structure of supply is monolithic and vulnerable; the seamless web of consumption, when starved of either its product or the product's image, does not so much fragment as dissolve. Community is gone, only wealth conceals atomisation. (Pawley 1975, pp.26–27)

Or to express this in more musical terms:

> The fruit of over-availability and democratization – what I'd call the wall-to-wall music that's now available – is passivity. The listener is no longer active but enfeebled and passive, and probably does something else while listening to music, and ultimately this makes music into Muzak. (Alexander Goehr, quoted in Oliver 1999, p.208)

Whereas once music took place in the sub-communities which formed our social contexts, and had an important role in constituting and reconstituting those contexts, now it has to a large extent become an aspirational product sold to us, together with lifestyle implications, by multinational corporations. With money we can buy into it. Without money we are cut off from it, cast adrift.

To summarise then, both music and mental health provision have been 'commodified'. The value ascribed to community within these fields has therefore declined. People are no longer situated in supporting networks, but are individualised consumers. Yet as a musician I know the intense experience of healthy interaction that comes with making music with others: as someone who has moved in mental health circles for years, I know the irreplaceability of supportive social networks and the value of experiencing oneself in healthy mutually beneficial relationships with others.

Community: A word back in vogue

But amidst the commodification, the word 'community' is back in vogue. The political climate in Britain in the 1980s was perhaps defined by Margaret Thatcher's assertion that 'there is no such thing as society'. The election of 'New Labour' in 1997 ushered in a new discourse of politicised social-mindedness, with the word 'community' much used in many areas of policy, including those of the arts and mental health. Both fields have discovered that the word 'community' is used by many figures in public life to add a tinge of moral authority and popular legitimacy to their ideas (Pawley 1975, p.16). 'Community' can be the sheep's clothing around lupine policies.

For anyone who has been around the UK mental health scene during the last two decades, the word 'community' is likely to engender mixed reactions. This may seem strange: after all, for most 'ill' people, community is the opposite of hospital – it is where you go when you are sufficiently recovered that you no longer need inpatient treatment. It has to do with normality, with going home to where you belong, with things being on the up. It is uncomplicatedly 'a good thing'. But in UK mental health care, 'community' has been associated with some retrograde steps as well as with some forward thinking.

Government policy in the 1980s proclaimed the benefits of 'care in the community', and this seemed attractive to many at first. People were no longer to be incarcerated in long-term hospital 'care' unless there was a demonstrable need for them to be so: many hoped that this might herald a new era of respect for people's rights and freedoms. Instead, the reality proved to be characterised much more by loss of services and lack of support. People who until then had been part of a ready-made social setting which, to some extent at least, understood their needs and attempted to cater to them, found themselves turned out of what they considered to be their homes – their communities, in fact – and displaced into isolated, poorly resourced mini-institutions 'in the community'. 'Community', previously an almost utopian ideal of belonging and identity, had become transformed into a geographical location experienced as hostile, unsupportive and uninformed.

'Community' remains an ambivalent word in mental health circles. A forthcoming Mental Health Act (soon to be ratified by the UK parliament) introduces 'community treatment orders'. Essentially this is an extension of the powers of mental health professionals to administer treatment against the will of the patient so that it can take place not only in hospitals, as has previously been the case, but elsewhere, including in the patient's home. This has been opposed even by the Royal College of Psychiatrists, and yet the Government seems set to press ahead with its introduction, primarily in the name of 'protecting the public' (presumably from the assumed-to-be-potentially-violent mentally ill).

A new kind of provision for mental health

Nevertheless, the move towards community care for people with experience of severe and enduring mental illness has produced a number of identifiable benefits. Local authorities, charged with providing some kind of provision for people who were moved out of long-stay institutions, turned in many cases to the non-statutory sector. Significant within this sector were organisations which promoted the viewpoint of service users, and in some cases were actively run by service users. For the first time funded services were significantly influenced by people with direct experience of using them. Now it was possible to have non-psychiatric mental health provision which attempted to put users at its centre, not at the bottom of a medicalised hierarchy. This is not to say that all such services were professional-free or medical-free: certainly some aimed for this, but others sought to deploy the specialist skills of professionals in ways that users identified as beneficial. It is in this latter category that I would place the work I am about to describe.

Way Ahead

Housed in a former industrial building in inner London, Way Ahead describes itself as a non-medical community resource centre for people with experience of mental health problems. It is not part of statutory services, but is funded by yearly grants from the local health authority, social services, and some charities. It is run by a management committee which comprises service users as well as local people and representatives from funding agencies. No doctors or nurses work here. There is almost nothing in the way of paperwork. No banks of files on people who use its services.

Way Ahead's environment is not an easy one. Tower blocks loom over dreary housing estates; levels of unemployment, crime and incidence of mental illness are amongst the highest in the UK. One of the most ethnically diverse areas of the UK, with many recent arrivals from war-torn parts of the world, racism is an everyday part of life. Although many people are socially and culturally isolated in their flats, this centre draws them in. It is designed to enable people to experience their capacity for well-being rather than their propensity for medical illness, to challenge isolation through social contact. It's a place where people can value themselves as individuals, but also their culture and their sense of community, achieved in many cases against the odds. It is a place where, for me, music therapy seems to fit.

And yet it remains an unusual place to find music therapy. Here it coexists with forms of provision which are not always considered natural allies. There are classes in woodwork and English for speakers of other languages, courses in basic skills and café working, and welfare and benefits advice. There is counselling and an art group. There is a drop-in most days and at lunchtime everyone comes together to eat in the café, be they user, worker or visitor.

Places like this are often suspicious of 'therapies'. Therapists are seen as aloof people who do not roll their sleeves up, but instead import their own agendas, their own ideas of what is good and bad. They are middle class and fail to see the world from any other angle.

And therapists too are often suspicious of places like this. Where are all the 'normal' features of working in mental health? The rigorously observed boundaries between client and staff, the accumulated information gathered on clients' lives by staff, the authority of the consultant psychiatrist which each member of staff represents to the client? These things not only do not exist here, they are intentionally avoided. Yet in hospital settings these are seen as promoting safety, for clients as well as for staff. Some might also claim that these boundaries offer a containing environment which is a prerequisite for effective therapy.

So is Way Ahead unsafe? Does its ethos preclude effective therapeutic intervention? My answer to these questions is of course no. But this is a very different kind of place from others where music therapy is traditionally offered, and it has required of me a very different attitude to working. This could be seen in two ways – as an affront to the therapeutic norms imparted to me in my training, or as an opportunity to challenge and grow beyond constraints which might limit the usefulness and effectiveness of my practice.

Way Ahead has something very specific to teach me as a music therapist. Its description of itself as a community resource centre has two implications, one of place and the other of ethos. The place is 'community' in that it is not medical, even though it is concerned with people's mental health. But the ethos is also community in that it is not concerned simply with processing individuals through a system, but actively promotes a model of well-being which recognises the value of the communal and the contributions of each individual within the communal.

My role too, is different. A music therapist in a psychiatric hospital is an authority figure, whether he or she means to be or not. In interacting with patients, they carry something of the authority of the psychiatrist-led system. At Way Ahead, I do not carry this authority. I am someone with particular skills and training who is employed to deploy these in whatever way is most appropriate for the particular people I am working with. I lose some authority and status, but gain freedom and opportunity.

I will now give three examples of this kind of opportunity in my work at Way Ahead.

Lunch break

It is the middle of a hot summer's day. As I leave the greenhouse-like music therapy room and make my way outside, I can hear music. Somebody somewhere is playing the guitar. Hungry, I walk towards the café but before I get there a voice calls me over to a table just outside the café door. 'Simon, mate! What do you think?' The voice belongs to a man I remember from more than a year ago, when he attended a group I ran. He came just out of curiosity at first but became a regular member and as the end approached he talked about wanting to learn to play an instrument. I suggested going to the local college and getting stuck into some lessons.

He tells me that he's been going to guitar lessons at the college and putting in many hours of practice. I am impressed, not only by his tenacity, but also by his tangible musicality. I encourage him to play some more. He's struggling slightly with keeping a melody going at the same time as the chordal accompaniment so I run back to the music therapy room to get my fiddle. As I rush, a slight wave of worry washes over me. What would my professional association say about this? Am I doing this for my own pleasure or can I really get away with calling it music therapy?

When I return, I tune my fiddle to his guitar and we tentatively attempt our first duet. He's working hard to play what he has learned, so I let him lead while I improvise around what he's doing. It's a bit stilted at first, but by the second tune we're getting somewhere. It feels more fluid, more flexible, more enjoyable. And it's not just us enjoying it either. A small group is gathering by the café door to watch and the radio has been switched off inside the café so that we are now providing the background music for lunch in the café. Again I momentarily remember two of the 'norms' of music therapy – privacy from outside ears and eyes, and boundaries of role. And here I am playing publicly with someone who the last time we met was my patient in hospital. What am I doing?

The two of us are playing, but everyone around is being drawn into this musical happening. Some want to come and watch, others stay where they are and carry on their normal activities to it. But it is bringing all of us together. At the end of each tune there is a ripple of applause. This isn't just politeness: it's a real taking pleasure in what is going on amongst us and between us. It is a quiet celebration of music, of ourselves within community. And for my ex-client it is a powerful affirmation of his journey from 'patient' to fellow musician, from provided for to providing.

And I realise that in this there is tremendous value. It was this affirmatory power of music-making between people and amongst people that made music therapy seem sensible to me before I trained. And the people around me, my fellow community members, can feel this too. They, like me and my guitarist, are a part of it. Of the music, of our community. Community nurtures us: as musicking people, we also nurture community.

Excursion

Ten of us are off to an art gallery. We compare notes and find that for most of us a school trip to the National Gallery is the extent of our experience, although one or two have been to the local gallery. We're going out of east London today though – to north London, home of posh art galleries (and posh therapy). A small gallery there is holding an exhibition of sculptures which are also musical instruments. I mentioned it to people over lunch at Way Ahead a few weeks ago, someone designed a poster and quite a few people were interested. It's primarily people who do music therapy (either individually or in the group) and members of the art therapy group.

Everybody arrives at the underground station on time. We can do the journey with one change of train, or possibly faster with two changes. The group opts for the double change. We manage the changes fine. The faster ones wait for the slower ones and we all emerge at our destination together. With the aid of a map I have brought, we straggle across roundabouts and block the pavement for everyone else – but we're enjoying ourselves.

Once inside the gallery, we are impressed. This is real north London chic: shiny floors and everything really clean and sparkly! We are also impressed to see how much money we're not having to pay to get in (I have somehow arranged a free visit – I had no idea it would have cost THAT much to get in).

We are guided into the exhibition room. It's a lovely airy, cool space – again so different from what we are used to. The sculptures are beautifully presented and beautifully lit. We are drawn in amongst them. We want to touch, but at first even the most disinhibited amongst us isn't sure whether we should. The attendant raises no objections, however, and soon we are passing around sticks and beaters. People begin to explore the instruments – visually, tactilely and aurally. Some people do it quietly, alone, far from others. Others do it in collaboration, even in competition, with others. A couple of people wander around, watching others and trying different instruments as they go. I wander too, learning about the instruments, encouraging some people and mildly restraining others. As the collective confidence rises, so does the resulting cacophony. I am struck by the similarity between this and an orchestral rehearsal. The musicians have assembled in an unknown venue, and are just tuning up.

Like the orchestra, there comes a point where the tuning ends and the work begins. It falls to me as conductor to indicate this, to draw people to order. I call out above the noise and the instruments gradually fall silent. All eyes are on me and there is a real sense of expectation – of impending performance. This is different from what we get week in and week out – but why? It must be the place: its specialness, the sense of something being created. Even the lighting is focusing us on our task as musicians.

I invite people to play for us, one by one. The rest of us listen, gradually learning the palette of sounds we have at our disposal. Then we improvise together, a few of us at first but gradually more and more of us. We are creating – really creating as if from nothing, from unfamiliar lumps of metal – extraordinary sounds. They twist and weave, interrupt, accompany and provoke. But most of all we are really listening to each other. Nobody is going through the motions here – the atmosphere is truly electric.

After 40 gripping minutes of this, the music brings itself to a close. There is a long silence at the end. Then people laugh, shout, sit. There is a feeling of real achievement and tiredness. We declare a tea break and head for the courtyard we can see through the window.

Revived, we gather once more amongst the instruments. Remembering my comparison with the orchestra, I invite people to take turns to direct the rest of us. It's a chance to create on a much larger scale, but also an opportunity to be in charge, to wield real power. And everyone has a go. Some people are restrained, some conduct in an almost classical manner, and some are quite unconventional but entirely communicative as to what they want. But one person's directing strikes me most forcefully. He is a Somali man in his 50s, small and quiet, due in part no doubt to his lack of English. Mostly he shuffles around slowly with his head down. He seems institutionalised, ordered around by others. But with a stick in his hand, he is transformed. He becomes a man who knows what he wants and can communicate it. His directing is imperious: he makes us wait. His piece is full of strong silence, all eyes trained on him for cues. At the end he grins in a way I have never seen before. We are astounded.

At the end, somebody pulls out a camera and we gather round to have group photographs taken. They will be souvenirs, pinned up in the Way Ahead café, not just of a good day out, but of a remarkable excursion into another world, one where we have created anew, and listened afresh.

Is this music therapy? I believe that it is. We were a group brought together by involvement in mental health services in a particular area. We travelled together out of our normal environment – geographically of course and socially too, but also certainly beyond the boundaries of the consensus model. And in doing so we deepened our own experience of ourselves as individuals, of our peers as our fellow community members, and of our community in relation to others. Some might dismiss this as the kind of jaunt more appropriately run by a nursing or occupational therapy assistant. I disagree: I needed all my musical skills combined with my understanding of people and mental health. This was a radical, political and musical act. An act of Community Music Therapy.

Back in the room

Josie arrives at music therapy at the suggestion of the computer class facilitator. She seems ill at ease and unwilling to play, so we talk about music instead: the solos she sang in church as a child, the pieces she learned in piano lessons and the music she enjoyed with friends as a teenager before her breakdown at college. I remark that her musical biography seems to stop with that breakdown. 'Yes,' she replies, 'there hasn't been much music lately.'

Over the next few weeks we start playing together. At first she is dismissive of her own playing, as if whatever she does can have no value. And if I suggest otherwise, she is dismissive of me too, using the kind of formal, critical language used in music journalism to rubbish performances or recordings. It is as though the whole world of music, once a gateway to social interaction, has become her isolating oppression. For a while, deterred by her reluctance to play and her continual trashing of our music, I am tempted to try to engage with her verbally rather than musically and find that I am spending almost half the session talking rather than playing. But perhaps I am being drawn into her belief that music can only be a bad thing when what she needs is the experience of successful music-making with me, not my collusion in avoiding it. So I suggest to Josie that for the next ten sessions we just play, without necessarily talking about it. Then we can review our work to date. Seeming a little reluctant, she agrees.

Our music-making begins to develop. Our improvisations get longer. Josie's playing seems to become less dependent on mine for its content and structure. After ten sessions, I ask Josie how she feels things are going. She says she enjoys coming 'in a weird sort of way', even though she considers herself a far from ideal candidate for music therapy.

We agree to continue. In all we work together in one-to-one sessions for nearly two years. As I listen back each week to the recordings of our sessions, I note the development of her spontaneity, her expressiveness, her sheer revelling in music-making. One day, after a lively and protracted improvisation in which both of us move freely between many instruments and she also sings, she spontaneously exclaims, 'Wow, that was amazing!' This feels like a real change: Josie is beginning to be able to take pleasure in our music-making. This pleasure encourages greater freedom, which in turn leads to greater pleasure. The role of music in Josie's life, formerly a force for failure, seems to be changing and allowing her to be more fully herself. She is taking pleasure in being herself, and in being herself with me. Towards the end of our work, we talk about what she will do afterwards. I suggest joining a choir, but she is cautious about such an organised way of making music. Then a few weeks later she arrives at the session, clearly very pleased with herself, and tells me that she has joined a theatre group where she will be able to sing and dance as well as try out acting for the first time. A year later, she invites me to watch her in performance. 'I enjoy myself with other people,' she said. 'I'm not ashamed of myself any more.'

On the surface, this vignette may seem to resemble 'consensus' model music therapy. Certainly this work was done in private over a lengthy time span. But I would argue that it lies on Ansdell's continuum of Community Music Therapy. Although we worked one-to-one, the process was one of Josie rediscovering a new, more healthy relationship with music (i.e. her musicianship) which ultimately enabled her to share this with others as she chose. Music therapy brought musicking back into Josie's life and permitted her to 'perform' herself more fully, freeing her from some of the limitations that her experiences of mental illness and music had imposed upon her.

Community Music Therapy – a haven from the consensus model?

Just as Way Ahead is for many of its members a haven from psychiatric orthodoxy, so for me it might also be described as a haven from music therapy orthodoxy, described by Ansdell (2002) as the consensus model.

Before playing in public with the guitarist, I worried about what my colleagues might say about this abandonment of the convention of privacy. Before taking the group to the art gallery, I wondered about the required shift in my role. And many colleagues would have criticised me for playing rather than talking with Josie, accusing me of failing to support her in verbal thinking about the causes of her isolation. Yet in all three cases I believe that what I did was appropriate for those people in that setting. The consensus model was inappropriate because it neglected not only the particular community within which I was working, not only the situations of the individuals within that community, but even the whole idea of music. In all three cases, it was my knowledge of the power of the experience of music-making which led me to depart from the consensus model, and my musical skill, experience and understanding which enabled me to do so effectively.

I have contended elsewhere (Procter 2002) that music therapy's almost total absence from non-medical mental health services is due partly to its own reluctance to abandon old ways of thinking which enable it to enjoy the power associated with psychiatry, and partly to reluctance on the part of user-led services to deal with what they (reasonably) fear comes as the baggage of 'therapy'. Often, non-therapist musicians are employed in such settings because they seem more willing to offer the sort of service that is valued by users than music therapists who seem to insist instead on 'doing therapy' the way they have been taught.

But music therapy has not always been this way. Music therapists working in the 1950s and 1960s were not averse to considering their work to be very practical, communally focused work, even when working within psychiatric institutions. Since the 1970s, however, there has been a gradual restricting of what is and is not considered to be 'music therapy', particularly in the UK. This has coincided with a period of professionalisation, and it is understandable that at such a time music therapy has been trying to convince the world of its professional status by claiming rigorous and clearly defined ways of working. These are generally couched in language borrowed from psychotherapy (apparently regarded as 'one step up' in terms of professional prestige) and concern themselves largely with what music therapy is not. This portrayal is propagated initially via training courses and subsequently via professional regulation.

The response of music therapists unhappy with this state of affairs has tended to be 'anti-establishment'. We rebel against imposed 'norms' of working, all the more so if these are presented as ethical rather than ideological issues. We are disturbed by attempts to link professional advancement with adherence to limiting ideology. We feel that we need to push at the boundaries of our profession and do whatever seems to be most appropriate for the people we do it with, even if this provokes criticism from our peers. These theoretical and practical concerns are conveyed in Ansdell's formulation of 'Community Music Therapy' with its continuum of practice, which promises to liberate music therapists from the notion that there is a single right way to work, a universally applicable set of norms. Not only will the norms be determined by the community in which we work, but they will move to and fro along the continuum.

A new kind of thinking for music therapy: 'Health musicking'

Community Music Therapy, like non-psychiatric mental health provision, needs to go further than simply pushing the boundaries of conventional practice. Instead, we need to provoke and develop new thinking about how music in general and music therapy in particular promote relational health and well-being in community – the broader area of what Stige (2002) calls 'health musicking'.

And the time is ripe: in recent years there has been an explosion of fascination in related fields with exactly the kinds of things we find ourselves doing. It is ironic that it is left to new musicologists and sociologists of music to examine the fluid, dynamic and social possibilities of music therapy. Music therapists seem extraordinarily unwilling to engage with this thinking (Ansdell 2001), and yet it is only through such engagement, by offering others our experience as well as learning from their insights, that music therapy can hope to develop indigenous thinking which enables us not to wrap ourselves defensively in theory, but rather to illuminate the social and musical (and hence personal and therapeutic) meanings of the interactions we share with our clients. I would advocate exchange with all those whose work impinges on ours. Rejection of the consensus model as inappropriate need not preclude any particular ways of reflecting on the work we do.

Community Music Therapy as a cultural enterprise

A powerful way of thinking about our work is as a cultural enterprise. Like 'community', 'culture' is a difficult term because of its plethora of meanings and implications. In using it here, I mean that music therapy must be immersed in the culture of the community whose health it works for. This will impact deeply on its understanding of what it is there for and hence on its sense of values. The 'consensus' model seems to have at its heart a non-negotiable set of values, to be a one-size-fits-all culture in its own right. Much of what I have described of my work at Way Ahead offends against those values: I choose to work this way because I feel that the values of the consensus model conflict with those of Way Ahead. But more than this, I suspect that the whole notion of a consensus model is anti-cultural. It seems bizarre to try to lay down universal rules about how people should make music together, be it in hospital, on the street or in a rehearsal space. It seems to fit more in hospital than elsewhere because it puts authority in the hands of therapists that music itself does not, thus making them feel on a par with medical professionals. Outside such a setting it seems simply to be a means of steamrollering the indigenous culture.

As I outlined at the outset of this chapter, most people's experience of both psychiatry and music is dominated by 'top down' culture – in psychiatry, by the controlling influence of the multinational drug companies as well as by the Government-imposed focus on coercion alongside treatment, and in music by the multinational media corporations who control both supply and demand of popular culture, and in so doing wield an extraordinary influence over people's perceptions of themselves and their roles in society. The music therapy I have described in this chapter is an attempt to evade the 'top down' in both fields. Music-making can be not only a healthy human activity, particularly for people whose sense of themselves and their value is threatened by illness, but also a very powerful way of being themselves, of being heard and listened to and responded to – by me and others – as themselves. It is a way of enabling people to hear themselves as they perform themselves (Aldridge 1996), not a way of fitting them into an agenda promoted by outside interests, be they commercial, governmental or professional. And thus ours is not only a cultural enterprise, but a political one.

In the early days, music therapists were enterprising and spiritual musicians from outside any system who burned with conviction about the role of music-making in mental health. Something of this conviction seems to have been lost in the recent drive towards professionalisation and paramedicalisation. What are we trying to do? How are we trying to achieve it? What is music anyway?

The radical answer to these questions is – there cannot be any standard answer. To try to standardise what we are doing or how we are doing it is anathema to the principle of political engagement. And indeed the trend toward standardisation – nationally and now even internationally within the European Union – has the potential to neutralise our work still further by fixing it within medical and administrative frameworks of authority. The only possible answer to these questions is 'It depends'. It depends where we are music therapists, who we are music therapists amongst, why we are there at all. There need be no consensus on how we do what we do. But in order to realise the potential of music-making between and amongst people, we must be explicit about our political engagement.

Music therapy is a polyglot tradition, not simply an offshoot of psychoanalysis, psychology, musicology or community music. It operates in territories and deploys discourses which may impinge on all or none of these. It has enormous potential for challenging the status quo. It exists in many forms in many different places according to local tradition and history. To deny this in our thinking is to limit our usefulness.

Musical capital

Putnam (2001) has charted the decline in participation in American society. People do things together less and less: instead they observe others and become sidelined in society. Similar trends are observable in the UK. Drawing on a long heritage of sociological thinking, Putnam uses the concept of 'social capital' to describe what is missing, and emphasises that this can be to both public and private good.

Putnam's book is littered with references to the decline in musical participation in America over recent decades. He gives some very specific examples of how active musical participation can be shown to promote people's engagement in their communities, raising their expectations of each other and increasing the likelihood of collective action for change and improvement.

Putnam calls for arts and cultural activities to be promoted in order to build social capital. He stresses that the emphasis has to be on participation, not simply consumption or 'appreciation':

> Art manifestly matters for its own sake... Aesthetic objectives, not merely social ones, are obviously important. That said, art is especially useful in transcending conventional social barriers. Moreover, social capital is often a valuable by-product of cultural activities whose main purpose is purely artistic. (Putnam 2001, p.411)

This connection between musical participation and social capital is reminiscent of Even Ruud's requirement that music therapy should increase 'possibilities of action', a definition of music therapy unique in coming from a socio-cultural perspective (1998, p.5).

Social capital is accrued through musical participation. Perhaps then we could even talk of musical capital: inherently social in that it is of and between people and increases the chances of positive change within society, but also inherently musical in that it carries opportunities for aesthetic self-realisation and self-experience. It can be both public and private, communal and personal. It is about self-identity but also about being heard by others. It is above all about living performance, about grasping opportunities that promote well-being, as an individual but also as a member of communities. The role of the music therapist, then, must include offering people opportunities to steer a healthy musical course, to renew and develop their health-promoting relationship with music within communities.

In Community Music Therapy, aesthetic objectives *are* social objectives. Playing together increases possibilities for action. No translation or interpretation is required. But this can only be so where the therapist has skills, experiences, perceptions and understandings which permit it.

Out of community, into community

Music therapists arrive at trainings with their culture, history and experiences from their own communities. They need to hone musical skills, to build musical experiences, perceptions and attributes, and to have their assumptions confronted with alternatives, their minds opened to new possibilities. But then they need to return to their own communities with enough of their own values intact for them to be an integral part of the community.

So the ideal is for therapists to be of their community, to put their musical skills at the disposal of their community. This seems to conflict with a model of working dominated by constructs which may conflict with the values of the community. This leads to two conclusions: first, that therapists should be 'of their community', and second, that music therapy as a discipline should not demand that therapists override community values with 'therapeutic values'. Training courses should be encouraging students to find ways of developing their musical skills at the same time as exploring culturally appropriate ways of deploying these to the benefit of their communities.

In practice, this leads me to make some perhaps provocative suggestions. Why not recruit future music therapists less from the ranks of university music graduates and more from the fields and communities where they can later apply what they learn? Why are there so few music therapists with experience of mental illness? At present, UK courses employ psychotherapists to 'weed out' at interview people with suspected mental health problems. But these are exactly the people who know the mental health communities best, who are best placed to deploy their musical skills within them, and potentially most understanding of the needs of the people they will work with. Of course, all trainees need support and it is necessary to be realistic about people's ability to cope. But this does not account for what seems like a refusal to deal with people who are 'tainted' by being part of a scene, whereas therapists are supposed somehow to be above membership of any potential client community. And what about workers in the mental health sector? Musically skilled psychiatric nurses or occupational therapists often integrate music-making into their work in a natural way. They are well placed not only to learn specific music therapy skills but to apply them too. It is hard for such people to give up jobs to train when there is little prospect of finding equivalent work when they finish. Perhaps our response, then, should be to offer them training in relevant skills as they continue to work in the very places where those skills are most needed – their communities.

Our vision of the future should not be one of professional music therapists everywhere imposing therapeutic values. It should instead focus on the dissemination of high-level skills in the use of music for the benefit of people in the contexts of their communities. People should be able to access music therapy skills, whether from a music therapist or a nurse. It is the political work of music therapists to ensure that communities have such resources available to them, for the benefit of all.

It is time to stop trying to define music therapy prescriptively: it is simply musicking in pursuit of well-being, wherever, whenever and however it happens. It is absolutely musical, utterly social and inescapably political.

Acknowledgement

I would like to thank the governors and fundraisers of the Nordoff-Robbins Music Therapy Centre, London, whose commitment and farsightedness have made this work possible.

References

Aldridge, D. (1996) *Music Therapy Research and Practice in Medicine.* London: Jessica Kingsley Publishers.

Ansdell, G. (2001) 'Musicology: Misunderstood Guest at the Music Therapy Feast?' In D. Aldridge, G. Di Franco, E. Ruud and T. Wigram (eds) *Music Therapy in Europe.* Rome: ISMEZ/Onlus.

Ansdell, G. (2002) 'Community Music Therapy and the Winds of Change.' In C. Kenny and B. Stige (eds) *Contemporary Voices in Music Therapy: Communication, Culture and Community.* Oslo: Unipub.

Oliver, P. (ed) (1999) *Settling the Score: A Journey Through the Music of the Twentieth Century.* London: Faber and Faber.

Pawley, M. (1975) *The Private Future.* London: Pan.

Procter, S. (2002) 'Empowering and Enabling – Music Therapy in Non-medical Mental Health Provision.' In C. Kenny and B. Stige (eds) *Contemporary Voices in Music Therapy: Communication, Culture and Community.* Oslo: Unipub.

Putnam, R.D. (2001) *Bowling Alone.* New York: Simon and Schuster.

Ruud, E. (1998) *Music Therapy: Improvisation, Communication and Culture.* Gilsum, NH: Barcelona Publishers.

Small, C. (1998) *Musicking.* Hanover, NH: Wesleyan University Press.

Stige, B. (2002) *Culture-centred Music Therapy.* Gilsum, NH: Barcelona Publishers.

PART V

What has Culture got to do with it?

CHAPTER 11

Promoting Integration and Socio-cultural Change: Community Music Therapy with Traumatised Refugees in Berlin

Oksana Zharinova-Sanderson

A big church in former West Berlin. In the middle of its vast space, under the dome, a circle of 70–80 people are chanting a simple melody together, clapping and stamping and using the rhythm to send musical questions and answers to each other. On one side are the men, their voices strong and loud, united in the feeling of their masculine solidarity, on the other – the women – their voices softer and less confident, but beautiful in their feminine tones. I am standing in the middle of this circle, feeling over-whelmed by the energy in their music whilst trying to conduct and help the people to sustain and develop what they are doing. The people around me are traumatised refugees from all over the world, who have come to this Berlin church to a patients' party organised by the centre where they receive treatment, and where I work as a music therapist. Most of them speak limited German and do not understand each other's languages. Before we formed the circle they had looked like a dispersed gathering of unconnected individuals, each person sitting with his or her family, not talking to the people from the other ethnic groups, each in their own little space. But in this circle they become part of the energy, united into a community. I can see the recognition of this energy in their eyes. As the music stops, I observe their faces still lit up, waiting for the music to start again...

Introduction

With the political and cultural changes in modern Europe, one can observe fascinating processes of evolution in its communities, which confront its inhabitants with new challenges. One of these is that European society is no longer monocultural and thus has to find ways of accepting and integrating every new inhabitant, with their widely diverse customs, values, systems of beliefs (Taviani 1988; Thränhardt 1999). As a result, European music therapists are increasingly confronted with clients from different cultural backgrounds, an experience that often requires them to question their theory and practice (Wintour 2002; Horvat 2002). Whether struggling to meet new musical and cultural worlds, or having to deal with the very different expectations of the patients, we are coming to realise that music therapy in the context of the evolving community of Europe is itself developing and changing.

For over three years I have been working at the Treatment Centre for Torture Victims in Berlin, establishing a music therapy service there in a project organised by the University of Witten-Herdecke and sponsored by the German Nordoff-Robbins Charity. The work with this clientele has strengthened my belief in music as a valid therapeutic medium across cultures. It has also fostered a growing process in my thinking about what music therapy can mean for the community and has given me a forum for setting these ideas into practice. I heard the term 'Community Music Therapy' (Ansdell 2002) some time after I started this work in Berlin, but I immediately felt that it reflected well the processes that were occurring in my work and that I was trying to understand.

Contexts

In the music therapy literature there is an increasing awareness of the influences of the cultures and contexts surrounding our practice on the way we work and think about it (Aldridge 1996; Ruud 1998; Pavlicevic 2002; Kenny and Stige 2002). This does not only imply the various ethnic, social and cultural contexts of the patients but also all the contexts in which the work takes place – the therapist's background, the ethics of the institution in which the therapist is practising (Procter 2002), as well the wider context of the village/town/city/country where the client, the therapist and the wider community live (Pavlicevic 2002). I believe that if we are to see music therapy as a 'contemporary force for change' (Hartley 2002), then we have to make efforts to understand the societies in which we are practising. Such understanding will help us to identify the areas where we as music therapists can be instigators of such 'change'. Therefore, let us first look at the various contexts that I found important in trying to conceptualise my work.

Geographical context – Berlin and Berliners

Today, Berlin is at the heart of the German integration process, struggling to bring the people and the ideologies of the former West and East Germany together. Being a foreigner in Berlin myself, I have observed the effect that this city can have on newcomers. It often seems to be a rough city, with sharp edges and contrasts that are sometimes difficult to grasp. It can be unwelcoming for foreigners, especially in the former East Berlin, where traditional attitudes towards foreigners are exacerbated by the fact that they are seen as yet another problem in the already difficult social and economic situation in this part of the city. It is particularly difficult for refugees to integrate because of the lack of cohesion in the city's social structure and the heavy bureaucracy of the social and legal system. However, the refugees' role in this city's future can be seen as vital: they are the symbols of the new society's attitude to foreign ideas and its capacity to integrate these ideas in building the new German capital (Barenboim 2001).

Institutional context and the context of trauma

Behandlungszentrum fuer Folteropfer (The Centre for the Treatment of Torture Victims) in Berlin is one of the most well-known organisations in Germany in this field. It is also one of the few such institutions where a full-time music therapist is engaged. Music therapy was introduced to provide a non-verbal therapy to complement the verbal therapies that rely on the help of an interpreter and to provide the patients with a direct unfiltered way of communication.

At the start of my work it was felt that the idea of music therapy was quite foreign to the well-established culture of this institution. Many of my colleagues in the therapy team felt that what music therapy was offering missed the main issue of the work – the trauma itself. Thus I had to discover and establish the place of music therapy in the treatment model of the institution and to share with my colleagues what benefit music therapy could have for these patients. My explorations were informed by the argument in the literature about trauma that suggested that trauma work alone is not sufficient in rehabilitating traumatised people. Grenadier (1995), van Dijk (2001), Pavlicevic (2002) write about the danger in this work of being solely preoccupied with trauma (however necessary such work can be). Pavlicevic suggests that looking at the whole person, 'managing and evoking the difficult, frightening, playful and creative feelings and tapping into the (client's) own potential for healing' (2002, p.112) is an effective way of working with this clientele. As my work progressed I witnessed a clear movement of the therapeutic model of the institution towards integrating new creative aspects of work with these patients into the necessary work on the past traumatic experiences.

The medical model of work, as well as the initially strong emphasis on trauma in the treatment approach of the institution, was exacerbated by the fact that the therapists were caught up in an endless process of attesting to the patients' traumatic experience. Diagnosing post-traumatic stress disorder (PTSD) and trying to fight for the traumatised patient's rights to receive asylum and social help in Germany dominated the reality of every therapist's work (Graessner and Pross 2002). That was one of the reasons why music therapy, not being able to play much of a role in this process, initially did not fit into the culture of the institution and had to create a new space for itself.

The patients

The patients[1] who come to music therapy range greatly in age, culture, nationality, education and degree of traumatisation. All of them are either survivors of torture and/or political persecution or traumatic events during wars. I came across people from a huge variety of backgrounds – from a Kurdish political activist to an African woman who lost her husband and children, from a bank manager from Chechnya to a Kosovo orphan. It may seem surprising that torture and traumatic experiences are generally not their biggest concern. Instead, their insecure residential status and unhappy life in exile without money, freedom of movement and employment, and fear of East German neo-Nazis – these are the most burning issues that are shared by every patient. Because of their refugee status there is very little help available for them in the German health and social services, so they flood into our privately run centre for all the help that they can get. Underneath these issues from their present daily life in Berlin lies the suffering caused by the symptoms of PTSD, such as acute insomnia, nightmares, extreme psychosomatic pains, phobias and communication problems (van der Kolk 1996; Hermann 1992).

---

1   I decided to use the word 'patients' as well as 'clients' in this article because the former is used in the institutional context in which I work. The BZFO was founded by and is still led by medical doctors and the institutional use of the word 'patients' highlights the medical ethos of their model of thinking. Talking about my music therapy work using such a 'medical model' term creates a certain tension with my own model of thinking. However, I pragmatically chose to use it as it reflects the reality of working in such an institution.

Case study – Herr A

The case I present here is one of many learning experiences that highlighted the significance of the ideas of integration and community in my music therapy practice. I aim to focus on:

- the evolution of the framework of the therapy and its effects for the patient, for the institution and for the wider community

- the effects of music therapy on the lack of trust and sense of isolation resulting from experiences of trauma and forced migration

- the integrating effects of the music therapy processes on the person in the community

- the variety of roles that I as a therapist had to adopt as the therapy developed.

First impressions

Herr A, a Kurdish man from Turkey, was imprisoned many times, beaten and tortured. After years of living in hiding, he escaped to Germany, whilst his wife and children decided to remain in Turkey. He lived alone in a refugee hostel outside Berlin, being generally very depressed, drinking and spending most of the time alone in his room. Herr A was referred to me by one of the centre's social workers. She said that he was always unhappy, complaining about his life situation and could not see anything positive in what she was trying to do for him. He often did not listen to her and sometimes got very angry blaming all his helpers for not doing enough. He mentioned to her that his rescue from his 'bad thoughts' was often his music, and that he played the Kurdish instrument, the saz.

In the initial music therapy sessions he played his instrument and sang whilst never looking at me and relating very little to any of my efforts to join his music. Then, for a long period he did not come again. From the social worker I found out that the reason for his absence was that he was too embarrassed at being alone with a young woman. He said that the only woman he had ever been alone with was his wife. Looking at a woman directly he felt was too close and disrespectful to her. The social worker suggested that I ask his interpreter, whom the patient trusted, to join us, in order to help him to overcome the feeling of awkwardness with me. I had never worked with interpreters before, believing in the power of direct communication through music, but I agreed, as it was my only chance to continue working with this patient.

The presence of an interpreter put me in the position of an outsider in their verbally based relationship of trust and masculine solidarity as Kurdish men. The patient still did not look at me and I often had a feeling he did not notice I was there at all. When we were playing drums together, the patient would take and pass the rhythmic patterns to the interpreter, but would avoid giving direct drumming answers to me. When he played songs from his culture, the interpreter would drum with him in the Kurdish style and whatever I played and sang did not seem to become a part of their music. At this point I made the conscious decision of working with what I was offered, without imposing any expectations of what music therapy should be like, and allowing the process that was already taking place to develop. So I let them play together and sometimes just listened. I believed that eventually, if I listened accurately enough, I would find a way in and a role for me in their music and a chance to connect with the patient.

Two plus one and the emergence of the trio

The first real feeling of the patient's acceptance of my presence came a few sessions later. He wanted to try out a new instrument and since it was nothing to do with familiar Kurdish music, the interpreter stayed silent. It was the first time I connected with the patient so directly. He played marimba standing with his back to me. It felt as if in this music we were being close without needing to face each other. Then we played a Kurdish song together. After we stopped he said that he thought I was a proper musician and sounded good accompanying his song. He then smiled and said that all three of us were like a group and that one day we would become famous and would earn lots of money with our concerts. From this time on the three of us worked as a group – a singing and playing trio from which I was no longer excluded. He recognised the musician in me and related to me as a person, not just a woman.

Eventually we had a repertoire of songs, with me playing the piano, the interpreter a drum and the patient a guitar, which he decided to play instead of his saz. He would play the melody line on the upper E string and just strum the rest without any particular chord, just as he would do it on his native instrument. When I asked why he had chosen the guitar, he said that the guitar tuning fits the piano sound better than the scale of a saz.[2] In my experience it was unusual that the Kurdish saz player would exchange

---

2   A saz tuning can have quarter tones in its scale and can sound out of tune when accompanied by a well tempered instrument, such as a piano.

his instrument for another. The saz is normally very meaningful for a Kurdish person; it is a symbol of Kurdish culture and the political aspirations of statehood. Here however his concern for the quality of the musical relationship between us became more important. Whilst before he was interested in what he was doing, now he was concentrated on what we were doing – a real shift in his perception and actions.

A few times, when the interpreter was ill, Herr A still came to music therapy. I was surprised that he did not mind us being alone. 'We are not alone any more', he said, 'the music is there with us'. I liked his personification of the music as a living organism. I suddenly remembered the first sessions we had together, and the feelings of exclusion and helplessness I had experienced because of his cultural attitudes that did not allow us to meet. I thought how lucky I was to have music on my side to help him trust me as a musician and as a person, in the safety of a musical dialogue.

The dancing four

The initial joke of the patient about us being a group became a reality when I was asked whether any of my patients would like to perform for the official ceremony dedicated to the 10th anniversary of the foundation of our centre. I asked Herr A what he thought about performing in front of other people and he said: 'Why not, we are a group and we have got something to show them, haven't we?' I was aware of the pressure that such an event can put on a patient (Turry 2001), so I told Herr A that if he did not feel comfortable in any way about this performance we could always cancel it.

This new task made a constructive change in our work – it gave us a clear aim. We had to choose a few of his songs, arrange and rehearse them. It was a difficult process of balancing three different players with very different ideas. The verbal function of the interpreter became redundant so he had to readjust and try to grow in his musical confidence – a process in which he was encouraged and supported by Herr A. Advising the interpreter on this or that aspect of playing, he had exchanged roles with the interpreter: Herr A now became the expert.

One of the songs that we were rehearsing had a catchy refrain, which in Kurdish tradition is sung communally. I suggested that we could sing this refrain together with the audience at the concert. Herr A liked the idea, adding that in this way the German audience would be able to experience the Kurdish spirit. In our rehearsals, we were certainly moved by this spirit – by now we were dancing as well as singing. However, the asymmetry of three dancers did not feel right. We needed another person. I asked a colleague of mine to join us so our group became a group of four. The dance had a strong musical impact on our singing. The rhythmic accents became more defined and the patient's whole musical expression became more authentic and exuberant. His movements became freer, he bent his body, swayed to and fro and when approaching another person in the circle he communicated with his movements and inspired us to dance in that way too. It was difficult to match the authenticity of his expression.

Herr A had the role of a leader in many aspects of our rehearsals, including, for example, starting the first line of the song alone and thus tuning us in. I noticed the change in his body language. The feeling of responsibility made him look straighter, stronger and more alert. While sometimes he still came in quite depressed, he always left the room energised and focused. He also seemed completely aware of others in the room. All four of us were working immensely hard together, sweating, exchanging ideas and arguing – all natural aspects of the creative process. Along with this process came a feeling amongst us of acceptance and belonging.

The final stage

Unexpectedly for me, some members of my team found the idea of trying to engage the audience not appropriate. The audience was going to consist of politicians and other VIP centre supporters, who were not expecting to be asked to sing! They were there to hear the speeches. The organisers expected that the patient would perform to make the programme less dry, but they did not expect us to involve the audience actively. They warned me that the patient and I might feel very embarrassed if the audience did not get inspired to join us. Eventually they agreed to put this song at the end of the evening, before the reception.

At the same time, as the rehearsals went on, some colleagues said to me that the sounds coming out of my room were so inviting that they could hardly resist coming in and joining us.

The big day of the concert arrived. As we finally got to sing and dance in front of an audience, many people clapped and joined us in the rhythm of the music. It felt natural and it did not conflict with the agenda of the evening, in fact it added meaning to it. After the concert the patient was congratulated and thanked many times by the guests. There was a look of pride in his eyes. His doctors and social worker were impressed with his calm and healthy performance. Many guests speaking to me afterwards said that seeing a person share his soul and culture with them was a moving experience, something that turned the concept of 'a traumatised refugee' into a real person with real feelings that they could empathise with. To me this was a confirmation of the need for building bridges between refugees and their host society, and that music can and should be used as a building material for creating such bridges.

The work with Herr A is continuing. He has expressed his wish to play some new music – 'something that we can perform together again'.

Discussion

The re-establishment of trust in humanity

An important issue in the work with Herr A was his capacity to trust. The suffering of a person, caused by the inhuman behaviour of another human being makes trusting difficult and sometimes almost impossible (van der Kolk 1996; Jaffa 1993). This is exacerbated by the experiences of hostility and racial antagonism that refugees have in their host communities (Lin 1986; Athey and Ahearn 1991). In therapy with traumatised people one observes that this lack of trust is a source of many other problems, particularly their social isolation, which I will talk about in the next commentary. The re-establishment of trust in another human being is one of the main aims in therapy with traumatised refugees since it can facilitate the processes of change in many other aspects of their life. Dixon (2002) suggests that music therapy has a particular role to play here, since the processes inherent in musical interaction are strong antidotes to the inhuman experiences of torture, helping the clients to connect with the core of their humanity and establish connections with other people.

Often when I first meet my patients, like Herr A, they show clear signs of mistrust. I personify everything unknown and foreign to them. However, as the music unfolds, they often seem to experience a basic grain of trust in the music itself, as if their mistrust gives way to the qualities of 'humanness' inherent in music. Through musical activity, they can recognise humanity in another person, humanity that extends beyond their culture and experience of trauma. Martin Buber describes such moments of people confirming each other's humanity as measurements of the extent to which a society can be called human (Buber 1951). In my experience, confirming each other's humanity by 'being music together' can facilitate the natural processes of connecting, healing and evolving, and in turn can impact upon a person's way of relating to himself and to the people around him.

From isolation to integration

Social isolation is one of the major problems that refugees face. The social support system from their homeland is disrupted and, finding it difficult to form a new one, they become isolated and withdrawn (van der Kolk 1996; Herman

1992). Such isolation and the lack of a sense of belonging makes the process of recovery very difficult (Lin 1986). 'The individual who is victimised cannot recover in isolation' (Ochberg 1993, p.778). Therapy has to focus on recovering their sense of belonging in order to help individuals to adapt and find a place in their new society (Ochberg 1993; van der Kolk 1996; Herman 1992). My argument is that music, being essentially a communal form of expression in most of these people's cultures, is a particularly effective medium in promoting their acculturation and integration. In my patients' cultures music is nearly always sung, played or listened to with other people. In music therapy we can help our patients to use this communal repertoire of expression that they are already equipped with by their home cultures to reconnect with their ability to be a creative part of a community (Zharinova-Sanderson in Ansdell 2002, p.25).

The process of a refugee's integration into a new society goes through several stages. During the initial ones the refugee has to decide whether his or her own cultural identity is of value and should be retained, and whether the contacts with the new society are of value and should be sought (Berry 1991). Integration 'implies some maintenance of the cultural integrity of the group… as well as the movements to become an integral part of a larger societal frame-work' (Berry 1991, p.24). The music therapy of Herr A included elements of such an integration process. On one hand, his cultural input was supported and celebrated by the group. On the other hand, he clearly developed the desire to fit into our joint music-making, adopting new instruments and ways of playing.

Throughout the whole process of therapy the issue of accepting and being accepted was important. The therapy room became a practice room where these ideas were being tried out, discussed and perfected in a mutual process of respect, understanding and acceptance. We had to grow in acceptance of each other's differences, whether cultural, musical or ability to dance. The patient was given opportunity to direct and make decisions, but he was also challenged to accept our ideas as co-musicians and people from different backgrounds and cultures.

His role evolved from being a withdrawn, isolated individual to somebody whose cultural expertise in music and dance was affecting and moulding our group's creative potential. His music evolved from being a solo expression that was impossible for me to meet, to being shared and co-created with a group of people. I have observed many times the natural process that happens when people 'musick' together – that of sparking off their creative potential and creating new connections between them. Whilst initially needing the safety of a protected therapeutic space, I often feel that the music therapy setting has to open up to include other frameworks for music-making in which the client would be able to participate. It is important not to be scared to follow up the paths along which music-making takes us, as they can shed new light on the patient's creative potential and allow the healing aspects of his musical heritage to work. I feel it is our responsibility as music therapists to stay open to the various therapeutic opportunities that music offers, even if it means leaving the safety of the usual therapeutic space and concepts.

On musical performance

Performance as a part of music therapy has been, and continues to be, a contentious issue (Turry 2001; Maratos 2002). Whilst the arguments about the ethical aspects of performance in therapy will continue, I want to focus on the issues of performance in work with clients from non-Western backgrounds. In my experience with Herr A I became aware that for him musical performance was not seen as an imposed task, but it was rather a natural conclusion of our musical explorations. Music in his culture is quintessentially about *sharing* and *connecting* with other people. In many non-Western cultures performance is not understood separately from the act of music itself (Small 1998). This results in the fact that performing music *with* and *for* people is not at all unnatural to many of my patients – on the contrary, it is an integral part of their cultural identity. For them, in their home countries, this is how music-making always happened. I feel therefore that a music therapist working with these clients has a responsibility to create spaces where such valuable communal aspects of music-making can be re-established and used therapeutically.

Kenny and Stige (2002) find it necessary and enriching for the music therapy profession to ground its evolving therapeutic concepts on its awareness of the clients in their social and cultural contexts. I have found that this is the best way to connect with the 'musical selves' of non-Western clients. It helps music therapy to be understood and validated through the experiences from their own cultures and not to be seen as a foreign Western idea. Individual music therapy is normally a necessary initial step in establishing a trusting relationship with a traumatised refugee. But, if we only work in the framework of an enclosed individual music therapy session, there is a danger of missing the clients' musical cultural resources, simply because this setting is unnatural for music-making as they know it. It does not mean of course that I encourage each client to perform publicly. What it does mean is that I have learned to be especially open in looking for clues from the clients that show that he or she would like to share their music with others and is ready to do so. The aim-directed process of the performance can activate the re-establishment of the traumatised refugee's feeling of self-worth, which is so often stolen from them by their experiences of trauma and exile. For example, for Herr A performance was an important affirmation of his worth and identity as a Kurdish person to be accepted and celebrated by a German audience.

Whether entering a music group, sharing music with the other refugees who live in the hostels, playing at a patient party in the Centre or at official events organised for the fundraisers and Centre supporters – I believe that these moments of sharing, and especially the process of preparation for them, can meet some of the fundamental needs of a traumatised refugee.

The therapist in process

What happens to a music therapist trained in a European context, and in an approach based on Western preconceptions about music and relationships, when faced by non-Western clients who do not necessarily share these ideas, and have their own different but equally valid ones? In the case material above I tried to describe the process of growth of not only the patient, but also of me as a therapist. Throughout this therapy my roles encompassed the usual music therapist's tasks in the individual and group settings, but also those required for facilitating musical performance, as well as specific roles which evolved as a reaction to these patients in this context and which put new emphases on my practice. I now want to focus on these roles.

Therapist as musician-ethnographer: learning to access the therapeutic value inherent in non-Western clients' music

At the beginning of my work with traumatised refugees I sometimes felt helpless – unclear how to bridge the gap between their practice and understanding of music and my role as their music therapist. In the early sessions with them my first real experience of their music was when they sang their ethnic songs to me. At first I tried to accompany their songs, to sing with them, but (as with Herr A) I often felt that I could not match the authentic flavour of their singing. Eventually I felt that my involved and intent listening was more important therapeutically than accompaniment that was stylistically flawed. I was trying to listen phenomenologically, not from the point of view of my musical background, but trying to feel rather than understand what they were doing. Listening intently and being inquisitive about the customs, texts or dancing patterns that go with the music helped me to win their trust and empathise with the spirit of their culture. I found myself in the role of a musician-ethnographer, who is exposed to the full gamut of human musical culture. I use this image as one that encapsulates listening abilities, sensitivity, respect and openness to music and culture. It also implies a desire to encourage the clients to re-establish and affirm their relationship with the cultural and communal values inherent in their music. Unlike the ethnographer however, the focus of my work as a therapist is in enabling these clients to use their powerful cultural heritage to facilitate their inner journey of renewal and healing.

The music therapist as campaigner for music as a 'force for change' in the community

As music therapists we can get overwhelmed and disempowered by Western society's perception of music as an object that is given to us by professionals and does not require active, spontaneous involvement (Small 1998). These attitudes permeate our society through to our therapy institutions. As a result, music therapists face the task of helping their colleagues to develop belief in the enlivening potentials of music, its capacity to move people's spirit and to bring people together.

There is an interesting juxtaposition in the way music is seen by Herr A, and by my colleagues. Herr A had no doubt that people would be moved by the music and would join in with it, whoever they were. In his culture, a spontaneous response is an expected reaction to musical action, and the audience is as much a part of the performance as are the musicians. He recognised that as a musician *he* had 'the responsibility for the whole social progress of the event, for its success as a human encounter' (Small 1987, p.295). My colleagues however, regarding the politicians as a particularly 'stiff' social class, doubted their capacity and openness to respond to this music. It took our conviction and their own experience of our music, initially through the (thin) walls of the music therapy room and finally in the performance itself, to dissolve their doubts. If we combine such conviction in music as 'a force for change' with the patients' cultural belief in 'musicking' as a communal act, music therapy can become not just a treatment profession, but 'a socio-political work' (Edwards 2002, p.1), that facilitates cultural movement and affects society (Ansdell 2002).

Conclusion

The space that music therapy has in the treatment model of the Berlin Behandlungszentrum fuer Folteropfer has gradually expanded. It evolved from the private space of the therapy room to include also other settings for engaging the patients' (and therapists') potential to develop through playing music. Both patients and therapists are using this 'music space' more actively, bringing more life into this Centre, where the tragedy of trauma and exile is constantly in the air, and making it a better place to work in and to be treated. Taking it one step further, the music therapy space evolved to include the use of music in community development and integration. One could say that in this way the community itself can also be seen as a 'patient'.

I started this article with a description of a community 'musicking' experience that made me feel the special uniting energy that music can evoke. Such moments are powerful and tell us a lot about the medium that we as music therapists are using. They also highlight for us the need to acknowledge such experiences and to reflect upon them, finding appropriate discourses to explain and validate their place within music therapy practice.

Music therapy is continually evolving, challenged by the needs of the clients and communities with whom the therapists work. When working with people from non-Western cultural backgrounds we are constantly stretched to the limits of our musical resources and have to extend them, as well as widen the horizons of our understanding of the meaning of music in different cultures. As musicians we are challenged to open our ears and 'go with the flow' (Pavlicevic in Ansdell 2002), to keep 'the doors' open so that we do not miss the opportunities of learning and using new ideas of 'musicking' (Pavlicevic 2001). As therapists we have to find new ways of thinking about and explaining what we do, since our experiences do not always fit neatly into accepted models of work. We also have to grow in our daring – daring to affect the ecology of our communities without fear of losing our professional integrity as therapists.

Acknowledgements

I would like to acknowledge Avni Avnioglu for his sensitive work as an interpreter and a musician as well as Rachel Verney and Professor David Aldridge for their inspiring and challenging ideas. I also want to thank greatly my husband and colleague Richard Sanderson for his loving support throughout our time of growth in Berlin and for his inspiring intellectual input into my work and this article.

References

Aldridge, D. (1996) *Music Therapy Research and Practice in Medicine – From Out of the Silence.* London: Jessica Kingsley Publishers.

Ansdell, G. (2002) 'Community Music Therapy and the Winds of Change.' *Voices: A World Forum for Music Therapy Vol.2,* 2, 2002. http://www.voices.no/mainissues/

Athey, J. and Ahearn, F. (1991) 'The Mental Health of Refugee Children: An Overview.' In F. Ahearn and J. Athey (eds) *Refugee Children. Theory Research, and Services.* London: The Johns Hopkins University Press.

Barenboim, D. (2001) 'Ein Leben in Deutschland. Warum Soll es nur eine Identitaet Geben? Die Deutsch-juedischen Beziehungen und die Versoehnende Kraft der Musik.' *Die Zeit* 5, 25 January 2001, 41.

Berry, J. (1991) 'Refugee Adaptation in Settlement Countries: An Overview with an Emphasis on Primary Prevention.' In F. Ahearn and J. Athey (eds) *Refugee Children: Theory, Research, and Services.* London: The John Hopkins University Press.

Buber, M. (1951) 'Distance and Relation. The Hibbert Journal.' *Quarterly Review of Religion, Theology and Philosophy 49*, 105–113.

Dixon, M. (2002) 'Music and Human Rights.' In J. Sutton (ed) *Music, Music Therapy and Trauma*. London: Jessica Kingsley Publishers.

Edwards, J. (2002) 'Response in "Debating the Winds of Change in Community Music Therapy".' *Voices: A World Forum for Music Therapy*. http://www.voices.no/discussions/

Graessner, S. and Pross, C. (2002) '10 Jahre BZFO – Einleitung.' In A. Birck and L. Pross (eds) *Das Unsagbare. Die Arbeit mit Traumatisierten im Behandlungszentrum fuer Folteropfer Berlin*. Berlin: Springer.

Grenadier, S. (1995) 'The Place Wherein Truth Lies: An Expressive Therapy Perspective on Trauma, Innocence and Human Nature.' *The Arts in Psychotherapy 22*, 5, 393–402.

Hartley, N. (2002) '10th World Congress of Music Therapy.' *Voices: A World Forum for Music Therapy Vol.2*, 1, 2002. http://www.voices.no/mainissues/

Herman, J.L. (1992) *Trauma and Recovery*. New York: Basic Books.

Horvat, J. (2002) 'Musical Meetings across Cultures: Investigating Multicultural Issues in Creative Music Therapy.' Proceeedings of 10th World Congress of Music Therapy, Oxford, England.

Jaffa, T. (1993) 'Therapy with Families who have Experienced Torture.' In J. Wilson and B. Raphael (eds) *International Handbook of Traumatic Stress Syndromes*. London: Plenum Press.

Kenny, C. and Stige, B. (eds) (2002) *Contemporary Voices in Music Therapy. Communication, Culture, and Community*. Unipub: Förlag.

Lin, K.M. (1986) 'Psychopathology and Social Disruption in Refugees.' In C. Williams and J. Westermeyer (eds) *Refugee Mental Health in Resettlement Countries*. Washington: Hemisphere.

Maratos, A. (2002) 'Response to Discussion Paper on Community Music Therapy.' *Voices: A World Forum for Music Therapy*. http://www.voices.no/discussions/

Ochberg, F.M. (1993) 'Posttraumatic Therapy.' In J. Wilson and B. Raphael (eds) *International Handbook of Traumatic Stress Symptoms*. London: Plenum Press.

Pavlicevic, M. (2001) 'Open Door.' *Voices: A World Forum for Music Therapy*. http://www.voices.no/columnist/

Pavlicevic, M. (2002) 'South Africa. Fragile Rhythms and Uncertain Listenings: Perspectives from Music Therapy with South African Children.' In J.P. Sutton (ed) *Music, Music Therapy and Trauma. International Perspectives*. London: Jessica Kingsley Publishers.

Procter, S. (2002) 'Empowering and Enabling: Improvisational Music Therapy in Non-medical Mental Health Provision'. *Voices: A World Forum for Music Therapy Vol.1*, 2, 2001. http://www.voices.no/mainissues/

Ruud, E. (1998) *Music Therapy: Improvisation, Communication, Culture*. Gilsum NH: Barcelona Publishers.

Small, C. (1987) *Music of the Common Tongue: Survival and Celebration in Afro-American Music*. London: John Calder.

Small, C. (1998) *Musicking*. Hanover, NH: Wesleyan University Press.

Taviani, H. (1988) 'Perspectives of a Host Country.' In D. Miserez (ed) *Refugees – The Trauma of Exile. The Humanitarian Role of Red Cross and Red Crescent*. Dordrecht, Netherlands: Marttinus Niyhoff Publishers.

Thränhardt, D. (1999) 'Integrationsprozesse in der Bundesrepublik Deutschland – Institutionelle und Sozialle Rahmenbedinungen.' In *Integration und Integrationsförderung in der Einwanderungsgesellschaft.* Foschungsinstitut der Friedrich-Ebert-Stiftung. Abt. Arbeit und Sozialpolitik. Bonn.

Turry, A. (2001) 'Performance and Product: Clinical Implications for the Music Therapist.' musictherapyworld.net

van der Kolk, B.A. (1996) 'The Complexity of Adaptation to Trauma: Self-regulation, Stimulus Discrimination, and Character Development'. In van der Kolk *et al.* (eds) *Traumatic Stress: The Effects of Overwhelming Experience on Mind, Body and Society.* London: Guilford.

van Dijk, R. (2001) 'Culture, Trauma and the Lifeworld of Refugees.' In M. Verwey (ed) *Trauma and Empowerment.* Berlin: Verlag für Wissenschaft und Bildung.

Wintour, E. (2002) 'Conversations about Culture: An Investigation into the Importance of Cultural Identity in Music Therapy.' Proceedings of the 10th World Congress of Music Therapy, Oxford, England.

Zharinova-Sanderson, O. (2002) 'Therapie in Musik: Entdeckungen, Problemen und Ideen aus der Musiktherapie mit Folterueberlebenden und Traumatisierten Fluechtlingen.' In A. Birck, C. Pross and J. Lansen (eds) *Das Unsagbare. Die Arbeit mit Traumatisierten im Behandlungszentrum fuer Folteropfer Berlin.* Berlin: Springer.

CHAPTER 12

Community Music Therapy and the Challenge of Multiculturalism

Dorit Amir

Introduction

When I view my work as a music therapy clinician, educator and supervisor, over the past 25 years, I see a steady shift in my thinking. I approached my early clinical work with what I would like to call 'individualized music therapy', meaning music therapy with very clear boundaries between inside and outside, between 'therapy life' and 'community life'. Subsequently, working with immigrants and people from various and diverse cultures has forced me to pay more attention to cultural issues and to see my work as taking place along a continuum ranging from the individualized to the communal. It seems to me that over the past 25 years, the goals of my work have not changed. What have changed, rather, are my ideas about my role, and the means to achieve the goals.

In my work with students and supervisees I became increasingly aware of their uneasy feelings when working with clients from different cultures. Jewish music therapists working with Arab clients, and non-religious students working with extremely religious children often experience strong feelings of inadequacy and confusion as to how to approach the other, how to build trust and make connections. I found that many students and supervisees deal with these differences by trying to focus on the purely clinical aspects of their work, and ignoring the cultural ones. By doing so, the risk is that '...they fragment themselves and leave aspects of their own identities behind' (Stige and Kenny 2002, p.26).

The purpose of my clinical as well as educational work has always been to maximize the emotional, physical, cognitive, intuitive and spiritual potential of each client and student, to empower people in times of crisis and in dealing with issues of everyday living and to strengthen self-identity, all this in order to enhance quality of life. Working in a multicultural society, with clients and students from various ethnic and religious groups and clients and students who immigrated to Israel from the former Soviet Union in the past 15 years, I began increasingly to focus on questions such as:

- In order to improve health and quality of life, do individuals who came from different cultures need to 'forget' their roots and completely adopt the new cultural identity? In other words, does past tradition have to be preserved or rejected?

- What is the right balance between 'keeping the uniqueness' and 'assimilating into the culture'?

- How can music therapists use music in order to build and strengthen the identity of clients who suffer from cultural loss and shaken identity?

- How can music therapists encourage clients to become part of the community and enhance their sense of belonging to society in order to feel less isolated?

- What does it mean for music therapists to work in the community? Do music therapists have a responsibility for the 'musical life' of the clients beyond the therapy room? Can there be a continuum between music therapy behind closed doors and communal music-making?

My questions are concerned with culture, identity, multiculturalism and the role of the therapist. In order to deal with each, I first describe my understanding of individualized music therapy (IMT) and Community Music Therapy (CoMT). Then I state my beliefs and ideas concerning culture, identity, quality of life and multiculturalism, and link these to CoMT using examples from my work.

Individualized Music Therapy versus Community Music Therapy

I would first like to make a distinction between the two approaches. When I am talking about IMT, I refer to what is usually called 'individual music psychotherapy': its purpose is to help identify, understand and resolve intrapersonal and interpersonal conflicts, unresolved emotional issues and enhance personal growth. An IMT approach looks at and treats the client as an isolated being behind 'closed doors'. Confidentiality and privacy are important for both therapist and clients. As a result, clients returning to everyday life can experience a gap between what happened in therapy and how to make use of it in the family and community contexts. There is no active connection between therapy and community; the therapist does not leave her room (physically) to accompany clients' creative and social activities in the community. In fact, therapists often feel embarrassed when they meet clients outside of therapy. In IMT therapists generally do not encourage clients to take things (cassettes, songs that were written during the session, etc.) out of the room. Everything remains in the room in order to make sure it is there when clients return. This is done for the sake of keeping the therapeutic process uninterrupted and maintaining strict bound-aries. In case clients want to share the music they make in therapy with parents or friends, or to perform for others, therapists usually do not welcome this, and may try to interpret this need according to their psychological model (e.g. not being able to keep boundaries, etc.).

Therapists working in the IMT mode generally do not encourage perfor-mances outside therapy and do not see performances in schools or in the community as their responsibility. IMT often addresses issues to do with the isolation that clients experience within society in isolation – therapists explore with clients the reasons and causes as to why clients feel isolated, but rarely suggest or come up with practical solutions concerning their clients' more active participation in the community.

A Community Music Therapy (CoMT) approach offers something in addition to IMT. CoMT explores the universal human need for self-expression and creativity, addresses cultural and musical identity in order to enhance the quality of life. Working in a multicultural society means that in this approach, the therapist deals with some of the questions I posed earlier, since the concern here is to help clients to achieve a better sense of belonging and participation in their community life. Therefore, the therapist wants '...to help clients access a variety of musical situations and to accompany them as they move between therapy and wider social contexts of musicing' (Ansdell *et al.*, in Ansdell 2002, p.120). CoMT looks at clients as cultural as well as musical beings, and as persons whose place within the community needs to be taken into consideration in music therapy.

CoMT requires the therapist to pay attention to cultural and identity issues, especially in a multicultural society where people suffer from a shaken identity and cultural loss. Music plays an important role in building and strengthening self and cultural identity, and therefore helps both therapist and clients in dealing with issues concerning the balance between past and present tradition, between the new culture and the old one, and between 'keeping the uniqueness' and 'assimilating into the culture'.

In CoMT, one of the therapist's tasks is to encourage clients to make music not only inside the therapy room for clinical purposes but outside as well, for fun and well-being. The idea is that it is important for clients to share their music with their families and friends, and to take part in performing and making music in the community. The therapist's role is to accompany clients psychologically and sometimes physically, to help them find their place in the community. This suggests that the music therapist may need to share and participate in the musical activities of their clients in the community, such as choir singing, recitals, concerts and plays, in order to share clients' participation and celebrate their success in their community. In this way, clients benefit, as so do others in the community and community life itself.

My understanding of CoMT is similar to what Bruscia (1998) calls 'ecological music therapy'. Here the therapist believes that facilitating a change in the individual will lead to a change in the ecological context: 'Helping the individual to become healthier is not viewed as a separate enterprise from improving the health of the ecological context within which the individual lives' (p.229). CoMT can be also seen as related to 'holistic music therapy' (Amir 1996), where the client is viewed as a whole within a bigger whole – namely family, community and society.

Although this dichotomy between IMT and CoMT probably exists only in theory while in practice therapists are more flexible, it is our perceptions, ideas, values and belief systems, as well as our theoretical orientation, professional and personal experience that shape our approach as music therapists. I would now like to state my own beliefs and ideas concerning human beings, culture, identity, quality of life and multiculturalism, and link these to CoMT.

The connection between culture, identity, multiculturalism and Community Music Therapy

1. Human beings are cultural beings; human beings are musical beings; both culture and music play an important role in building and strengthening cultural self-identity.

People are cultural beings. Modern human beings do not live in an empty space. No matter where we live, we are influenced by whatever surrounds us: nature, civilization, technology and other human beings. Our inner worlds, inner beings, personalities and self-identities are shaped in the course of our relationships with the outer world and through communicating with others (Ruud 1997a; Sagi 2000; Taylor 1992). Factors such as music, life experiences, culture, community and society play an important role in keeping and maintaining good health and quality of life.

Sagi (2000) explains the connection between culture and people as follows:

> People have a culture in the same way as they have a face. Culture is not a mere addition to their existence as human beings – they are not human beings without it. People are born into a culture. Culture establishes their identity as

> concrete entities, as well as their language and most of the mechanisms through
> which they experience existence. It provides both the materials of memory and
> its conscious parameters, and plays an important role in shaping their hopes
> and their future. (Sagi 2000, p.167)

Culture gives meaning to our lives. It may be understood as a certain strategy to
interpret symbols or signs, a way to give meaning to the world around us (Ruud
1997a). Thus, culture is not only a field of society or a certain type of activity,
which we engage in, but is intimately linked to our personal identity. From birth,
our self-identity is inextricably linked with group identity (Isaacs 1974). This
means that group identity recognizes each individual as 'speaking from a particular place, out of a particular history, out of a particular experience, a particular
culture' (Peake and Trotz 1999, p.4). Our self-identity is not a fixed,
pre-existing entity, but is being shaped through living in different societies and
cultures. We all communicate and learn from each other, and we adopt and internalize whatever is suitable for us from the 'culture of the other', and reject
whatever is unsuitable. We can define self-identity from a cultural perspective: it
is an inner entity, core being that is being constructed and re-constructed over
the course of living based on intra and interpersonal connections and on
cultural existence.

People are musical beings, born with culture as well as a built-in musical
capacity. Nordoff and Robbins (1977) believe that each human being, even the
most handicapped, has an innate ability to sense, experience and appreciate
music. They call this phenomenon 'the music child'. Christopher Small's idea is
even more radical; he talks about 'musicking' (1998) and thinks that there is no
such thing as music as a noun, only as a verb: every human being is born with a
capacity to music. Music is an activity, something that we all do, and its primary
meanings are not individual but social. Music can be used to maintain and
strengthen identity on a social level (Forrest 2002; Ruud 1997a, 1997b); it can
define social identities and boundaries; teach aspects of social organization, and
transmit a group's history and heritage from one community to another
(Magowan 1994, in Forrest 2002). On an individual level, music enables individuals to negotiate, strengthen and transform the boundaries of their identity
(Baily and Stokes, in Forrest 2002).

Even Ruud (1997a) suggests that music continues to play an important role
in the construction of identity throughout life. He defines 'identity' as a
'metaphor for self-in context' and states that 'music can be used and experienced
in a way which positions people in relation to time and place, other persons or
transcendental values' (p.3). Music can trigger thoughts and memories associated with a specific time, place and other people (Stokes 1994).

In the context of CoMT, music and culture are linked together. By making and experiencing one's own and others' music both inside the therapy room and outside in the community, clients strengthen their cultural identities, come to understand themselves and others, find a place in society and feel less isolated.

2. Musicking contributes to the quality of life; understanding musicking is part of understanding ourselves and our relationships with other people.

As already stated, music has an important role in building and strengthening cultural and self-identity, thus contributing to the quality of life. Even Ruud suggests that music helps build our sets of values and life orientations, helping not only to build identity but also contributing to the quality of life in four areas: music can increase feelings of vitality, music provides opportunity for increased sense of agency, music-making provides a sense of belonging and communality, and experiences of music create a sense of meaning and coherence in life (Ruud 1997a, 1997b).

Improving quality of life means that as persons we feel better about ourselves, less isolated in society, we keep the 'right' balance between our roots (past tradition) and our present life; between our uniqueness and the group's identity. When we gather together, share and make music with each other, we feel less isolated. Musicking covers all participation in a musical performance, whether it is active or passive, sympathetic or antipathetic, constructive or destructive, interesting or boring (Small 1998). There is no question in Small's mind that taking part in a musical act is of central importance to our humanness. He believes that only by understanding what people do when they are involved in a musical act can we understand its nature and the role the musical act fulfils in human life.

In the CoMT approach musicking is the main activity. Improving the client's participation in any kind of musicking is the goal of therapy – the therapist forms her relationship with the client and learns to know, understand and help her client through the shared activity of music. Small (1998) claims that understanding musicking is part of understanding ourselves and our relationships with other people. Through musicking we can bring into existence relationships in our world as we experienced them in the past, and as we wish them to be.

3. Multiculturalism is an integral factor in dealing with the question of identity and quality of life issues.

Multiculturalism can be defined as 'a state of affairs in which many cultures in a given society engage in a mutually meaningful relationship' (Gutmann 1993, p.172). Sagi (2000) elaborates on that definition and suggests that '... a multicultural reality emerges when people from significantly different cultural worlds live within a given social framework' (p.170). He explains that multiculturalism involves establishing relationships, closeness, and associations between groups or individuals living in a society; it also involves significant variations between the groups or the individuals. These variations are highly important to them because they are expressions of their uniqueness. For individuals and groups in a multicultural society, music is an important factor in maintaining 'a sense of shared ethnic and historical identity' (Allen 1988, p.20). And yet, music is an important factor in reaching 'the other'. By sharing their music with each other, both therapist and client, who come from a different ethnicity, religion, cultural group or age, create a bridge, and enlarge each other's identity.

I work in Israel, which is a multicultural country, like many other countries in the world. In a multicultural society, where there are many ethnic and cultural groups, and continuous immigration, the identity of my clients is often shaken, confused, fragmented and even destroyed. Some suffer from cultural losses and radical changes in lifestyle, any of which can cause difficulties in interpreting cultural symbols and signs, thus interfering with their ability to give meaning to the world around them.

Since I am mainly concerned with clients' health and quality of life, I need to consider their cultural perspectives instead of only focusing on the individual as independent of outer influences. This, for me, is what CoMT means. Taking this perspective I need to study the concept of multiculturalism and understand the cultural patterns of clients' identities.

I will now address the questions posed at the beginning of this chapter, using examples from my work.

The balance between preserving past tradition and adopting the new cultural identity

Some students and clients who immigrated from the former Soviet Union tend to preserve their past traditions. Their parents' traditions become a source of comfort, pride and confidence. In times of discomfort, pressure or personal crisis, they revert to their native language (Russian), and sing Russian songs from their childhood. Others reject their tradition, will not speak Russian or sing Russian songs because they do not want to emphasize feelings of being an outsider, a foreigner and being ashamed. They want to erase any sign of their past in order to become 'assimilated' into being an Israeli. Such students present themselves musically only with music that they identify as Israeli, or present themselves only with classical music or songs in English that can be identified with liberation and with being a cosmopolitan, worldly citizen. The vignette below is a case in point.

> Ana[1] is a 22-year-old MT student who immigrated from Russia five years before enrolling in the program. Her Hebrew is quite good, and she has almost no Russian accent at all. She is a talented classical pianist, a good improviser, has a lovely voice, and loves to sing. Her musical presentation[2] at the beginning of the program consists of classical music and no songs at all. When the students question her about this, she says that she does not want to sing Russian songs because she feels embarrassed, and she can't sing any songs in Hebrew because she is not familiar with those yet. The group decides to sing for Ana a Russian song in Hebrew, and Ana smiles because she knows the song. The group then encourages her to sing the song in Russian. She sings the song while the whole group hums the melody. It is a beautiful experience of welcoming her.
>
> Later on, while doing her internship, she has to sing Russian songs with her Russian-speaking clients and also has to learn many Israeli songs that her native clients want her to sing and play with them. For her, being a part of the music therapy program and having to learn a big repertoire of Israeli songs speeds up her process of becoming an integral part of Israeli culture.

In my music therapy clinical work and training program, singing Israeli folksongs is a main contributing force to the creation of the 'Israeli identity' that, for a moment, overshadows all ethnic variations and cultural conflicts. We see this happening with Ana, when the group sings the song for her. Ana had chosen to reject her past in order to feel a sense of belonging. She thinks that in order to become part of Israeli society she needs to forget her roots and completely adopt the new identity. Will Ana have to give up aspects of her authentic self that are to do with her national and individual history, in order to adjust to the new country, to the more suitable, accepted and successful ways of becoming Israeli? Will she go all the way assimilating into Israeli society until she won't even ask the question of who she is and what her real will is? And what is my role as the teacher/therapist here? I love the warm welcome of the group and the way they accept her. I also want her to keep her own individual-

---

1   Names in this chapter are fictitious to protect identities and respect privacy.

2   At the beginning of the first year, each student has to present him/herself musically in front of the group. The presentation consists of several pieces – songs and/or classical pieces that last approximately 20 minutes and can be recorded or presented live.

ity, not to give up important and integral aspects of her whole identity – past traditions as well as her present experiences.

If I encourage Ana to sing in Russian, I am forcing her to share with the group part of her cultural self-identity that she does not want to expose at this time. If I accept the fact that she does not want to sing, then perhaps I participate in the conspiracy to deny her true voice and risk not offering her the possibility of adjusting in a more balanced way into Israeli society. The student group finds a nice way to integrate the two cultures for Ana – they sing a Russian song in Hebrew. By doing that, the group encourages Ana to share part of her Russian identity. The group's message is: there is room for your home culture among us, you don't have to reject your past tradition in order to be accepted.

The question of how much past tradition has to be preserved or rejected is a very personal one. There is no simple answer. By dealing with such questions, concerns and dilemmas, rather than avoiding them, I am practising CoMT instead of IMT.

The balance between 'keeping the uniqueness' and 'assimilating into the culture'

Working in a multicultural society means dealing not only with people who come from different ethnic backgrounds, but with people who belong to various religious groups, who are conflicted within themselves and do not live in harmony with each other. In Israel there is a group of extremely orthodox Jews that has its own inner conflicts; another group is the 'Gush Emunim' – religious Jews who are politically located in the extreme right wing and occupy the settlements in the West Bank (Jews who believe that the West Bank is an integral piece of the land of Israel that was released in the 1967 Six Days War, and it is the Jews' right to live there). And of course there are Jews who do not consider themselves religious at all.

Singing Israeli folksongs in my music therapy groups often becomes a mirror of the tensions connected to complicated issues of Israeli society. Specific Israeli folksongs have become political symbols. Such songs have become identified with left or right wing politics, and elicit strong positive or negative feelings and emotions, depending upon my students' or clients' political opinions. Specific folksongs that are closely identified with religion and nationalism bring up powerful, sometimes negative associations in certain students. Singing these songs can cause arguments among members and may bring up the tension between religious and non-religious people in Israel. Political discussions that we experience so often in our lives enter the therapy room and can become very intense. The songs open the door to issues we all have in common from the very fact that we all live in a small country that struggles for peace, identity, meaning and a better quality of life.

> Fifty per cent of my students are religious. Among the religious ones, some are more religious than others, and among the non-religious there are also students who are traditional (who keep kosher homes, go to synagogue on high holidays, etc.), and some who are atheists. Rosi is a religious student who lives in a Jewish settlement in Judea and Sumaria (the West Bank), and culturally – in her principles, ideas, behavior and belief system – she belongs to the right wing organization, Gush Emunim.

> Rosi's presentation (at the start of the year) consists mostly of Israeli songs, some of them religious songs that can be identified with the settlers (in the occupied territories). I find myself having a strong reaction to this presentation. Some of the Hasidic songs[3] give me a very spiritual feeling and yet, as the presentation continues, I start to feel uncomfortable. Her total immersion and identification with the right wing religious culture evokes uneasy feelings in me. I wonder, where is Rosi, as an individual, unique human being? Group members have mixed feelings about Rosi's presentation. Several group members say that they cannot relate to this presentation due to its heavy religious and right wing song repertoire. Others share that even though they have a similar belief system, they cannot identify with Rosi. They feel as if she has lost and even erased her individual identity for the cultural identity. All of this results in a very heated discussion. The group becomes a microcosm of the torn and split Israeli society. The discussion focuses on questions such as: what is the right balance between 'personal identity' and 'cultural identity'? What happens if the two are extremely unbalanced?

Rosi presents me with specific challenges: can a student who is so extremely attached to one style of music and who cannot identify herself with other styles work with people who have different taste and other political opinions? Or maybe she can only work with a very limited population and not with others? I feel that Rosi needs to find her own authentic voice before she can become a

---

3   Hasidic songs are considered to be the richest among all Jewish folksongs. The Hasidim are members of a mystic Jewish sect which flourished in eastern Europe, originally in the eastern Carpathians, in the middle of the eighteenth century. The Hasidic songs are unique in character and form. 'Niggun' is the Hasidic term for a tune. 'Most niggunim are sung without any words, with the frequent use of carrier syllables such as Ah, Ay, Oy, Hey, Ya-ba-bam, etc.' (Hajdu and Mazor 1972, p.1423). The tunes are mystical in character, and usually have a prayerful mood.

music therapist who can work with various ethnic groups. She has to learn to be open to and tolerant of other individuals. I hope that as the students continue their training, Rosi will be able to open herself up to other types of songs, develop a more personal taste by listening to other presentations, learn new songs and remember songs from her childhood. Working with her was very difficult and challenging, for us both.

Some of my students or clients consciously or unconsciously choose not to sing Israeli folksongs. They prefer to sing other musical styles that appeal to them and they can identify with. Refusing to sing Israeli folksongs can be understood as a rebellion against nationalism, protest against what is going on in the country in terms of political and cultural tension, and as an act of anti-patriotism, a declaration of being a citizen of the world.

In any of these scenarios we see how Israeli folksongs can become symbols of patriotism, extremism and fanaticism, and enlarge the gap between sub-cultures of religious and non-religious Jews, between right and left wing Israelis.

My role in building and strengthening the identity of my clients who suffer from cultural loss and shaken identity

In addition to having adjustment problems in all aspects of life, many clients and students who immigrated to Israel in the last ten years exhibit conflicts between generations, when parents and grandparents want to keep the old ways and their children and grandchildren want the greater freedom generally open to their school friends and contemporaries who were born in the new country. As Bright (1996) points out, conflicts arise even for those children of migrants who were born in the new country while their parents 'adhere closely to the ways of the past' (p.87). More than that, the children of the new immigrants quickly learn Hebrew, and then the weight of family responsibilities transfers to them. They understand what people are saying about the new immigrants, they see what is written in the municipality's letters to their parents, and they decide what to tell and what not to tell their parents, so as not to cause them pain. They take upon themselves the functions of adults, and it often makes them confused and ashamed. To be immigrant is a weak place. The removal and the replanting are breaking points. Some survive the crisis and get stronger; others give up and return to their previous country or emigrate to other countries.

Some Russian clients come to music therapy because they feel insecure and suffer from low self-esteem and low self-confidence. Some are good musicians, but have difficulties in pursuing a career in music, playing music in the community or even just playing with friends. Some come to see me, an Israeli 'sabre' (one who was born in Israel), because they want me to help them adjust better to Israeli society. How do I do that? What is my role? How can I encourage clients dealing with these kinds of issues to become part of the community and enhance their sense of belonging to society in order to feel less isolated? Do I, as a music therapist, have a responsibility for the 'musical life' of my clients beyond the therapy room? Can there be a continuum between music therapy behind closed doors and communal performance? How can I help my clients access a variety of musical situations, and accompany them as they move between therapy and community; between musicking in therapy and musicking in the community? The vignette below presents such a scenario.

> Tamara is a forty-year-old woman who came to Israel from Russia eight years ago, with her six-year-old-son, Arcadi. Her husband did not join her and decided to stay in Russia. Her fifteen-year-old-daughter, Natasha, stayed with the father in Russia. Tamara's parents came with her to Israel, and she has been living with her parents and her son in a small apartment in one of the big cities in Israel.

> Tamara is a good pianist. She studied piano in Russia and finished the music conservatory with high grades. In Russia she worked as a pianist, gave recitals and solo performances with local orchestras. She also gave piano lessons to children in her area. At the beginning of a long process of migrating from one society to another she had a lot of difficulties settling in and adjusting to the new life here. She did not know the language and could not find her place within the musical-cultural life in Israel. She found work as a cleaning woman in private houses, but even though she was able to earn a living, she felt humiliated by this job and lost her confidence as a proud independent woman. Later on, her knowledge of Hebrew improved and she started giving piano lessons to a few children in the local conservatory. Since it was not enough financially, she continued cleaning houses as well. This had a big influence on her self-image; she could not really regain her confidence as a pianist. She could not practice the piano at all since she was tired, and her hands became swollen. Arcadi, her son, was going to first grade in elementary school and adjusted fairly well. He picked up the language rather quickly and started making friends. The gap between his adjustment and hers caused her mixed feelings: on one hand, she was very happy for him. On the other, she was ashamed of herself and felt guilty for working as a cleaning woman and for not knowing Hebrew as well as he did – she needed his help in translating teachers' notes to her and in her dealings with governmental and municipal offices. They switched roles: he had to help her and her parents in their adjustment to the new community. She felt inadequate as a mother, not only towards her son but also towards

her daughter, whom she missed terribly and felt as if she had deserted. She could not help her parents and felt helpless and hopeless. She lost her confidence and started thinking seriously of going back to Russia.

She came to music therapy as a last resort before doing this. As I heard her sad story I immediately knew that I had to help her come back to her piano playing and regain her confidence and pride. It became clear to me that the process of working with Tamara had to re-awaken her musical self not only in therapy behind closed doors, just her and me, but also in her local community. When she first came to me her musical self, her 'music child' (Nordoff and Robbins 1977) was not accessible. Even though she had been giving piano lessons, she felt that her music was dead and that her life circumstances made it hard to bring it to life.

From the very beginning I asked her to play the piano in my presence. At first she played from the music books I had in my room, and later on she started to bring her own music. She told me that she never improvised, and I suggested to her that we play the piano like two children playing games: chasing, hiding, racing, building together, etc. At the beginning it was awkward for her, but later on she started to enjoy it and became freer in her expression. This helped her play the classical music she loved so much. Her playing improved and she started to practice at home and to regain her technical ability.

She told me that she had not been taking part in any of the community activities. I suggested that she perform a piano recital for her friends and neighbours in the local conservatory. After hesitation and doubts, she agreed to do it. In therapy we combined practicing the compositions for the recital and talking about her emotional difficulties in living here. She also practiced at home and when she felt ready she set up the date for the recital.

I attended the recital together with 20 other people. The principal of the conservatory was there together with several other teachers. It was very successful and as a result Tamara got more students and could quit her cleaning job. With my encouragement, she became more involved in the conservatory's activities. She arranged chamber music groups with some of the teachers, and with students who studied wind and string instruments. They practiced under her guidance and performed on holidays and at the end of the year. She became more involved in the musical life of her city, and she and her students received invitations to perform in other settings. We ended therapy after one year. Her Hebrew continued to improve and her professional and social life centered around her musical activities. She felt better and decided to stay in Israel.

It became clear to me in our work together that I needed to help Tamara find a way to bring her back to her music, not only in the therapy room but further than this – to help her establish herself in social life through contributing to the musical activities in her community. My therapeutic thinking was to focus on the music as a central factor in her emotional health and quality of life. My interventions went in this direction: making sure she felt secure in the small music therapy room at my home, and establishing a good and trusting relationship with her so she could start playing the piano, first for herself, later for her friends and neighbours. All this led to her getting more involved in the musical life of the community. It was not only that she personally benefited from 'gaining back' her musical self, the whole community gained from her active participation. I, of course, gained too: Tamara allowed or even forced me to widen the way I see my role as a music therapist and the way I perceive therapy.

Working in the community – extending the music therapist's role

Supervising music therapy students and music therapists who work in special education within the educational system in Israel has prompted the question of how music therapists can encourage clients to become part of their community and feel less isolated. It has become clear for me that the IMT approach is not appropriate for dealing with these kinds of issues.

In the educational system, students and supervisees often find themselves responsible not only for therapy, but also for the music life of the school. They are asked to be responsible for holiday rituals and for other musical activities such as conducting a choir and a band. There are music therapists who refuse to do such activities since they do not think that it is part of their role. Others handle this issue differently, as in the following example.

> Michal[4] is a music therapist who works in a high school for adolescents and young adults who suffer from severe emotional problems. Most of the students/clients have been hospitalized at least once in psychiatric hospitals, for various durations, and some have pervasive developmental disorder (PDD). Most of the students come from low socio-economic and difficult family backgrounds. From the beginning of her work there, Michal has developed a unique working model: during the year, from September to March, she does individual and group clinical work with the majority of the students. In April, immediately after Passover vacation,

---

4   At Michal's request, this vignette retains her name. The author wants to thank Michal Zilbermintz for the interview that was conducted in 2002.

Michal ends 'regular' therapy with the groups and begins to use therapy time rehearsing the students for their end-of-year performance. For approximately six weeks the students learn to play and sing specific songs, learn dances and commentaries and at the end of the year they perform the show in front of staff, families and other guests.

Since Michal has been working like this for several years, I interviewed her to ask her what brings her to do this. Why does she devote precious therapy time to do rehearsals? Is musical performance in front of an audience more important than doing clinical work?

Michal feels that the end-of-year show has definite benefits for all of the people involved. The show brings out the students' (clients') inner, sometimes hidden creativity and talent. Performing in front of an audience connects them to a 'healthy place' within. Suddenly, staff and parents see them differently, more like regular human beings. The students gain self-respect, they have increased respect for their friends and receive respect from others. The students' self-image improves. Rehearsals offer the opportunity to work hard, while also addressing difficulties they may have with concentration and focused attention that rehearsals demand.

As a result of this project, the students have become more independent: they have initiated new activities in school such as a students' club. Students who usually sit outside and don't attend classes have changed their habits and have started entering classes. For example, a student who used to be shy and anti-social, felt differently after participating in the show. He now feels that people believe in him and accept him the way he is. As a result, he has started believing more in himself and has found his place among others.

The school also feels proud of the students. The last performance was held in a club outside of school, a regular club in the community with many guests coming to see it. It gave the school not only good public relations, but also the possibility to be seen as an integral part of the community. As a result, the school hired more therapists and Michal, the music therapist, got more recognition of her work. Last year she was invited for the first time to participate in parents' meetings and to take part in interviewing new students. She also got a full-time job instead of a part-time one. That, of course, gives more students the chance to benefit from individual and group music therapy. The project was a dominant factor in bringing a change in the school's perception and attitude. The school's principal, the psychologist and other staff members started seeing that music can bring out the best in these students. This awareness changed the school's orientation from a purely educational one to a rehabilitative one – finding more and more opportunities to integrate the students into the community: in working facilities, in various learning activities for further developing their talents, capabilities and social skills. The school's approach has changed – it is seen as a passage to community life instead of a closed educational unit.

The project also made it possible to improve connections with the families. Some of the parents who came to the end-of-year performance felt proud of their children, a feeling they do not often experience. Parents who never came to school started to show interest and get more involved in school life. They now come to parents' meetings, donate things and participate in support groups. Parents who usually experienced a lot of anger towards the school started to have a more positive attitude towards it.

There are also difficulties. Some staff members see the project as taking away precious time from therapy, study time and other school activities. There are students who experience too much tension and pressure in connection to performing and who do not show up for the performance. There are parents who do not come and their child feels hurt and ignored.

And yet, the performance brought out part of what has been done in therapy in the closed room so that the staff, especially the educational staff, could understand better what are the benefits of music therapy for their students. The results of individual and group music psychotherapy that focus on group dynamics and intrapersonal understandings could be seen in these end-of-year rehearsals and performance.

In Michal's working model there is a clear and important continuum between therapy and performance, between musicking in therapy and musicking in the community. The intimate psychotherapeutic work that is done behind closed doors for six or seven months is the first stage of the model. It helps build trust and develops relationships between Michal and her clients, and among the clients themselves. This framework allows work on personal issues in order to gain more self-confidence and better self-image. In the second stage, therapy is viewed differently; the rehearsals and the performance increase the students' ability in choosing, making decisions and taking responsibility. Together with Michal and other people from the school they choose the themes, the songs and the commentaries. They make a commitment to come to rehearsals and to participate in the final product. Many of the issues that are being worked out and dealt with in the first stage prepare the students to deal with other issues. The knowledge that at the end of the year there is going to be a performance in front of an audience brings strengths that could not be seen in the first stage. The last stage is the performance itself. Out of the closed room, out of school, and in the community. Most of the students feel proud and more accepted. Some of them come back to therapy the following year, others graduate and try to find their place in the community. Many of the graduates stay in touch and come back every year to the end-of-year performance.

Summary

The work with Ana and Rosi, Tamara and Michal has resulted in many questions, and has challenged many of my beliefs concerning my work. As I said at the beginning, I started my professional work believing that for best results, music therapy has to be done only in the closed room in order to establish clear boundaries between therapy and life, between me and my client. It was my perception that I should not get involved in any activities that take place outside the room because it can confuse the clients and lead to mistrust and failure in therapy. Cultural questions were not very important to me and even if I asked them, I did not let them 'interfere' with the way I did my work.

Both Ana and Rosi alerted me to issues concerning the tension between the individual and the communal, self and cultural identity, 'keeping the uniqueness' and 'assimilating into the culture', past and present traditions, old and new experiences. They helped me to see that music can bring creative answers and resolutions in dealing with such issues.

Tamara has taught me that as a music therapist who works privately with a client and is concerned with her well-being and quality of life, I also have responsibility for her 'musical life' outside the therapy room. Michal feels that she has the same responsibility for her student-clients, since she works in a school and cannot separate the individual from the social-communal aspects of her student-clients' lives. It has become clear to me that it may be our responsibility, as music therapists, to help our clients access a variety of musical situations, and to accompany them as they move between therapy and community, between 'musicking' in therapy and 'musicking' in the community.

> An important aspect of the everyday therapy work is trying to help the clients to find their authentic voice... The more a society includes in her more life models and more kinds of cultural experiences, the better chances the individual has to find his natural place within the society. (Strenger 1999, p.8)

As I see it, among the tasks and challenges of music therapy in a multicultural society is helping clients to find their authentic voice and to find their place within society. The more we are able to be open to, and value, clients' cultural, communal, musical, social and artistic experiences, the better chance clients have of finding their natural place within society.

All of this invites us to widen our view of music therapy, to see our work on a continuum between music therapy behind closed doors and communal musical activities. Community Music Therapy includes clinical as well as communal, social, and cultural aspects. Community Music Therapy attends to the health of the individual as well as that of the community. The bridges being created between individual and community give us all hope for a better future.

References

Allen, R. (1988) 'African-American Sacred Quartet Singing in New York City.' *New York Folklore 14*, 3–4, 7–22.

Amir, D. (1996) 'Music Therapy – Holistic Model.' *Music Therapy 14*, 1, 44–60.

Ansdell, G. (2002) 'Community Music Therapy and the Wings of Change – A Discussion Paper.' In C. Kenny and B. Stige (eds) *Contemporary Voices in Music Therapy*. Norway: Unipub Förlag.

Bruscia, K. (1998) *Defining Music Therapy*. (Second Edition) Gilsum, NH: Barcelona Publishers.

Bright, R. (1996) *Grief and Powerlessness: Helping People Regain Control of their Lives*. London: Jessica Kingsley Publishers.

Forrest, L.C. (2002) 'Addressing Issues of Ethnicity and Identity in Palliative Care through Music Therapy Practice.' In C. Kenny and B. Stige (eds) *Contemporary Voices in Music Therapy*. Norway: Unipub Förlag.

Gutmann, A. (1993) 'The Challenge of Multiculturalism in Political Ethics.' *Philosophy and Public Affairs 22*, 171–206.

Hajdu, A. and Mazor, Y. (1972) 'The Musical Tradition of Hasidism.' In *Encyclopedia Judaica, Vol. 7*. Jerusalem: Keter.

Isaacs, H.R. (1974) 'Basic Group Identity: The Idols of the Tribe.' In G.E. Pozetta (ed) (1991) *American Immigration and Ethnicity – Ethnicity, Ethnic Identity and Language Maintenance, 16*. New York: Garland.

Nordoff, P. and Robbins, C. (1977) *Creative Music Therapy*. New York: John Day.

Peake, L. and Trotz, D.A. (1999) *Gender, Ethnicity and Place – Women and Identities in Guyana*. London: Routledge.

Ruud, E. (1997a) 'Music and Identity.' *Nordic Journal of Music Therapy 6*, 1, 3–13.

Ruud, E. (1997b) 'Music and the Quality of Life.' *Nordic Journal of Music Therapy 6*, 2, 86–97.

Sagi, A. (2000) 'Identity and Commitment in a Multicultural World.' *Democratic Culture 3*, 167–186.

Small, C. (1998) *Musicking*. Hanover, NH: Wesleyan University Press.

Stige, B. and Kenny, C. (2002) 'Introduction – The Turn to Culture.' In C. Kenny and B. Stige (eds) *Contemporary Voices in Music Therapy*. Unipub: Förlag.

Stokes, M. (1994) 'Introduction: Ethnicity, Identity and Music.' In M. Stokes (ed) *Ethnicity, Identity and Music – The Musical Construction of Place*. Bridgend: WBC Bookbinders.

Strenger, C. (1999) *Individuality: The Impossible Project*. Tel Aviv: Am Oved.

Taylor, C. (1992) *Multiculturalism and the Politics of Recognition*. Princeton, NJ: Princeton University Press.

PART VI

What has Context got to do with it?

CHAPTER 13

Music, Space and Health: The Story of MusicSpace

Leslie Bunt

Introduction: A space for music

The UK Government's 'care in the community' policy developed in the late 1980s presented new challenges to a gradually evolving music therapy profession. We had worked consistently during the late 1970s and early 1980s to develop music therapy within the statutory services with a growing presence in the large institutions for adults with learning difficulties or mental health issues. The award of a career and grading structure for music therapists within the National Health Service in 1982 was regarded by many as the successful culmination of years of hard lobbying. How was our service to develop once patients and clients were transferred from these large institutional settings into a myriad of community-based small units and homes? Some music therapists responded to the challenges by setting up peripatetic services, following their clients out into the community. Others became part of community-based teams, linking with other creative therapists or local paramedical services. Setting up MusicSpace was another response: a community-based project providing a network of spaces for music for people of all ages and needs. Such spaces were to become specifically designated to provide settings for individual and group music therapy, as well as provide bases from where therapists could go out to create spaces in other community-based settings be they nurseries, schools, day centres or hospital wards. MusicSpace would also be the focus of support for communities of music therapists, trainees and researchers. In addition, other communities would inhabit the spaces, the work not being possible without the support of administrators and volunteers. The nature of a space for music for all was fundamental to the vision of MusicSpace and this also included encouraging all kinds of musical performance with links to wider cultural and social contexts.

MusicSpace: The first centre

Students on the 1989 music therapy course at London's Guildhall School of Music and Drama helped in the final selection of the name MusicSpace. The MusicSpace Trust was established as a registered charity in 1989 and the founding group of trustees signed the charity's memorandum and articles. As Director, I became the first therapist to be employed by the Trust. The project was to be music-centred; the name was considered to be flexible enough to embrace all aspects of a space for music for all people, both disabled and able-bodied alike. In retrospect we can see how this search for a wide-embracing name integrating music and space linked to features of Christopher Small's now well-known notion of 'musicking' (Small 1998; Stige 2002, and see Ansdell in this volume). MusicSpace implies: a physical space for listening to and making music, a public space, a private and personal space, a psychological space, an emotional space, a space encompassing relationships between people and one with the potential to move beyond. The decision not to have the word 'therapy' in the main title provided sufficient creative freedom to develop areas of training, teaching, research and performance. However, as music therapy was to be at the hub of the activities an extra line 'Communication and Therapy through Music' was included in the MusicSpace logo.

The Southville Centre, a community centre in south Bristol, became the base for the first MusicSpace. There was sufficient space for a downstairs therapy room, waiting room and toilet and upstairs some office space and a small kitchen. Additional facilities of the adjoining Southville Centre included the café for use by staff and visitors, disabled toilet and larger spaces for training sessions. A local business firm sponsored the production of a promotional video used in the official launch of MusicSpace in September 1991. At the launch a steel band and a brass quintet from local schools also performed; music-making of all kinds has been a feature of many profile-raising and fundraising events for MusicSpace. Such events also connect the work of MusicSpace to the wider community. A van was purchased, with funds from a television appeal and a local business firm. Work continued to be set up in local day centres for people of all ages, schools, etc., and a waiting list of individuals and potential settings established. By the end of 1992 the growing members of the Bristol team were seeing over 200 children and adults per week. A year later, the Bristol centre was employing six therapists. During 1993, MusicSpace was one of the first recipients of a *Building a Better Bristol* award, at the request of members of the local Chamber of Commerce.

Funding MusicSpace

We made the decision early in the development of MusicSpace that funding would be provided from a mixture of sources:

- contracts with local statutory bodies: National Health Service, local education authority, social services (all three aiming to be developed over time as the main sources of revenue)
- contracts with local voluntary groups
- grant-making trusts funding specific projects
- private sessions
- donations from local businesses, including Gift Aid
- private donations, covenants and legacies
- donations of equipment
- fundraising events (performances of all kinds of music given by staff, supporters, patrons and other professionals to raise funds for a music-based project being attractive to potential audiences and sponsors).

Here is a hypothetical example of how work can move from being primed with initial set-up costs from a grant to becoming contracted and more firmly established.

> A MusicSpace therapist approaches a local children's centre and, after an introductory workshop, the staff request some regular music therapy input. The centre's management can only make a small contribution to the full costs of providing a therapist for one day a week. MusicSpace applies for a grant to make up the difference and is successful in securing funding for a year. The work begins and parents and staff observe the benefits for the children. A successful case is made to the management to continue the funding from the next year's budget. MusicSpace is contracted to sustain the weekly service.

The MusicSpace Model

The objectives of MusicSpace can be summarised so:

- the provision of community-based music therapy for individuals and groups of all ages as part of both in-house and outreach work
- the provision of training ranging from workshops on a therapeutic approach to music to specialist postgraduate music therapy training

- the development and supervision of research

- the encouragement of performance: MusicSpaces as performance spaces.

The MusicSpace model places at its hub an emphasis on in-house and outreach work in clinical spaces that maintain all the established boundaries of time and space regarded as essential for the practice of conventional music therapy. In relation to this volume's definition of Community Music Therapy, this feature of the MusicSpace model does transport 'conventional music therapy approaches into community settings'. Links are, however, maintained with the other caring communities surrounding the central client–therapist relationship, that is, parents, other carers and members of the multi-disciplinary team (some therapists choosing to develop joint approaches with other therapists or working with parents and carers). When appropriate, referrals to members of other communities such as music teachers or local community musicians are made.

A short example illustrates these processes at work.

> Jane was referred for music therapy because of her complex social communication needs. She attended Bristol MusicSpace for individual therapy for three years. At various stages in the therapy both her mother and professionals in the multi-disciplinary team observed the sessions so that all involved could discuss and understand more about Jane's needs and how a more holistic and collaborative approach could help her. As the therapy moved to a natural ending with a change of school in sight, a transition stage was arranged in the form of individual piano lessons. The lessons included improvisation, the proposed local teacher having trained also as a music therapist. The recommendations in the final music therapy report played a significant role in the selection of Jane's senior school.

At the root of this vignette and in all other MusicSpace clinical work is a pragmatic action-based response to the needs of any one client, at any one time and in any one context. This may mean organising sessions in a variety of community-based settings while keeping in place all the features of standard music therapy practice (described recently as the 'consensus model': Ansdell 2002). The work encompasses a range of activity, for example, from working in intensive individual sessions with young people in crisis through to composing songs together with a day patient in a hospice or arranging pre-composed music for a group of children in a special school. Such flexibility is nothing new and connects to the adaptable approaches of much music therapy practised in the early years of the profession in the UK.

From the beginnings of MusicSpace we were open for this flexible model to develop in other communities around the UK. However, a central tenet of the philosophy was that requests should come from a local group of therapists identifying local needs. In this way the unique qualities of the different communities could become central to local plans. A group of therapists from Nottingham were the first to approach MusicSpace with a wish to create a new centre in their community. The setting up of new branches outside Bristol has presented new and exciting challenges.

The establishment of new branches within other communities

The setting up of new branches after Bristol[1] was supported by more grants, including two awarded by the Department of Health for national community-based projects. This enabled MusicSpace to respond to requests from other groups of therapists in different communities and to provide initial financial and administrative support in their early plans. This support included help in:

- creating a business plan
- finding members for the local management group
- making an initial application to the trustees for branch status
- securing some funding for a branch co-ordinator (a role by this stage felt to be crucial in the evolution of any new branch)
- setting up early work.

At the time of writing over 50 employed and sessional therapists in these six branches are seeing over 1000 children and adults per week. A small number of paid administrative staff give support to the therapists with additional help from the members of the local voluntary groups. One of the strengths of the semi-autonomous nature of the branches is that each can reflect the local context, while maintaining links with the overall philosophy of MusicSpace. The different spaces created by the different branches are filled with different elements, for example, the therapists in Hampshire focused their early work on running a cross-county peripatetic service, for the most part for pre-school and school-aged children. The size of the county of Hampshire necessitated setting up spaces in a variety of locations. More recent developments in Hampshire, aided by a grant from the Community Fund (part of the UK's National Lottery

---

1   Nottingham (1994), Hampshire (1996), London (1999), North West (Liverpool) (2001), West Midlands (Worcester and Birmingham) (2001).

scheme), have included renting highly accessible and neutral spaces in local
health centres in inner city areas so as to develop more adult work.

A community of music therapists – a space for the teams

Setting up and maintaining a practice is often isolating and difficult for the
sessional music therapist. The work and travel can be both strenuous and tiring
and in addition there are the administrative and business requirements of
keeping careful accounts, invoicing regularly, promoting the work and its continuation. Finding regular supervision and ongoing training and support are
further responsibilities.

MusicSpace wanted to take some of these pressures away from the music
therapist allowing full concentration to be given to music therapy work itself;
thus the branch co-ordinator and administrative staff of MusicSpace take care of
all the business and administrative concerns (even if management has, by
necessity, to be at a distance). The MusicSpace model also provides the flexibility for therapists to develop their own special interests. For example, a therapist
may be interested in developing work in the local hospice. Contacts can be
made, meetings arranged, some mixed sources of funding sought, a pilot project
set up and after the initial period of work, moves made to create a more established locally situated service.

In addition to administrative support, MusicSpace is committed to funding
regular monthly supervision for all members of its therapy staff who choose
their own clinical supervisors. The senior therapists (the Trust's structure
parallels the music therapy grading structure used within the statutory bodies)
and branch co-ordinators provide managerial and, when appropriate, clinical
supervision for the colleagues in their teams. The Trust is enriched with
graduates from all the current training courses in the UK working in the local
teams, involving a wide cross-section of approaches to the work. Some therapists also seek supervision from other professionals, for example, from a psychotherapist or other arts therapist. As Director, I am responsible for overseeing the
quality of the music therapy work carried out by members of staff as a whole. An
enormous pleasure of this role is the regular visits to the different branches to
facilitate group supervision and supportive peer group discussions. At these
meetings it is clear to see how MusicSpace therapists grapple with the complex
issues of working in different localised contexts. Social, political and environmental issues are never far from the discussions. We continue to address the
central action-based response to the needs of clients (as exemplified by Jane's
vignette above), maintaining this central emphasis of boundaried music therapy

practice while being open to the appropriateness of other individual and communal initiatives.

Therapists working for MusicSpace point out regularly the positive aspects of meeting to discuss work: sharing knowledge, ideas and problems, making music together and recharging batteries. They feel part of a bigger whole, particularly if several therapists are engaged to work on one large project, for example, a large education contract. The local team of therapists is one part of the community of support surrounding the therapist.

Working as a MusicSpace branch co-ordinator involves a variety of tasks encompassing leadership, management and business and promotional skills in addition to therapeutic and supervisory expertise. There are meetings to attend (sometimes in the evenings), workshops, presentations and teaching sessions to prepare (particularly if the therapist wants to develop as a teacher and presenter) and fundraising events to help organise, promote and attend. A branch may also find that a particular staff member has, for example, well-developed public relations or information technology skills. Such skills benefit the local branch and filter through to the steady evolution of the charity as a whole.

Eleanor Tingle, branch co-ordinator of MusicSpace West Midlands, has suggested that, as therapists, our external and internal needs must be met, including physical, social and emotional needs. In a joint presentation to the Oxford World Congress of Music Therapy, she proposed the following community of support which neatly summarises this notion of a space for the therapy teams (Tingle *et al.* 2002):

- the music therapy team, that is, regular contact with colleagues from within the same discipline
- the multi-disciplinary team, that is, the multi-agency team of professionals involved with the patient/client
- clinical and peer group supervision
- personal therapy
- continual professional development – CPD (MusicSpace encourages branches to set up a training budget to enable staff to take up courses; the charity also arranges its own programme of CPD-type events)
- management framework (co-ordinator, administrator, local management group)
- encouraging joint music-making and performances within various spaces and involving other local musicians

- maintaining wider links with both other local music therapy groups and the national organisations.

Towards communities of trainees

It was always intended to support the music therapy work with training at all levels and research. It took a surprisingly short period of time to set up a part-time, two-year postgraduate course in music therapy at the University of Bristol. The first group began their training in January 1992. The part-time nature of this training course reflects the overall community-based nature of MusicSpace. It enables mature musicians to train and at the same time continue in their professional work, be it as performer, teacher, leader or composer. This balance of skills exemplifies the changing life pattern of the contemporary musician. Interestingly, these four areas are identical to some findings in a report commissioned by the Higher Education Funding Council for England, *Creating A Land with Music: The Work, Education and Training of Professional Musicians in the Twenty-first Century*. This report notes the varied nature of current training opportunities for the musician and the

> cross fertilisation between art forms and between academic and professional disciplines being created by a growing number of musicians seeking to redefine and extend the artistic territories in which they work. This is, for example, generating developments in music therapy and healing... (National Foundation for Youth Music 2002, p.17)

Other branches have made institutional links with universities and local teaching centres. London and North West branches were developed in conjunction with the Guildhall School of Music and Drama and the Department of Music at Liverpool Hope College respectively. Music therapists at the Nottingham and West Midlands branches run introductory modules for music students at their local universities.

Many of the branches also include workshop and training programmes as part of their activities. Our response to running workshops on the more therapeutic aspects of music can be seen as extending the boundaries between therapy and community music, between developmental approaches to therapy and teaching. MusicSpace staff might be involved in devising a series of workshops for a group of parents, carers or other professionals. In many ways this clarifies the specific contribution of music therapy to health care whilst supporting the development of a more therapeutic approach to the use of music in many different contexts. An example that seems to stand on these cross-over points illustrates this.

Several years ago I was invited to help create short courses on music-making for care staff working within the children's hospice movement. This initiative came from the founders of Jessie's Fund, Jessie being the inspiration for the setting-up of this charity in her memory by her parents who are professional musicians. The challenge was to bring together into a teaching team a community-based musician well-known for his educational work with musicians, music therapy colleagues specialising in hospice work and groups of highly motivated carers all interested in music but at different levels of ability and experience. There have been three cycles of these short training courses with increasing clarity on the specialist contribution of the music therapist for certain children and contexts and the use of the music therapist within the hospice as a kind of consultant.

There are also clear areas of shared expertise that can be developed and explored by the carers. The increase in confidence is almost palpable in the members of these courses. MusicSpace has recently organised further short courses on therapeutic music-making that have brought together musicians, teachers and carers. There is a great deal of sharing of multi-disciplinary skills and different experiences on these courses.

Developing a community of researchers

As early as 1991 Bristol MusicSpace received a commission from the then Wessex Health Authority to carry out an investigation into the effects of music therapy with elderly mentally ill patients at one of the region's hospitals. This was the first properly funded research project and the appointment of the first part-time researcher a further development of the MusicSpace model.

A major donation enabled the development of further research work (alongside the teaching and national development work) to be housed in a different location from Bristol MusicSpace at the Southville Centre. In 1998 MusicSpace collaborated with the University of the West of England (UWE) in setting up a new space on the university's St Matthias campus. The link with another academic institution provided more access to research possibilities. The work of MusicSpace within the Faculty of Health and Social Care at UWE also balances the connections with the Music Department and Faculty of Arts at the University of Bristol. Current opportunities are for music therapists:

- to apply for research degrees (MPhil/PhD) with present research being undertaken in the areas of group work with adults with learning difficulties and individual work with an autistic young person

- to apply for funded research fellowships and associates (at present one member of the research group is being supported by funds from the Music Therapy Charity)
- to be engaged in collaborative research projects (at present there are three projects involving collaboration between different universities and local health care and community settings in the areas of cancer care, dementia care and hydrotherapy)
- to present work as part of research seminars and small symposia (at time of writing we have just completed a second series)
- to be supervised by a team of academics, involving both music therapists, health care and other specialists
- to be part of a larger academic community, including innovative plans for the use of information technology in distance learning and support.

UWE added its support to the development of the research by inviting me to be visiting professor in music therapy and linking this into a part-time research contract. The faculty at UWE encourages the evolving research group to submit material for publications and supports work being presented at both national and international conferences.

Developing internationally

In 1998 the Trustees of MusicSpace granted a licence to MusicSpace Italy to use the name for the development of the MusicSpace model in Italy. There had already been negotiations to run an Italian version of the Bristol Music Therapy Diploma in Bologna. Plans to develop a cohesive and academically sound course had been emerging for many years with workshops and teaching sessions both in Bologna and other Italian cities. To date over 40 trainees have passed through the Bologna/Bristol course, based on the same part-time model as the UK course but delivered over three years with weekend and short residential meetings.

Past graduates of the Bologna course have decided to set up music therapy projects in their own communities and there are currently MusicSpace branches in Bologna and Genoa. MusicSpace Italy has its main administrative centre in Bologna where the co-ordinator runs the branch with the emphasis on clinical work and the Bristol diploma. There are also academic links with the University of Bologna. The branch co-ordinator in Genoa is developing links with the cultural activities of the city, organising seminars, performances, and forging connections with other therapists, as well as providing opportunities for music therapy.

Future challenges

The primary aim of MusicSpace is the provision of a music therapy service for people of all ages. It accomplishes this through its network of community-based branches, which establish boundaried therapy spaces both within dedicated centres and as part of the burgeoning outreach service. New challenges present themselves with different client populations and settings, for example, working effectively with the non-Western musical traditions of those multicultural communities encompassed by our branches. Further development of branches (both in the UK and overseas) will continue to be in response to requests from local communities of music therapists. We need to ensure that the therapists at each branch can access appropriate professional and personal support and that they feel part of a greater whole. As the charity grows so does the need to run an efficient business with all the additional legal, financial and statutory responsibilities. There are further challenges of supporting the therapy work with research and a variety of training initiatives, including the challenges of training more musicians from non-classical music traditions and becoming a focus for training in guided imagery and music (GIM).

MusicSpace has been in existence for over ten years. As we move forward we need to acknowledge and listen to the organic and dynamic shifts between the various elements within the organisation. As in the life of any young teenager, we need to find a way of holding various tensions in balance. There is a case for more standardisation and regulation as long as it is held within the creativity that the practice of music therapy induces. I would like to see MusicSpace becoming available to more people with the kind of attitude to music-making implied in Small's musicking. One plan is to create a MusicSpace in a country setting, a space for creative and health-giving nourishment for all aspects of the project: individual and group therapy, support for staff, training and teaching, research and performance.

Conclusion

In some ways the whole evolution of MusicSpace can be viewed as a series of interlinked cycles of action research. Stige refers to the stages in action research as identified by Kurt Lewin (1948). These stages pass through the cycle of: defining an objective, fact-finding, making a plan, action and evaluation. The organic growth of MusicSpace reflects the way in which each cycle influences the next, adapting and modifying as necessary. Some of Stige's features of participatory action research in music therapy also fit the processes in the evolution of MusicSpace. The   project is: community orientated, focused on solving problems of clients and practitioners, orientated towards improving 'situated practice', sensitive to musicking, creative and flexible and 'guided by critical awareness and collective reflections' (Stige 2002, p.291).

We need to continue to reflect how these different communities – clients, therapists, trainees, researchers and volunteers – all connect to the broader communities of music-makers and larger social, cultural and political issues. These connections through music and these different spaces run very deep, connecting us all to the root of what it is to be human.

> Oh, you transformation of
> feelings into…audible landscape!
> You stranger: Music. Space that's outgrown us,
> Heart-space. Innermost ours…
> (from To Music by R.M. Rilke)

Acknowledgement

To Eleanor Tingle, Emma Wintour, MusicSpace colleagues; and to Sue Pontin for helpful suggestions on early drafts of this chapter.

Further information about MusicSpace can be obtained from our website at www.musicspace.org

References

Ansdell, G. (2002) 'Community Music Therapy and the Winds of Change.' http://www.voices.no/mainissues/

Lewin, K. (1948) 'Action Research and Minority Problems.' In K. Lewin *Resolving Social Conflicts. Selected Papers on Group Dynamics.* New York: Harper and Brothers.

National Foundation for Youth Music (2002) *Creating a Land with Music: The Work, Education and Training of Professional Musicians in the Twenty-first Century.*

Rilke, R.M. (1964) *Selected Poems.* J.B. Leishman (trans) Harmondsworth: Penguin Books.

Small, C. (1998) *Musicking.* Hanover, NH: Wesleyan University Press.

Stige, B. (2002) *Culture-Centred Music Therapy.* Gilsum, NH: Barcelona Publishers.

Tingle, E., Read, B. and Bunt L. (2002) *A Space for Music: Community Music Therapy – Ideals and Realities.* Unpublished presentation to the 10th World Congress of Music Therapy, Oxford.

CHAPTER 14

Narratives in a New Key: Transformational Contexts in Music Therapy

David Stewart

Introduction

This chapter is about transformation, in particular the transformative power of context. It is the story of my journey as a music therapist through different contexts – personal, professional and social – and the view that these contexts offered of myself and my relationships. A central storyline is that different places on a personal–professional journey offer particular ways of 'seeing' and finding meaning in experience. Each stopping point is a new context of time and place within which the world of ideas, experience, actions and interactions can be shaped and transformed.

This story holds that transformation is not always experienced as a change from one thing *into* another. It can also be felt as a more subtle process, a shift in the overall template for perceiving and understanding the world. In this narrative then, transformation is about the constantly shifting colours, textures, modulations and key changes that compose the many 'contextual scores' of our lives and which, at various moments, offer us the opportunity to see, hear and experience ourselves in new ways.

The first section of the chapter charts the evolving *context of ideas* that has surrounded my practice for a period of 13 years. Various shifts in my theoretical template are outlined, from an original psychodynamic framework to one that draws on post-modern, social constructionist ideas without any specific alignment. This section highlights how a change in context can generate funda-mental questions concerning not only therapeutic roles and responsibilities, but also the intentions, commitments and motivations underpinning practice. In my experience, engaging with these questions has led to a richer repertoire of ideas and practices.

The focus of the second section is the *personal context*. Here I share snapshots from two transformative life experiences – a trip to South Africa and the birth of my first child – that reflect the ways in which personal and professional contexts co-exist and can co-relate. Both events were instrumental in helping me to re-evaluate music's ability to evoke and transform experience.

Section three concerns the *context of therapeutic practices*. It narrates three different stories about transformation that have emerged over time and in different places. They are stories of how music can transform the relationship between self, illness and health; how an experience of transformation for the therapist can help enrich the narrative possibilities within music therapy; how a particular socio-cultural context can shape how music is used in a therapeutic group.

The context of ideas: Towards a 'no-labels' music therapy practice

Widening the template

In this section I will outline my developing ideas about therapeutic role, responsibility and intention over 13 years' practice. I will chart a move, instigated largely by changes in personal and professional context, from within psychodynamic music therapy (Sobey and Woodcock 1999) to a place where I am currently less and less willing to align with one school. I am now more interested in finding a practice that works for a particular person or group in their particular context. I am working towards being a 'no labels music therapist'!

While I could not currently call myself a psychodynamic practitioner, this framework has nonetheless proved a rich resource over a number of years and, in a strange way, its particular grounding has given me the means to think beyond its limits. It gave a particular meaning to the first eight years of my work which was in the contexts of learning disability and chronic mental health difficulties. In the early days it also increased my sense of professional identity. With few music therapists in my home country on returning from training, the psychodynamic character of my practice linked me with a strong and growing tradition within UK music therapy. It also helped me to connect with other professionals who worked within this frame.

I have always maintained somewhat of a 'lover's quarrel' with psychodynamic theory, however, (or some versions of it at least)! Seeing little value in directly mapping ideas from one context onto another, my interest has consistently been for a theory that is practice-led and which honours the unique contribution music makes to a therapeutic encounter. Winnicott has been a crucial companion on this path of 'creative dissent' (Stewart 2002a). A rebel himself within the psychoanalytic world, Winnicott's developmental-interactional model emphasises the quality of the external environment and the primary importance of play and creativity to emotional health (Winnicott 1971). These concerns spoke to my own experience of the crucial role played by environment and context and what different environments could allow a person to be or do through shared musical play.

I continued to find voices within this tradition, which helped me to think outside the 'psychoanalytic box' and keep me closer to practice experience. Considering my particular work contexts at the time, most spoke with a developmentally-attuned accent; many were also independent, 'outsider' voices. Alvarez's influence was strong (Alvarez 1992). Reinstating the role of *pleasure* in therapy – tragic how strange that concept is to all schools of psychology – and the achievement value in creating and maintaining 'good feelings', Alvarez has turned around many of the cherished psychoanalytic ideas about dealing with loss. She also sees the importance of play not only as a means of communicating the way things are, but also that 'which may be, that which ought to be, that which could be and even that which will be' (Alvarez 1992, p.182).

Alvarez values the more active, enlivening therapist too alongside the more classical adaptive-receptive role. She has also reframed the thinking on defences, often seeing them as an achievement for a particular child in a particular situation. She has taught respect for defences and their value in giving a child a sense of mastery. And all this in a way that helped me make sense of my practice and how music therapy might offer an enlivening space for an experience of the pleasure of play and creativity.

Views from within attachment theory (Holmes 1998; Hurry 1998) further provided a research-led answer to my growing unease with the traditional insistence on the primacy of 'transference' and 'working through' old relationship patterns. Here I found validation for the fundamental value of presenting someone with a *new* experience – being a 'new object' in psychodynamic language – and helping create alternative templates for relating.

But how did music fit into this ever-widening view? Surely it was central to this 'new experience', offering the crucial extra ingredient, the 'something more'? In Christopher Bollas's (1987) concept of the 'transformational object' I found a satisfying resonance with my evolving views on music's role – and mine – within the music therapy context. The timing of this discovery was crucial for me, helping to clarify a struggle to understand some group work with people who had chronic mental health difficulties (see second example in the 'Context of Therapeutic Practices' section and also Stewart 2002a).

Bollas (1987) locates the beginnings of transformational experience in our earliest days, a time when the mother is primarily a transformer of her infant's experience. She acts as a 'forming and transforming idiom' (*ibid.* p.36), as she 'manipulates the environment to make it correspond to human need' (p.36) in her repertoire of caring, soothing and enlivening behaviours. Bollas sees this as an essentially aesthetic process: 'an experience of being rather than mind' (p.32), and one which I think links with the now accepted musical aspect of preverbal/protoverbal communication and interaction (Stern 1985; Trevarthen and Marwick 1986). Bollas goes on to say that we seek these experiences throughout life, where something/someone in the environment evokes a promise of transformation. He sees the arts as the great mediators of these early memories of self-transformation and describes how we can experience ourselves 'uncannily embraced' (Bollas 1987, p.4) by an aesthetic encounter. It is this kind of embrace that I recognise in the everyday listening to music, for instance, where a particular piece 'hits the spot', resonating with an important aspect of our lived experience but also transcending or transforming it.

Shifting the template

At times these various ideas and influences came together gradually. There were other times when a change in the environment of ideas and practices had a greater urgency, as when I made a significant change in work context. After eight years' freelance music therapy practice, I decided to train as a social worker. After graduating I worked as a child therapist for two years in a community counselling service in an area of high socio-economic deprivation. More than ever I found a need to embrace the role and impact of environment and context. Developmental concerns due to organic damage or deficit were no longer my bread and butter; these were 'real problems' with symptoms and reactions that required a clear resolution.

Going somewhat against the psychodynamic grain, my work focus shifted towards honouring the achievements of pleasure and good feelings as well as exploring difficult experiences. In doing so, I observed a benefit in getting away from old patterns and helping a child or family enjoy a new experience. Far from being a diversion, this was a way of putting something new against the old, of contextualising well-worn patterns within a larger template. While recognising the primary need to attune to clients, I also saw a need to draw on music as a source of transformation.

These ideas grew in strength as I made a move to my current work environment, a Barnardo's project offering a community trauma counselling service to children, families and communities affected by the Northern Ireland 'Troubles'.

Here I was expected to work with people in their own homes or other community venues. I needed to find a way of renegotiating my role in this new environment. There is nothing like the challenge of working in people's homes to compel a re-evaluation of cherished ideas about roles, responsibilities and practices! In doing so I found the focus and intentions of my work naturally altered too, in particular, the need for an explicit acknowledgement of the power differential between therapist and client.

I was discovering that a change in context affects what you do and how you do it; that context ultimately influences the narrative frameworks you draw on to find meaning for your actions and interactions. To help me in this task I was able to draw on the strong culture within the agency, which valued the social and community dimension of people's experience. I found this particularly important in working with Troubles-related trauma, itself a form of community trauma. Individualistic models of practice proved of little use to the people I worked with, whose experience was as part of communities facing low intensity 'continuous trauma' (Straker 1987).

My growing interest in systemic theory and practice – in particular a narrative therapies approach (White and Epston 1990; Freeman, Epston and Lobovits 1997) – also proved useful in this new context. I was fortunate to rub shoulders with family therapists in my work as a child therapist and enjoyed their challenge to include the social and cultural meanings of experience in my work. Of course, my schooling in social work was an important push in this direction too, with its focus on socio-economic and wider cultural influences. A final strand of influence is my most recent training in brief therapy (Griffen and Tyrell 2003). This plays a central part in my current work for Barnardo's (each of my colleagues has a similar training), further increasing the 'wide-angled lens' I can now bring to different aspects of my work.

Embracing a social constructionist[1] view of people and their problems has been a basic component in this shifting template. In doing so I found myself freed from the constraints of maintaining the preordained – and highly prized – 'boundaries' which had been a crucial part of my previous practice. I have by no means given up on the idea of boundaries, however; all work needs parameters to keep it safe and productive. However, I have found that what I do naturally

---

1   My current interest in a social constructionist view was prefigured in my reading of psychoanalytic thinkers such as Adam Phillips (1994) whose vision of psychoanalysis is of a means of constructing a more helpful story or metaphor for living. Similarly, Christopher Bollas's ideas on the 'transformational object' seemed to me to point to the ways in which the world could be co-created rather than discovered and 'known'.

changes from context to context and that I actively want to collaborate with people in making boundaries that are meaningful to their particular situation. I was beginning to see error in a therapy that validated itself more on adherence to therapeutic doctrine – and sometimes against many odds – than on making people's lives better, more satisfying and liveable.

I discovered that, in committing myself to the latter view, the onus for change was as much on me and my practices, as on the therapy participant. Similarly, work in the trauma[2] context continues to open my eyes to how illness and health are themselves constructions, reliant on the meanings people attach to certain events and experiences. This raised fundamental questions about my role and responsibilities: who decides what constitutes illness and health; what will the process of recovery involve; what will recovery 'look like'?

One of the exciting experiments in my current post has been to embrace this evolving context of ideas in my music therapy practices. Although I am employed as a social worker-psychotherapist, my manager was keen for me to develop a music therapy input in tune with the project's broad community focus. This has led to the initiative I call *Music for Health*, a group music therapy provision helping community groups manage trauma and stress reactions. It has been stimulating for me to link the developments I have made in this area with those within wider UK discourses on 'Community Music Therapy' (Ansdell 2002). I found I was calling my work 'Community Music Therapy' before hearing of these broader developments (Stewart 2002b)! Receiving retrospective validation in this way has been an interesting experience, highlighting once again how particular ideas and practices make themselves available at certain times and within certain contexts. Perhaps current Community Music Therapy discourses represent a response to wider debates within UK social policy on partnership, social inclusion and community-based care.

Reading musicologist Nicholas Cook (1998) has provided vital connections between the three worlds inhabited by the *Music for Health* work: music, music therapy and psychotherapy. Writing from a social constructionist standpoint, Cook views music as a 'means of personal and social transformation' (p.128). In a vision remarkably congruent with music therapy, he understands music essentially as a form of action and interaction. Whether listening, performing or composing, it is about what music *does* to our view of ourselves and

---

2   DSM IV (American Psychiatric Association 1995) recognises that the experience of a life-threatening event does not in itself constitute a trauma or lead to post-traumatic stress disorder; the person must also have a reaction of terror or helplessness. Thus an experience of trauma involves the event itself but also the meaning the person assigns to it.

others that matters. Music *is* important as a means of representing or reflecting 'the way things are', but it also presents an opportunity for reshaping realities. Music – along with the other arts and verbal language – can be used to construct and reconstruct a 'narrative of identity'. It can enable us to make meaning, shape more helpful metaphors for living.

The different applications of music within *Music for Health* continue to develop with each new group experience. However, the following represent a range of emerging commitments within the *Music for Health* ethos:

- collaborating with participants in defining what 'health' and 'illness' mean in their lives and what increased health would be like for them;

- increasing emotional health and well-being through music and verbal conversation;

- recognising mind–body connections and their impact on well-being;

- maximising music's capacity to increase healthy mind–body connections, e.g. using music to relax the body–mind, including a use of music and visualisation;

- emphasising music-making as a 'social meeting ground': using improvised group rhythmic play – 'rhythmic attunement' – to counter the social isolation experienced after trauma;

- using individual improvisations as a way of giving voice to personal experience and receiving support from other participants, e.g. members play 'how my week was' on their chosen instrument and receive feedback from others, 'your week sounded…';

- using improvised music to construct 'aural metaphors' for the experience of stress and recovery: finding '(re)solutions in sound' to stress-related problems;

- presenting/performing music for other members of the community as appropriate.

Opening up to a shift in the template of theory and practice is a challenging experience. It is a leap into the unknown. While it is very much an evolving process, there are moments when it can feel as if the next step might invalidate the past and its commitments, its successes and failures. Ultimately, however, this has been a creative experiment for me which has enlarged and enriched my therapeutic repertoire. Happily, I have found that the process can happen without present 'knowledges' necessarily cancelling out the past; indeed it has been interesting to chart how past theoretical preferences anticipated many of my present concerns and commitments.

In many ways, my overall experience is of a shift in the 'figure and ground' of what I do and how I do it, rather than a change from one thing into another. It is a shift that has made a real difference, however. In keeping my practice more alive to the social and cultural context, I find my work more genuinely respectful of people's participation in the recovery process, honouring their own knowledges and expertise as well as professional knowledges.

In terms of a shift in commitments within my music therapy practice, this reconfigured template has helped me keep alive two crucial ideas about using music with others. When working out of a psychodynamic label, I was primarily drawn to the single idea of co-improvised music as attunement (Stern 1985), as reflection of the 'internal world'. I remain convinced that an experience of attunement is essential to all therapeutic work and that music is itself a form of mind–body resonance. However, I am also now interested in the more active, generative components of music. This is the second idea then: that music, music-making and music therapy are opportunities for facilitating 'acts of transformation'. Together these two ideas – music as attunement and as transformation – bring a balance that is, to my mind, more in tune with music's inherent plurality.

The personal context: Valuing different 'knowledges'

Much therapeutic training implicitly and explicitly encourages the idea that what we learn in our professional work and personal therapy can be useful in 'real life'. There seems little acknowledgement, however, that personal experience can or should influence the nature of what we do professionally. I have found that this one-way learning street holds true between different types of professional knowledge too where, for instance, the 'deeper knowledge' of psychology is valued over more instinctive or social-relational knowledge.

I have experienced the allure of professional knowledge myself, particularly in work as a community musician. While I was enthusiastic to translate music therapy expertise into my community music work – and with some good success – I gave little serious thought to what community music might have to offer music therapy! Perhaps community music seemed to me too 'unprofessional' as a discipline at that time and thus I missed the potential for reciprocal learning. However, in moving beyond the influence of this idea I am now for the de-professionalisation of some of my knowledge; I am for giving personal knowledge its voice and influence on professional practice.

The two brief snapshots of personal experience below show how important it was for me to allow a flow between personal and professional knowledges, how they can interact and transform one another. Both are examples of times when personal experience actively taught me something valuable about what I came to see as a missing element in my own professional practice. Both are examples of the evocative, transformative potential in music, something which my previous professional knowledge about music therapy did not always give its due.

Music for the wonders and terrors of a brand new world

It is June 2001. My son is five days old and I can but marvel at the determination he shows for greeting the strange new world he finds himself in. I imagine it a place of bright new intensities: new colours, new sounds, new aroma, new warmth. I try to picture the slow definition of light and shadow, the sudden clarity of sound and silence, the brand-newness of air on skin. How can it be to leave the sequestered safety of your watery universe for the light and heat of day? I reflect on bridges between these worlds: the muffled yet recognisable voices, the daily patterns of activity and rest, the absorbed rhythm of his mother's living.

It is indeed a world of wonders and terrors. He is in my arms. Terror has suddenly taken hold. I walk with him, rock him, try to soothe him. It seems we cannot get into step; we are out of rhythm with each other. A South African song (Ladysmith Black Mambazo, 1997) enters my mind and I play it to him.

This music does something. It restores our soothing mind–body rhythm. We step together once again and life's continuity returns for a while. It has been the first of many moments when music has given us both a way of putting my son's world back together again. I wonder about the music, the way it suggested itself to me, its powers of transformation. I feel its pulse, how it wants to lift and rock you; I hear its steady emotional intensity and harmonic structure – rich and sonorous, voices set closely and moving together – and how they cradle and hold you.

Music for community healing

It is September of the previous year. I am on a working visit to Cape Town, South Africa, and have agreed to go to a church service in one of the townships. Immediately I am struck by the extent to which music is woven into the whole pattern of the ceremony. It often comes unexpectedly as someone spontaneously begins a song with which the others soon join.

Here is music to dance to, to stomp with, music that is sung standing still, music to sit quietly with: a richly elaborate yet spontaneous use of sound and movement.

It is time for the sermon and three young people get up in turn. They walk around the church, talking in an impassioned and rhythmically stylised way in the Xhosa language. Later I discover they were speaking about drugs and gang violence and HIV in the community. The second speaker becomes visibly distressed soon after she begins. Members of the congregation articulate a soothing 'ahh' and she begins to speak once more. She becomes distressed again and the soothing utterance urges her on a second time. It is not enough. She begins to weep. Suddenly a song starts up, quietly to begin with and then building in harmonic intensity. Soon we are all singing and continue for some moments. The music stops. It has done its work, for the young woman begins to speak again with renewed clarity and fluency.

I am left with a sense of having encountered something new. I come away with fresh thoughts about music; about music therapy (I feel I was witness to a powerful indigenous form of Community Music Therapy); about what you can do with music; about music's capacity for personal and social transformation.

The context of therapeutic practices: Stories of transformation

In this section I share three examples of work from different times and contexts in which the theme of transformation is central. I begin with an example from early in my career with a man with a chronic muscle-wasting condition. I continue to draw on this particular work as a model for the way shared music-making can reshape and transform the relationships between self, illness and health. The second example comes from group-work with adults with mental health difficulties in a therapeutic community context. It illustrates how a transformation in the therapist's understanding of the group's use of the music can open up new repertoires of communication and interaction. The final example comes from a *Music for Health* group and outlines how the wider socio-cultural context of practice can shape its form and purpose.

Example 1: Re-sounding relationships between self, illness and health

Kevin and I began working together early on in my career. He has a chronic muscle-wasting condition known as Friedreich's Ataxia and was 35 when he began his individual music therapy which spanned four years. Kevin was the first person I encountered with a life-limiting illness. He had a hunger for improvised music and it is the passion and directness of Kevin's playing which have stood as a consistent reminder to me of music's capacity to transform experience. This is work I have revisited on many occasions and each time I become increasingly aware of Kevin's capacity to use our music-making to rewrite or re-sound the relationship with his condition.

> Kevin's music is driven by opposition: the crashing blow of a cymbal, the poignant line of an African flute, the faltering melody of a metallophone. It often comes in bursts of barely controlled sounds and silences, crashing its way into the next phrase or change in instrumentation. This music wails, cries out, rages. It is existential music that both screams at the illness attacking Kevin's body and conveys a vulnerability to its impact. It is expression and transformation, a statement of 'the way things are' and a shift in the way things are.

The music medium itself essentially provides this shift for Kevin. As he literally absorbs the impact of the music he receives powerful somatic feedback, a bodily resonance that he has created. Music can help him feel more physically and psychologically alive. Here is an integrative force to put against the experience of bodily fragmentation. Here is music as psychosomatic transformation and integration.

> There is another dimension to Kevin's experience of music therapy, however. He uses the time available after playing to create verbal meaning for the music. Together we play with words, create a verbal aesthetic for our wordless music. Kevin talks about the music as his 'lifeline'. He refers to the 'battle' between the instruments he plays but also how they 'must learn to play together'. In the metaphorical vision we create the cymbal – the instrument that affords him the most powerful body resonance – becomes his illness. But not just that, for each cymbal crash also turns into a form of hitting out at illness and its impact. Life and aliveness are in this music too then, and find a voice in other instruments such as the metallophone, bells and African flute.

Here, Kevin and I are moving into the 'second human aesthetic, the finding of the word to speak the self' (Bollas 1987, p.35). Nicholas Cook (1998) would say we were enlisting words to give 'specific expression' (p.125) to the music, adding that

> music is pregnant with meaning; it does not just reflect verbal meaning. But words function, so to speak, as music's midwife. Words transform

latent meaning into actual meaning; they form the link between work and world. (Cook 1998, p.125)

Here, then, are music and words coming together to make emotional and verbal meaning of an experience of extreme physical and psychological stress. Here are words and music challenging helplessness and reinstating personal agency, making the unbearable more bearable and liveable: reflecting and transforming.

Example 2: Therapist transformation and enriching music narratives

This second example is from a group music therapy context with adults with mental health difficulties. It charts my own experience of transformation, specifically my evolving understanding of the group's use of music during a particular period, and how this helped make a more varied repertoire of communications and interactions available to all participants. Being open to the potential for transformation and surprise by the group helped me to make a crucial shift towards seeing their music more as a communication of health than pathology.

> It is the beginning of a group session and members are sharing their solo improvisations. Tony is the first to play. He chooses the bongos today and plays for about four minutes. He is intently involved in this characteristically lively and rhythmic music. Some way into the piece he changes his way of playing, dragging the nails of his left hand over one drumhead while continuing with a steady pulse on the other with his right. The rest of the group note this change and look over at him. This playing intrigues me. An image enters my mind of the day-to-day Tony pacing the floor of the community house; an almost silent Tony, apparently oblivious to the world outside. I enjoy the contrast it makes with Tony now – so engrossed in and connected with his music. I wonder about the impact of this difference on Tony, how it affords him an opportunity to hear himself in a completely different way.

> After the whole group has played we have a few moments to talk. I remark about how long each member took to introduce himself – between three and four minutes each – and comment on how this contrasts with the general silence held by many group members when in the wider community. I look at Tony and comment on how much I enjoyed his playing. Tony looks back, smiles and, pointing to the drum, says 'different!' [probably the third word I have heard Tony say in the course of the group!!]. I talk about how music can give us a different view of ourselves.

It is later in the session and we are improvising as a group. We are playing in a slow tempo using two bass chime bars, a metallophone, large Chinese drum, gato drum and tambourine; I am playing the piano. The overall effect is one of rich musical sonority and a steady emotional intensity. At one point Tony – an almost silent group member – initiates a clear crescendo that the others follow. It comes to a peak after which the group allows the music to fall back to its earlier dynamic. The conversation that follows runs like this:

Bernie: Isn't it surprising?

Therapist: What's surprising Bernie?

Bernie: That we can play together!

Therapist: Mmm – yeah! A good surprise!

This particular mode of music played an important part in group improvisations for many months. Characterised by a strong, unified pluse, members frequently mirrored each other's subdivisions of the basic beat. I have a keen memory of looking from the piano on many occasions to see arms rise and fall onto instruments with exact precision. In this strongly cohesive music members seemed fused together musically and emotionally. Tony's opening solo is full of this connection too, a strong subjective affinity with both the instrument and the music he is creating. He is in a state of musical 'flow'.

To my ears this is the music of self- and group-transformation, evoking a resonance with an earlier, preverbal mode of living. I hear it as a sounding of Bollas's (1987) 'aesthetic moment' (p.16), an experience distinguished by a 'deep subjective rapport' and 'uncanny fusion' (ibid. p.16). As one group member frequently remarked, it is music 'where we are all harmonising'. It is absorbing, this harmonious fusion of sound that provides a form of self- and group-transformation, a new way for the group to hear and experience itself, both individually and collectively.

Not that I always heard it this way! When this form of playing first emerged I wondered – from a more traditional psychodynamic viewpoint – whether it was more an 'avoidance' of loss than a developmentally useful experience of togetherness. As the group persisted, though, I began to hear an implicit appeal to alter my understanding. I felt I was really missing the point! As a result I found myself thinking of Alvarez (1992) and how finding an object and delighting in it – 'harmonising' with it – can be a developmental achievement. In reading Bollas I encountered a further resonance between the group's music and a search for a transformational object that is 'associated with ego transformation and repair' (Bollas 1987, p.18).

Here then was a process of transformation for *me*, as well as the group. Like Bernie, I found a way to be 'surprised' by the music-making and what it could do. This experience nurtured an important new meaning for me. In my original therapist-centred deduction about the 'meaning' of the group's music, I found myself drawn into a discourse about illness and pathology (an often all-too-available insight within psychodynamic thinking). For me, these therapist-inspired thoughts of 'illness' actually closed things down between us. Dislodging myself from the language of pathology helped me stay closer to the group and open to its surprises. In doing so we were all able to create a more valuable narrative about what music was and could do for us.

Example 3: A cultural meeting place for social transformation

The last example focuses on a group of community volunteers in Northern Ireland and their use of music-making during a period of heightened community tension. The volunteers live and work in an area of high intensity community conflict, tension that builds as the annual summer 'marching season' approaches. Community centre staff identified their volunteers as a group that often misses out on support. As a result, it was agreed to offer a music therapy input between Easter and summer taking the form of a *Music for Health* group.

From the outset it has been important to consider how music therapy would fit within the cultural context of the community centre and the wider Community Trust of which it is a part. I see this as a process of acknowledging and working with the implicit structures and values of the context, with its emphasis on community development, self-definition of need and the offer of various holistic health and social care resources. The Community Trust employs a community health worker with whom I collaborate closely and I was also invited to sit on the Trust's community health panel. In this way the *Music for Health* group is seen as a clear response to expressed needs as well as something new and creative.

In actively acknowledging and responding to the group's particular context, I find that its boundaries naturally differ from groups I have run previously in other settings. For instance, although the music-making takes place in a room with a closed door, it can be heard by other people in the centre. This has generated much out-of-session discussion about the music-making and the group's increasing confidence and skills and after several sessions I have heard members talking to staff and other visitors about the group. Here confidentiality takes on a different form, one that is more negotiable than absolute. Similarly in the final session, which took place during school holidays, we negotiated that the members make a music presentation to their children who came in at the end of the group. Collaborative boundary-making is central to this group then, whether in relation to the matters above or the question of how mobile phone calls might be responded to within sessions!

As my most recent work, the *Music for Health* group represents my latest research into how music can be both a reflection of reality and a forum for creating it. This is echoed in the group aims, which focus as much on helping to generate a relaxed body and mind as on offering the opportunity to voice feelings of stress and tension. The group emphasises the pleasure in the act of playing music together as a challenge to the isolation experienced by some participants. It is a forum for creating verbal metaphors that link the experience of music-making to everyday life and in ways that emphasise personal agency and problem-solving.

Here is a group that spends time tuning in to each other's rhythm each week and, in playing together, has found ways to challenge their 'stress rhythms'. A group where you can be heard and understood as members give sound to their week in solo improvisations and hear others respond: 'your week sounded...hectic...lonely...celebratory'. Here, improvised group narratives offer a way of gaining insight into life experience. A group where relaxation and visualisation come together with improvised music-making to soothe mind and body. Here, metaphor can be used to help make more sense of life. The 'dead beat' of an exhausting week – as one member put it – can transform into what she called a 'lively rhythm' in the opening music. A carved wooden fish, the focus for a group improvisation, that appears to have a different facial expression depending on where you sit, has evoked a metaphor for how music-making allows you to look at life stresses from a different viewpoint.

Conclusion

This chapter has focused on the different stories we can tell about our therapeutic practices and the contexts within which they grow and develop. It has charted my own evolving contextual narratives over a 13-year period and how these have shaped and transformed what I do, how and where I do it, and the passions and commitments that drive my work. My experience is that different stories are meaningful at different times and in different places. Rather than asking whether a particular story is right or wrong, I now find it important to think about what use it is to the person or group I am working with. Does it make a difference to their lives? Does it help them feel heard and understood? Does it change the view they have of themselves and their difficulties?

This chapter has narrated three 'stories within a story' and how each enriches the overall plot: the story of ideas and theory, the personal story, the story of therapeutic practices. The central narrative thread in each is the music story. An account of music's inherent plurality, this story verifies that music can do many things, express many things, mean many things. Music is its notes, rhythms and harmonies, the patterns that find a resonance in our minds and bodies. It is also something that we *do*, something that is a part of us whether we are listening, playing or composing. Music is also latent with meaning; it engages our emotional and metaphorical mind. We tell stories with and about music.

Above all, this chapter has provided a way of honouring a quite simple, yet to me significant, observation: music can create a world as well as represent it. It can both reflect and shape experience. Music can be a source of attunement and transformation. In embracing this view of music – and letting it embrace us – we are donning the role of artist and composer. We are creating narratives in a new key. With this in mind, perhaps music therapy, indeed psychotherapy in general, could be seen less in terms of re-composing the past and more as a means of composing a future, creating something new with what is available to the person within his or her context.

References

Alvarez, A. (1992) *Live Company*. London: Routledge.

American Psychiatric Association (1995) *Diagnostic and Statistical Manual of Mental Disorders (DSM IV)*. Washington: APA.

Ansdell, G. (2002) 'Community Music Therapy and the Winds of Change.' *Voices*. 2(2). http://www.voices.no/mainissues/

Bollas, C. (1987) *The Shadow of the Object*. London: Free Association Books.

Cook, N. (1998) *Music: A Very Short Introduction*. Oxford: Oxford University Press.

Freeman, J., Epston, D. and Lobovits, D. (1997) *Playful Approaches to Serious Problems: Narrative Therapy with Children and their Families*. New York: Norton.

Griffen, J. and Tyrell, I. (2003) *Human Givers: A New Approach to Emotional Health and Clear Thinking*. London: MindFields Publishing.

Holmes, J. (1998) 'The Changing Aims of Psychoanalytic Psychotherapy: An Integrative Perspective.' *International Journal of Psycho-analysis 79*, 227–240.

Hurry, A. (ed) (1998) *Psychoanalysis and Developmental Therapy*. London: Karnac.

Ladysmith Black Mambazo (1997) *Spirit of South Africa*. Gallo Music International.

Phillips, A. (1994) 'Futures'. In A. Phillips *On Flirtation*. London: Faber and Faber.

Roth, S. and Epston, D. (1996) 'Consulting the problem about the problematic relationship: An exercise for experiencing a relationship with an externalised problem.' In M. Hoyt (ed) *Constructive Therapies*. New York: Guilford, pp.148–162.

Sobey, K. and Woodcock, J. (1999) 'Psychodynamic Music Therapy: Considerations in Training'. In A. Cattanach (ed) *Process in the Arts Therapies*. London: Jessica Kingsley Publishers.

Stern, D.N. (1985) *The Interpersonal World of the Infant*. New York: Basic Books.

Trevarthen, C. and Marwick, H. (1986) 'Signs of Motivation for Speech in Infants and the Nature of a Mother's Support for Development of Language.' In B. Lindblom and R. Zetterstrom (eds) *Precursors of Early Speech*. Basingstoke: Macmillan.

Stewart, D. (2002a) 'Sound Company: Psychodynamic Music Therapy as Facilitating Environment, Transformational Object and Therapeutic Playground.' In A. Davies and E. Richards (eds) *Music Therapy and Groups*. London: Jessica Kingsley Publishers.

Stewart, D. (2002b) 'Music for Health: A Community Music Therapy Initiative Supporting Children and Adults Affected by the Northern Ireland "Troubles".' Poster presentation at the 10th World Congress of Music Therapy, Oxford.

Straker, G. and the Sanctuaries Team (1987) 'The Continuous Traumatic Stress Syndrome: The Single Therapeutic Interview.' *Psychology in Society 48*, 8, 48–79.

White, M. and Epston, D. (1990) *Narrative Means to Therapeutic Ends*. New York: Norton.

Winnicott, D.W. (1971) *Playing and Reality*. London: Routledge.

Afterword

Mercédès Pavlicevic and Gary Ansdell

Two important questions remain in respect of Community Music Therapy...

Is it dangerous?

In responding to Community Music Therapy many people have asked: *is client safety risked?* Also, *is therapist sanity risked?*

Our answer to this is backed up by most authors in this book: the safeguards for both client and therapist and the assurance of effective practice are no different from those for any other music therapy approach – namely, training, awareness, research and a good match between theory and practice. We resist and challenge the assumption that client safety is somehow guaranteed by a theory rather than a practitioner.

Concerns with client and therapist safety typically flow from how the consensus model links safety to the therapeutic frame: the conventions of space, time and person which many authors talk around and challenge, in respect (usually) of these being transgressed in various ways. This might involve taking clients out of the therapy room; putting them in more public and performance situations, where necessarily the therapist's role and relationship to the client also shifts (the dreaded 'dual relationship'); seeing them at different times, in different places – the possibilities are endless. Because these aspects of the thera-peutic frame, inherited from psychotherapy, seem like rules, then Community Music Therapists feel like rule-breakers, and can think that they *may* indeed be damaging clients and themselves.

But we hope that this book and its so-varied situations have made one message loud and clear: the only rule is that there are *no rules* in this game. From a culture-sensitive and reflexive position on music therapy, all the 'rules' are up for reflection and rethinking, according to context.

This is of course not to be interpreted as a licence for irresponsible practice. On the contrary, we would argue that genuine reflection on the real needs of music therapy in context – which would vitally include reflection on safety issues – in fact *increases* professional accountability and responsibility. This is demonstrable by the fact that a high proportion of chapters spend quite a bit of time talking about just these aspects.

Let's take an example where these problems might look quite acute. In Stuart Wood's 'three-stage model' not only do clients leave the therapy space, they also sometimes leave the therapist (or at least the therapist steps into the background). You will find careful discussion of how clients and musicians were prepared and trained, the key point being that the project was deeply *reflexive*, and therefore responsible. This is a point also made by Mercédès Pavlicevic in her chapter. She talks about how, even when in the unconventional situation where she is unsure of her role, what to do, etc., she nevertheless still operates in what she calls a *meta-therapeutic mode*. That is, she still *thinks* as a therapist, brings a reflexive awareness to the situation, rather than just giving in to it. And this of course is one of the main professional tools we have, and which we can thank our rigorous trainings for, not the models and the theories, but the creative *thinking-in-action* that is the mark of the true professional.

A characteristic of the authors in this book is their humility in letting situations and people teach them what is needed. It may well be uncomfortable, but if honestly faced this can also be a way of ensuring safety in the sense of not imposing what to you is the right answer, but waiting with the situation until the music or the person leads.

On a more practical level, Kenneth Aigen ends his chapter with some reflections on the new issues which Community Music Therapy brings up: thinking about new and different ethical issues on the risks of performance, on client confidentiality and so on. He also hightlights the new challenges that Community Music Therapy poses for the therapist, both practically in terms of the additional skills potentially needed, and for the expansion of the knowledge base of a music therapist into cultural and social issues and politics, and the connection between music and these. Trygve Aasgaard is, as usual, honest with the situation newer practices put the therapist in:

> Any music therapist who gets involved in sessions like The Musical Hour works without a safety net: not only is the setting rather uncontrollable, but the therapist's incomplete musical skills and (not the least) failures are heard and seen by 'everyone', not the least by other members of the hospital staff. It is an understatement saying that I am not always proud of my own therapeutic, musical or dramaturgical 'solutions'.

Trygve's work suggests that the gains justify the risks. To repeat, we would urge that nearly all of these potential 'problems' with Community Music Therapy can be tackled by: the legitimation of broader practices and ways of thinking about them, appropriate training to cover the skills required, appropriate means of reflexive thinking and research to deepen theory and knowledge.

Which takes us to a last point: perhaps the 'danger' in Community Music Therapy is not for clients or therapists, but for the discipline and the profession of music therapy. Although Brynjulf Stige assures us that 'Community Music Therapy [is] complementary and not contrary to more conventional practices of modern music therapy', he also adds this caveat:

> This proposal does not exclude the possibility of 'dangerous knowledge' being produced through the development of Community Music Therapy, that is, knowledge that may challenge taken-for-granted assumptions in established practices. (Stige 2003, p.446)

Radical thinking about music, people, society, culture and the relationships between these has peppered the chapters of this book. An example: whilst a conventional question might be whether it is 'safe' to 'expose' clients to 'less boundaried' work and to community and performance situations, exactly the opposite could also be argued. Is it really safe *not to?* That is, is it 'safe', in the long run, that music therapy should provide for clients an (over) protective refuge from the world for ever? Could that not be seen as simply artificially isolating clients with their problems? How 'safe' is it not to follow a client into the musical performance where he for once feels he is *not* a client, does *not* have a problem?

We hope Community Music Therapy provides a platform for reinvigorating music therapy's sense of what Simon Procter calls 'radical musicianship'.

Should you take it seriously?

We hope that this book has given an answer to one of our opening questions: *is there anything new under the bonnet?* We think the answer really has to be 'Yes'. We hope you agree.

Even given this, however, you may still be wondering whether you can safely ignore Community Music Therapy. Is it perhaps a dodo rather than a phoenix? Is it a flash in the pan, a five-year wonder, that will fade as quickly as it grew? Or is it just a 'big British balloon', as one delegate at the keynote forum on Community Music Therapy at the Oxford World Congress in 2002 suggested (with perhaps the additional suggestion that it be popped as soon as possible!)? Could it be, on the other hand, the beginning of a significant international movement in music therapy for the twenty-first century, the beginning of a third generation of music therapy, or even (to go one stage more radical, following the hints of some of our authors) perhaps a stepping-stone to something beyond music therapy as we now know it?

It may simply be too early to answer any of these interesting questions with authority or reliability. However, we enjoy asking them (as we think our authors have enjoyed posing some challenging and perhaps uncomfortable questions to current music therapy). In this final section we therefore review some of the achievements and flaws of this book in preparation for making what tentative conclusions are possible at this stage concerning Community Music Therapy's prospects.

How representative are the 14 chapters of this book? Are the authors marginal mavericks who can be safely ignored? We think not! The chapters, whilst not presenting anything like a comprehensive international picture, do, however, represent five international music therapy traditions and a variety of national contexts, many different trainings, a variety of client groups and working contexts. There is clearly something about Community Music Therapy that provides a 'broad umbrella' for a diversity of music therapists to sit under and exchange ideas and practices. However, we are equally aware of some gaps in this preliminary collection of chapters. Strangely, there is a predominance of work with adult clients (with only Amir and Bunt discussing work with children). Unfortunately, a planned chapter of work in a school for deaf children by Christine Rocca did not quite make the page – but this classic Community Music Therapy work we think is characteristic of much similar work going on today (but again, being under-documented, as we have noted). Another area not represented, but increasing on the ground, is that of music therapists using their Community Music Therapy skills to work musically in a variety of contexts where the work is not considered 'music therapy' as such. To cite just one example, Sarah Wilson runs a community choir in a non-medical setting for people with enduring mental health problems in the East End of London. This kind of work fits in neatly with Brynjulf Stige's comment that a music therapist may well do other things than 'therapy'.

A final anomaly in our book: there are too many men! The men write and... well, *you* complete the sentence! Why?

Concerning then how this book's representativeness reflects on the viability of Community Music Therapy as a notion: we think that as a preliminary survey it points to the possibility that Community Music Therapy should be taken seriously, if critically. The concept offers perhaps a useful umbrella for discussion of practices which are context and culture-sensitive, flexible and pragmatic and thoughtfully critical. We hope most of all, however, that this book encourages others to say what they do, and what they think – to dialogue and debate the panoply of ideas presented in this book.

Brynjulf Stige's recent work on tracing the origins of Community Music Therapy has shown how various its roots are. In his chapter in this book Stige writes of the 'banyan tree' of Community Music Therapy, suggesting the way in which, like the banyan, new roots are put down from already established branches, forming yet new trees. So whilst Community Music Therapy has several independent traditions, it may well put yet more roots down as it catches on. This would be nicely consistent with its emphasis on the importance of context and culture. There could never be *one* Community Music Therapy tree!

But to pursue another perhaps less palatable thought about the prospects of Community Music Therapy: is it a professional suicide bid? The Finnish musicologist Jaako Erkkilä comments on Community Music Therapy (in particular on Ansdell's (2002) version) in a review of the recent book *Contemporary Voices in Music Therapy* (Kenny and Stige 2002):

> we have had to fight for the status and approval of music therapy for years, and we all know that there is no other way to survive than the consensus music therapy. It would be professional suicide to change the track which links us with the other therapy professions. (Erkkilä 2003)

The argument by which Erkkilä comes to this conclusion relates to many points made by the authors in this book and, we suspect, to not a few which will appear in responses to it! Brynjulf Stige (2003) suggests one response to Erkkilä, along with an additional prospect of his own:

> it is just as plausible that Community Music Therapy may bring music therapy from a marginal position to a more central one in late modern societies, that is, from the relatively limited space of music for people with special needs to the enormous sphere of music for community development and public health. A third possibility is that Community Music Therapy will only grow for a time and then be marginalized, for instance because other and stronger professions rush in and occupy the broad field of music and health. (Stige 2003, p.465)

What do we think about the last of these options (which of course is related to the first, *professional suicide*, option)? Along with many authors, we agree that 'radical musicianship' may also need radical thinking and radical action. The tide is turning in many Western countries in terms of how higher education in music is organised, how 'cultural capital' is distributed, and how health services function. Would it really be a terrible thing if music therapy (with Community Music Therapy as an 'advance party') led to radically new ways of working musically with people in our communities? This may not of course be comfortable for any of us. Who said comfort was best?

Community Music Therapy, as witnessed in the preliminary survey of this book, seems to be offering several things to the current discipline and profession, and to individual music therapists uncertain about what they are doing and why they are doing it in the contexts in which they find themselves. Our authors seem to be suggesting that Community Music Therapy is offering:

- an enlivening of music therapy practice

- a freeing from (outdated?) norms and orthodoxies

- a space for critical reflection on the attitudes and assumptions of the consensus model, and for challenge to this when appropriate

- a space for critical reflection on the professional and institutional structures of music therapy, and for challenge to these when appropriate

- a space for the reintroduction of a discourse of music therapy that includes the social, cultural and political dimensions of working musically with people

- a space for thinking about how to break down the barriers between different professional groups working musically with people, leading to dialogue with these

- a laboratory for the development of practices and models which may be appropriate to developing countries, unconventional settings and totally conventional settings with changing social and cultural needs.

We have enjoyed working with a vibrant group of music therapists in order to produce this book: people who have had the courage to follow where people and music led them. We hope, therefore, that if Community Music Therapy does thrive, it still remains as much a question as an answer.

References

Stige, B. (2003) 'Elaborations towards a Notion of Community Music Therapy.' Unpublished Ph.D. thesis. Department of Music and Theatre, University of Oslo.

Erkkilä, J. (2002) 'Book Review of *Contemporary Voices of Music Therapy: Communication, Culture and Community* (Kenny, C. and Stige, B.)' *Nordic Journal of Music Therapy.* http://www.njmt.no/bookreview

Concluding Remark

Mercédès Pavlicevic and Gary Ansdell

Community Music Therapy is a pebble dropped into the music therapy pond. As an evolving idea, discourse and umbrella to characterise a wide-ranging set of practices, it seems to be making an impact.

Some people are excited by it, others would like to see the pond calm again.

We hope it will create waves: creative, energetic waves.

Contributors

Trygve Aasgaard is teaching music therapy at the Norwegian Academy of Music and at Oslo University College where he is Associate Professor. He has established and developed music therapy services at Hospice Lovisenberg and at the paediatric departments of Rikshospitalet and Ullevål University Hospital, Oslo, and is also a professional sackbut (renaissance/baroque trombone) player. He has published in the fields of funeral music, music in cancer care and on qualitative case study research. His doctoral thesis (Aalborg University, Denmark) is a longitudinal study of the 'life-histories' of songs made and performed by seriously ill children in hospital.
Email: trygve.aasgaard@su.hio.no

Kenneth Aigen is Co-Director of the Nordoff-Robbins Center for Music Therapy at New York University. Prior to this he worked for the New York City Board of Education, creating a pilot music therapy programme for autistic and emotionally disabled children and at the Creative Arts Rehabilitation Center (CARC) in New York City with music therapy pioneer, Florence Tyson. Since 1991, he has published articles in all the major music therapy journals, chapters in a variety of music therapy books, has co-edited *Qualitative Research in Music Therapy: Beginning Dialogues* and written *Being in Music: Foundations of Nordoff-Robbins Music Therapy, Here We Are in Music: One Year with an Adolescent Creative Music Therapy Group, Paths of Development in Nordoff-Robbins Music Therapy, Playin' in the Band: A Qualitative Study of Popular Music Styles as Clinical Improvisation* and *A Guide to Writing and Presenting in Music Therapy*. He is currently on the editorial board of the *Journal of Music Therapy* and the *Nordic Journal of Music Therapy* and is a trustee of the International Trust for Nordoff-Robbins Music Therapy.
Email: kenneth.aigen@nyu.edu

Gary Ansdell is Head of Research at the Nordoff-Robbins Music Therapy Centre in London and Honorary Research Fellow in Community Music Therapy at the University of Sheffield. He trained as a music therapist at the Nordoff-Robbins Centre, London in 1987, and later at the Institut für Musiktherapie, Universität Witten-Herdecke, Germany. He has worked with many client groups in the UK and Germany (currently in adult psychiatry). From 1994–7 he was Research Fellow in Music Therapy at City University, London, during which time he completed his doctoral thesis, *Music Therapy as Discourse and Discipline*. His book *Music for Life* was published in 1995, and he has co-authored (with Mercédès Pavlicevic) *Beginning Research in the Arts Therapies – A Practical Guide*.
Email: gja@dircon.co.uk

Dorit Amir has been Head of the Music Therapy M.A. programme at Bar Ilan University in Israel since 1982. She finished her music therapy M.A. and D.A. studies at NYU and has worked with a rich variety of populations. Dr Amir has taught and supervised students and professional music therapists in Israel, the USA, Norway and Finland. Her book, *Meeting the Sounds: Music Therapy Practice, Theory and Research*, was published in 1999 in Israel, in Hebrew. She has published many articles on various subjects in music therapy in Israeli, European and American journals. Her interests include supervision, spiritual and multicultural elements in music therapy.
Email: amir@mail.biu.ac.il

Jessica Atkinson graduated from the Nordoff-Robbins Music Therapy Centre, London, in 1999. She previously taught music and performing arts in mainstream and special education. Her current work includes violin performing and teaching and music therapy in palliative care.

Leslie Bunt has been a music therapist for over 25 years, currently working with groups of cancer patients and in individual guided imagery and music. He has trained students since 1980 and now directs the course at the University of Bristol (groups in the UK and Italy). He gained his Ph.D. in 1985 and is a Research Fellow in Music (University of Bristol) and Visiting Professor in Music Therapy at the University of the West of England. He has published extensively and is a regular presenter at conferences. Leslie is Director of the MusicSpace Trust, a past Chair and Vice-President of the British Society for Music Therapy and an adviser to the professional association. He is also a freelance conductor.
Email: leslie.bunt@uwe.ac.uk

Jane Davidson is Reader in Music at the University of Sheffield. She has published widely on musical performance including expressive and social aspects. She teaches a range of topics from musical development to music theatre, and supervises many masters and doctoral students. She was editor of *Psychology of Music* (1997–2001) and is on the editorial boards of five international journals. She is currently Vice-President of the European Society for the Cognitive Sciences of Music (ESCOM). Besides her academic work she directs music theatre, having just completed a project with Andrew Lawrence-King on the baroque Latin American opera, *La Purpura de la Rosa*.
Email: j.w.davidson@sheffield.ac.uk

Anna Maratos trained at Guildhall School of Music in London in 1996 and is currently Clinical Lead for Arts Therapies for a large Mental Health Unit in West London. She is undertaking a systematic review of the evidence for music therapy in the treatment of depression for the Cochrane Collaboration and is nearing completion of an M.Sc. degree in 'Psychodynamics and the Psychoses'.
Email: anna.maratos@nhs.net

Mercédès Pavlicevic lives and works in South Africa, where she heads the M.Mus (Music Therapy) programme, is Associate Professor at the University of Pretoria, and has been involved in Community Music Therapy projects for the past six years. She is also Research Adviser at the Nordoff-Robbins Music Therapy Centre in London, and has published extensively in music therapy.
Email: mercedes@postino.up.ac.za

Harriet Powell lives and works in north London where she practises as a music therapist with children and adults, and with older people with dementia. In the 1970s she worked as a community musician and children's songwriter with a pioneering community arts and education organisation. For 15 years as Spare Tyre Theatre Company's Music Director she initiated dozens of community-based drama and music projects with people of all ages. In the mid 90s she decided to combine her community musicianship and experience as a group worker with music therapy by taking the M.A. course at the Nordoff-Robbins Centre. She has two grown-up sons and a very supportive partner.
Email: harriet.powell@btinternet.com

Simon Procter works as a music therapist in both medical and non-medical mental health services in London, UK. He is also Research Assistant at the Nordoff-Robbins Music Therapy Centre, London, and assistant editor of the *British Journal of Music Therapy*.
Email: simonprocter@ukonline.co.uk

Even Ruud is Professor at the Institute for Music and Theatre at the University of Oslo and Professor II at the Norwegian Academy of Music. He is trained as a certified piano teacher from the Music Conservatory in Oslo and as a music therapist from Florida State University (Master of Music Therapy). Ruud studied musicology and education at the University of Oslo, completing a dissertation on music therapy. Ruud is trained as a certified psychologist and he is about to complete his further training in music psychotherapy (Guided Imagery and Music). Ruud has been working interdisciplinary within musicology and music therapy in relation to didactic theory, special education, psychology, cultural theory and media studies. He has been using approaches from the humanities and social science to understand musical influences within different contexts. Ruud has published some 15 books and 200 articles.
Email: even.ruud@imt.uio.no

Brynjulf Stige is Associate Professor and Head of Music Therapy at Sogn og Fjordane University College, Sandane. Stige worked for five years as a music therapist with a community-based approach before he published his first book in 1988 exploring community perspectives: *Med Lengting, Liv og Song* [With Longing, Life and Song] (written with Mette Kleive). He has continued to develop this area, most recently in the dissertation *Elaborations toward a Notion of Community Music Therapy* (2003) and

previously in books such as *Samspel og Relasjon* [Interaction and Relationship] (1995) on theoretical perspectives on inclusive music-making. The recently published *Culture Centered Music Therapy* (2002) and *Contemporary Voices in Music Therapy* (2002, edited with Carolyn Kenny) are his first books in English. Stige is editor-in-chief of the *Nordic Journal of Music Therapy* and co-editor (with Carolyn Kenny) of *Voices: A World Forum for Music Therapy*.
Email: brynjulf.stige@hisf.no

David Stewart has worked as a musician, therapist and trainer since 1990. He has trainings in music therapy, social work and brief therapy. Currently, he is senior practitioner with a Barnardo's trauma counselling project which provides therapuetic support to children, families and community groups affected by the Northern Ireland conflict. As part of this work David has established *Music for Health*, a Community Music Therapy initiative supporting community groups in managing the impact of trauma.
Email: davidstewart502@hotmail.com

Rachel Verney is Head of Outreach, and a senior tutor at Nordoff-Robbins Music Therapy Centre in London. She has worked as a music therapist and music therapy supervisor with a variety of client groups for 30 years. She is co-founder of The Speedwell Trust and has a rich background of music therapy research, practice and writing.

Stuart Wood graduated from the Nordoff-Robbins Music Therapy Centre in London in 2000. Prior to this he was a music teacher in Singapore and a lawyer in London. He works in a variety of settings including a neurological rehabilitation unit, a school for children with autism, and a residential nursing home.
Email: stuart@matrixmusic.org

Oksana Zharinova-Sanderson was born in 1973 in the west Ukrainian city of Lviv (Lvov, Lwow, Lemberg). She studied piano and graduated from the Lviv State Music Conservatoire. She completed her M.A. in Music Therapy at the Nordoff-Robbins Music Therapy Centre in London in 1998. Since 1999 she has been working for University Witten-Herdecke, Germany, on an outreach project in the Berlin Centre for the Treatment of Torture Victims. She is married to Richard and the mother of Anna Emanuela.
Email: oksanarichard1@compuserve.de

Subject Index

Author Index